W9-DFW-422

THE ENVIRONMENT AND ECONOMIC
DEVELOPMENT IN SOUTH ASIA

The Environment and Economic Development in South Asia

An Overview Concentrating on Bangladesh

Mohammad Alauddin
Senior Lecturer in Economics
The University of Queensland
Brisbane, Australia

and

Clement Allan Tisdell
Professor of Economics
The University of Queensland
Brisbane, Australia

First published in Great Britain 1998 by
MACMILLAN PRESS LTD
Houndmills, Basingstoke, Hampshire RG21 6XS and London
Companies and representatives throughout the world

A catalogue record for this book is available from the British Library.

ISBN 0–333–64027–6

 First published in the United States of America 1998 by
ST. MARTIN'S PRESS, INC.,
Scholarly and Reference Division,
175 Fifth Avenue, New York, N.Y. 10010

ISBN 0–312–21106–6

Library of Congress Cataloging-in-Publication Data
Alauddin, Mohammad.
The environment and economic development in South Asia : an
overview concentrating on Bangladesh / Mohammad Alauddin and Clement
Allan Tisdell.
p.   cm.
Includes bibliographical references (p.   ) and index.
ISBN 0–312–21106–6 (cloth)
1. Sustainable development—Bangladesh.   2. Economic development–
–Environmental aspects—Bangladesh.   3. Sustainable development–
–South Asia.   4. Economic development—Environmental aspects—South
Asia.   I. Tisdell, C. A. (Clement Allan)   II. Title.
HC440.8.A615 1998
333.7'095492—dc21   97–36092
                                                            CIP

This book is printed on paper suitable for recycling and made from fully managed and
sustained forest sources.

10   9   8   7   6   5   4   3   2   1
07   06   05   04   03   02   01   00   99   98

Printed in Great Britain by
The Ipswich Book Company Ltd
Ipswich, Suffolk

Contents

List of Tables   x

List of Figures   xiii

Foreword   xvi

Acknowledgements   xix

Preface   xx

1 Changing views and perspectives on the environment–development nexus   **1**

1.1   Introduction   1
1.2   Changing views and perspectives on the
       environment–development nexus   2
1.3   Issues considered and the plan of this volume   6

2 The environment, biodiversity and development in South Asia   **12**

2.1   Introduction   12
2.2   The importance of natural environmental resource stock
       and sustainable development: a digression   14
2.3   Demographic features   20
2.4   Utilisation of natural resources and environmental quality   22
2.5   Urbanisation, wastes and environmental problems   23
2.6   Protection of biodiversity   25
2.7   The human development index and a human
       development/conservation (or biodiversity)
       index applied in Asia   27
2.8   Concluding comments   33

3 Natural resources: Water and land-use in Bangladesh   **34**

3.1   Introduction   34
3.2   An overview of water resource problems in Bangladesh   36
3.3   Agricultural water use   39
3.4   Navigation   41
3.5   Fisheries including aquaculture   43

3.6	Some other considerations, especially income distribution and poverty	47
3.6.1	Health and other household problems related to water	47
3.6.2	Income distribution and poverty aspects	48
3.7	Forests and natural vegetation loss	49
3.8	Concluding comments	52

4 Rural employment, technological change and the environment **55**

4.1	Introduction	55
4.2	The data	56
4.3	Productivity, employment and labour intensity	57
4.4	Capital intensity, labour intensity and employment	60
4.5	Labour absorption in Bangladesh agriculture: Some further considerations	65
4.6	Growth of non-agricultural employment	73
4.7	Concluding observations and policy implications	78

5 Village perspectives on technology, employment and the environment **80**

5.1	Introduction	80
5.2	State of the rural environment: A brief overview	80
5.3	Some evidence at the disaggregated level	83
5.4	Farm-level analysis and overview of the survey villages	85
5.5	Employment creation in rice farming: Patterns and determinants	86
5.5.1	Overall employment: Family labour versus hired labour, labour intensity	86
5.5.2	Patterns and determinants of labour intensity	89
5.6	Environmental trends and the state of the rural environment	91
5.6.1	Environmental changes in survey villages	92
5.6.2	Environmental change: Implications for sustainability of employment and development	95
5.7	Concluding comments	96

6 Property rights, governance and the environment 98

6.1 Introduction 98
6.2 Property rights issues in a historical perspective:
A brief overview 99
6.3 Property rights: Different dimensions 100
6.4 Property rights issues: The Western view 102
6.5 Administration of resources by the state, local
communities and by co-management 103
6.6 South Asian perspective 106
6.7 Environmental governance in Bangladesh 108
6.7.1 An overview 108
6.7.2 Shrimp culture in Bangladesh: Property rights and
resource use 110
6.8 Concluding observations 111

**7 Impact on the rural poor of changing rural environments
and technologies: Evidence from India and Bangladesh** 113

7.1 Introduction: Some trends 113
7.2 Socio-economic assessment of 'green revolution'
technological change 115
7.3 Village surveys in West Bengal 118
7.4 Results from a village survey in Bangladesh 123
7.5 Concluding comments 124

**8 Agricultural sustainability in marginal areas:
Principles, policies and examples** 126

8.1 Introduction 126
8.2 Agricultural sustainability: Some principles 126
8.3 Sustainable agricultural techniques and systems of
land management 128
8.3.1 Normative and positive attitudes to agricultural
sustainability – what is versus what ought to be 131
8.3.2 Economics and sustainability of agricultural production 131
8.4 Agricultural sustainability in the Barind Tract,
Northwest Bangladesh 134

8.5   The sustainability of agriculture and related land-uses on
         the north eastern hills of the Indian subcontinent   139
8.6   Concluding Comments   145

9   Sustainability of rice–shrimp farming systems:
Environmental and distributional conflicts   **146**

9.1   Introduction and overview   146
9.2   A brief review of literature   151
9.3   The shrimp sector: A broad picture   152
9.4   Farm-level evidence   155
9.4.1   Data analysis for the *gher* owners   158
9.4.2   Data analysis for the land owners   161
9.4.3   Data analysis for the landless   164
9.5   Some further observations   165
9.6   Concluding observations   168

10   Energy resources in Bangladesh: Issues and options   **169**

10.1   Introduction   169
10.2   Energy use in South Asia: A broad overview   169
10.3   Sources and pattern of energy use in Bangladesh   170
10.3.1   Biomass   170
10.3.2   Electricity   174
10.3.3   Natural gas   178
10.4   Energy pricing   181
10.5   Energy, the environment and related issues   182
10.6   Concluding observations   184

11   Sectoral change, urbanisation and South Asia's
environment in a global context   **186**

11.1   Introduction   186
11.2   The relative decline of agriculture and the expansion of
         manufacturing and service sectors in South Asia   188
11.3   Urbanisation in South Asia   189
11.4   Urbanisation in Bangladesh and associated
         environmental problems   193

11.5   Transboundary and global aspects of environmental
        change in South Asia   196
11.6   Concluding comments   198

Bibliography   200
Index   215

List of Tables

1.1   Four major South Asian countries: Some selected
        indicators of socio-economic development   5
2.1   Rates of growth of production and population in
        selected South and East Asian economies   13
2.2   Estimates and predictions of population levels for
        selected Asian countries: Totals in millions   21
2.3   GNP per capita in 1992 U.S. dollars for selected Asian
        economies, its growth rate 1980–92 and the number of
        times by which GDP per capita would need to be
        multiplied to equal that of high-income countries   21
2.4   Land use in selected Asian countries, for Asia, Europe
        and the world as a whole – percentage change in area,
        1979–91   22
2.5   Urbanisation in Asia   24
2.6   Access of urban population to safe drinking water and
        sanitation in Asia, 1980 and 1990   25
2.7   Protected areas as a percentage of total land area and
        percentages of protected area totally and partially
        protected, 1993, for selected Asian countries   26
2.8   Number of species of threatened mammals, birds and
        higher plants in the 1990s in selected Asian countries   27
2.9   Human Development Index (HDI) 1992 for selected
        Asian countries   28
2.10   Conservation Index (CI), HDI, and value ordering,
        $V = 2/3$ HDI $+ 1/3$ CI, for selected Asian countries   29
3.1   Agricultural water use in Bangladesh, 1969–70
        to 1992–93   39
3.2   Waterways by season and type of navigability
        in Bangladesh   42
3.3   Movement of goods by means of transportation:
        Bangladesh 1980–81 to 1991–92   42
3.4   Sources of fish supply in Bangladesh: Percentage
        contribution in terms of weight, 1983–84 and 1990–91   44
4.1   Relationship between total employment in foodgrain
        production (IMDFG) and yield per net cropped hectare
        (INYFDT): Bangladesh, 1960–61 to 1990–91   59

4.2 Relationship between overall labour intensity per hectare (IMDPHA), overall and *rabi* season labour use (ITOTAL and IMDR) and capital intensity (FERT and IMODRMD) 62

4.3 Relationship between overall labour intensity per hectare (IMDPHA), overall and *rabi* season labour use (ITOTAL and IMDR), and fertiliser irrigation interaction (INDFIRRI) 66

4.4 Trend in difference in employment during the kharif and *rabi* seasons: Bangladesh 1960–61 to 1990–91 68

4.5 Relationship between area under various crops and seasons, and (total) labour use: Bangaldesh, 1960–61 to 1990–91 69

4.6 Relationship between labour intensity per hectare for different crops and relevant land areas under cultivation: Bangladesh 1960–61 to 1990–91 70

4.7 Non-agricultural employment and productivity growth: Bangladesh, 1974–89 73

4.8 Trends in agricultural and industrial real wages: Bangladesh, 1969–70 to 1988–89 75

5.1 Marginal revenues and costs of HYV paddy farmers in Bangladesh, by districts, season and labour input: District level data 1989–90 84

5.2 Employment in rice production: Three Bangladesh villages 87

5.3 Labour intensity per hectare of land cropped with rice: Three Bangladesh villages 88

5.4 Impact of yield per hectare on intensity of labour use per hectare for different rice varieties: Three Bangladesh villages 89

5.5 Impact of technology on overall intensity of labour use per hectare: Three Bangladesh villages 91

6.1 Pattern of ownership and management of forest in Bangladesh 109

7.1 Percentage improvement in economic situation expected by household heads in Durgapur, Bangladesh, 1992 from restoration of natural resources to their levels of 5–10 years prior to 1992 123

8.1 Land utilisation in Bangladesh (1989–90): Area in 1000s of hectares 137

9.1 Shrimp farming methods in Bangladesh 149

9.2 Shrimp in Bangladesh's export trade: 1972–73 to 1993–94 153

9.3	Structure, regional distribution of area and output and yield of shrimp in Bangladesh	156
9.4	Distribution of percentage of own land in *gher*	158
9.5	Distribution of percentage of size of *ghers*	159
9.6	Discriminant analysis for *gher* owners on groups defined by ECONOMY	160
9.7	Rice yields on and off shrimp farms and pre and post *gher* phases: *t*-tests of paired samples for *gher* owners	161
9.8	Distribution of land ownership pattern	161
9.9	Distribution of land area in the *gher*	162
9.10	Distribution of land area outside of the *gher*	162
9.11	Discriminant analysis for land owners on groups defined by ECONOMY	163
9.12	Discriminant analysis for land owners on groups defined by FAVOUR	163
9.13	Rice yields on and off shrimp farms and pre and post *gher* phases: *t*-tests of paired samples for land owners	164
9.14	Discriminant analysis for landless on groups defined by ECONOMY	165
10.1	Commercial energy use, consumption and industrial pollution in major South Asian countries	171
10.2	Biomass fuels in Bangladesh, 1981	173
10.3	Power generation and consumption in Bangladesh, 1972–73 to 1993–94	175
10.4	Total and sectoral consumption of electricity in Bangladesh, 1985–86 to 1993–94	177
10.5A	Trend in natural gas production and consumption in Bangladesh, 1983–84 to 1992–93	178
10.5B	Changing pattern of natural gas usage in Bangladesh, 1983–84 to 1992–93	179
10.6	Total projected energy demand for selected energy sources with and without conservation: Bangladesh 1995 to 2010	183
11.1	Labour force distribution in selected South Asian economies	188
11.2	Structure of production in selected South Asian countries	189
11.3	Urbanisation statistics for selected South Asian countries	190
11.4	The world's twenty-five largest cities, 1995	191
11.5	Coverage of urban water supply in Bangladesh: Per cent of population	194
11.6	Coverage of sewerage disposal in Bangladesh: Per cent of population	194

List of Figures

1.1 A generalised map of South Asia   4

1.2 A schematic representation of the poverty – environmental degradation problem   6

2.1 Economic links with the natural environment   16

2.2 Production of man-made capital usually draws on natural capital and makes use of human capital and labour. Man-made capital is subject to depreciation, but natural capital is not usually and the same is true for human capital   17

2.3 Weak and strong conditions for sustainable development and spectrum of views about those conditions according to Pearce (1993, Ch 2.)   18

2.4 Representation of valuation frontier incorporating human welfare and biodiversity conservation as considerations, trade-off possibilities and optimisation   31

3.1 Schematic representation of important environmental interdependencies in Bangladesh linked to water bodies and effected by economic change   53

4.1 Trends in foodgrain yield per gross cropped hectare (**IGYFDT**), crop sector employment (**ITOTAL**) and labour intensity per gross cropped hectare (**IMDPHA**): Bangladesh 1960–61 to 1990–91   57

4.2 Trends in foodgrain yield per net cropped hectare (**INYFDT**), foodgrain sector employment (**IMDFG**) and labour intensity per net cropped hectare of foodgrain (**IMDNHA**): Bangladesh 1960–61 to 1990–91   58

4.3 Relationship between capital intensity (indices of irrigated hectare per man-day of employment generated in the production of *rabi* crops, **IMODRMD**) and total *rabi* season employment (**IMDR**): Bangladesh 1960–61 to 1990–91   63

4.4 Relationship between capital intensity (indices of irrigated hectare per man-day of employment generated in the production of *rabi* crops, **IMODRMD**) and labour intensity per hectare of *rabi* foodgrains (**IMDHFR**): Bangladesh 1960–61 to 1990–91   64

4.5   Trends in indices (1969–70 = 100) of real agricultural
      (**RWINDEX1** and **RWINDEX2**) and industrial wages
      (**INDWAGE**): Bangladesh 1969–70 to 1993–94.
      RWINDEX1 and **RWINDEX2** are indices of real
      wages derived by deflating nominal wages and food
      commodities respectively. **INDWAGE** are indices of real
      industrial wages   76
5.1   Schematic diagram representing inter-relationships
      among technology, the environment and employment   81
6.1   Property rights and environmental outcome   101
6.2   Property rights issues in shrimp farming in Bangladesh   111
7.1   Anticipated improvement in the economic position of
      households for restoration of natural environment/resources
      of 5–10 years ago as a function of their relative economic
      position in the villages of Barakuli, Kamla and Maharajpur,
      India, September, 1992   121
8.1   Basic requirements for the sustainability of
      agricultural techniques. Only techniques or projects in the
      overlapping sections (dotted) satisfy all the requirements
      for sustainability   129
8.2   Illustrations of sustainable and unsustainable agricultural
      systems according to Conway (1985a, 1987)   130
8.3   Due to environmental spillovers or externalities, private
      and social benefits from economic projects may differ.
      This diagram indicates three alternative possibilities   133
8.4   Map of Bangladesh showing the general location of the
      Barind Tract   135
8.5   The seven North-East Hill States of India. They are
      Arunachal Pradesh (1), Nagaland (2), Manipur (3),
      Mizoram (4), Tripura (5), Meghalaya (6) and Assam (7)   139
9.1   Shrimp farming areas and locations of other sub-sectors
      of the shrimp industry in Bangladesh   147
9.2   Relative shares of different shrimp farming methods in
      Bangladesh   150
9.3   Shrimp in export trade: 1972–73 to 1993–94   154
9.4   Major shrimp farming countries with their relative
      contribution to world production (per cent)   155
9.5   Regional distribution of shrimp area and output, 1992   157
9.6   Schematic diagram of Bangladesh's shrimp industry
      showing sectoral linkages   166

10.1 Power generation and gross power loss: Bangladesh,
     1972–73 to 1993–94   176
10.2 Trend in production and consumption of natural gas in
     Bangladesh, 1983–84 to 1992–93   180
10.3 Changing pattern of use of natural gas in Bangladesh:
     1983–84 to 1992–93   180

Foreword

Environmental issues are important and, somewhat belatedly, they are now recognised as important. However, while the interaction of environmental change and development has received some lip service, the vital nature of that interaction is not well documented. In particular, there is inadequate recognition that in developing countries this interaction occurs substantially in rural areas. Given the neglect of the rural interactions between development and the environment, it is not suprising that little farm level data are marshalled and analysed to shed light on these interactions in the rural sector. Finally, one cannot view environmental development interactions without analysing poverty and its corollary of employment, and that in an urban as well as a rural context.

We now have a book that takes up all these requisites for meaningful analysis. Naturally an empirical approach must concentrate if it is to be down to earth and meaningful. This book uses South Asia to explore these interacting forces, and gives special weight to Bangladesh. The latter choice allows the authors to draw upon the wealth of specific knowledge from their earlier book on the Green Revolution and economic development. After all it is the green revolution that raises many of the environmental issues at the same time that it offers major prospect for accelerated growth and poverty reduction.

Thus this book represents a natural historical evolution from a stagnant, very poor economy to one engaged in the transition to development, and now one encountering the complex problems of interaction of environment and development. In this context the authors refer constantly to empirical data with a heavy emphasis on micro data from the villages.

While much of the pressure for environmental attention comes from the high income countries, that concern is generally not matched by knowledge of how the environmental problem differs in relatively poor countries. Sanitation, which is an environmental issue in both rich and poor countries, takes quite different forms in poor countries with very different health effects. The need to get over a hump of development – that is onto a track that will bring rapid increase in levels of living and reduction in poverty is also a problem of poor countries that is not shared by rich countries.

Thus, dealing with the externalities of global environmental problems requires a knowledge of differences and objectives and solutions. It is only from that knowledge that intelligent decisions can be made in the high income countries with respect to global problems that are strongly influenced by actions in developing countries.

Bangladesh is a particularly important case for protracted treatment to shed light on more general issues. It is still one of the poorest countries in the world. But, it has progressed immensely from the 'basket case' description by Henry Kissinger in the early 1970s. It seems squarely on track for soon achieving high growth rates. It is a potential major loser from global warming and its accompaniment of rising water levels onto a low flat country. It is encountering the problems of massive growth in urban areas, a series of problems associated with the green revolution, and is still significantly foreign aid dependent. It differs from the general run of African countries in having the basic processes of growth underway. It differs from the Asian front-runners in still facing high levels of poverty. Thus the treatment can draw upon mistakes of the earlier take-off Asian countries and benefit the still lagging African countries. And, of course, with a city in the top 25 in population size and an immense over-all population that is still growing rapidly it is of considerable importance in its own right.

Bangladesh represents a quite different water problem than that facing most countries. It is flooded almost every year, lying in the flood plain of two of the world's largest rivers. Even so, problems of salinity, declining water table in some areas and of course ground and surface water pollution are real and growing problems in Bangladesh.

In a world that pays far more attention than in the past to letting markets operate and to the private sector, it is useful to view how a poor developing country in which operation of the market may penalise very poor people and in which the private sector is still small, copes with the interplay of environmental and growth forces. Bangladesh is an excellent laboratory for treating these issues.

The developing countries have provided numerous demonstrations of the advantages of communal, or community organisation for management of natural resources. That favourable effect has generally been in comparison with public sector operation of resources and the associated corruption. The rule seems to be, get management of resources as close as possible to the people who depend on those resources if good stewardship is needed. Bangladesh and hence this book provide several illustrations of the incumbent issues. This treatment is particularly valuable for lessons to the developed countries as well as other developing countries.

Finally, a distinction needs always to be made, in the rural context, between low productivity, marginal resources and high productivity, resources. Not only is the nature of the environment problem different in the two situations, but the solutions are quite different as well. Bangladesh is generally a country of high potential rural resources, but it also contains marginal upland areas allowing illustration of the special conflicts between environmental stewardship and wresting a minimal living from those resources.

Thus, we have a feast of ideas well illustrated, by authors who have a deep understanding of the developmental problems and issues. They are then able to place those developmental issues in the context of contemporary very real concerns for the environment and provide solutions that have broad applicability.

John W. Mellor

Acknowledgements

The authors and publishers gratefully acknowledge the following for permission to reproduce copyright material:

Figure 1.2 comes from *World Development*, Vol. 19, No. 6, pp. 607–21, 'Sustainable Development: A Critical Review', with permission from Elsevier Science Ltd, The Boulevard, Langford Lane, Kidlington OX5, 1GB, UK.

Chapter 4 is a modified version reprinted from *World Development*, Vol. 23, No. 2, pp. 281–97, 1995, 'Labour Absorption and Agricultural Development', with permission from Elsevier Science Ltd, The Boulevard, Langford Lane, Kidlington OX5, 1GB, UK

Chapter 5 relates in modified form to pp. 221–55 and Figure 5.1 to pp. 69–92 of *Beyond Rio: Environmental crisis and sustainable livelihoods in the Third World*, by Ahmed, I. and Doelman, J.A. (eds). Copyright © International Labour Organization 1995. Published on behalf of the ILO by Macmillan Press Ltd, London.

Preface

The period encompassing the last two to three decades has witnessed prolific growth in the literature on the relationship between economic development and the environment. The concern about the environment has become one of the potent political factors that have shaped politics in industrialised countries and engendered a debate that concerns not only the environmental consequences of economic development through industrialisation, but also environmental degradation in non-industrialised economies. The question of environmental change has become a key element in discussion and analysis of Third World development. This volume explores the environment–development relationship in the South Asian context concentrating on Bangladesh. One might note that 1997 marks the 50th year of the end of British colonialism in South Asia and it is just more than a quarter of a century since Bangladesh achieved its independence from Pakistan.

This book is the product of several years of joint research funded in part by research grants from Australian Research Council (ARC), Australian Centre for International Agricultural Research (ACIAR) and International Labour Office (ILO).

We wish to thank Professors Muhammad Iqbal Zuberi and K.P Nath, and Drs Mustafa K. Mujeri, Kartik C. Roy and Raj Kumar Sen for supply of useful materials and for sharing ideas of assistance in the completion of this book. The usual *caveat* applies.

We wish to thank Mr Akhter Hamid for his excellent research assistance, and Mrs Jeannine Fowler and Mrs Robyn McDonald for typing assistance. We also gratefully acknowledge useful assistance from Ms Farzana Alauddin, Mr Faridul Huq, Ms Nilufar Jahan and Ms Tatjana Kehren at various stages. For primary materials for some case studies, Mohammad Alauddin wishes to thank Mr Shamim Hassan and his team, Mr Ataur Rahman and Mr Motaher Hossain Miah.

In relation to his contribution Clem Tisdell has benefited from seminar papers which he was invited to present at: the Department of Economics, the Research School of Pacific and Asian Studies, The Australian National University; the Centre for Migration and Development Studies, University of Western Australia; the Bangladesh Institute of Development Studies (Dhaka); Rajshahi University (Rajshahi); International Institute of Development Studies (Calcutta); The University of California (Riverside);

York University (UK); The University of Greifswald (Germany); Kiel University; Swedish University of Agricultural Sciences, Uppsala; and the Northeastern Hills University (Aizawl Campus), Mizoram (India). Mohammad Alauddin has benefited from seminar and conference papers he presented at: the Department of Economics, the Research School of Pacific and Asian Studies, The Australian National University; World Aquaculture '96 (Bangkok); ACIAR-Thai Department of Fisheries Workshop (Hatyai, Thailand); and the conference celebrating twenty-five years of independence of Bangladesh (Brisbane, Australia). Of course none of those mentioned above is responsible in any way for any short-comings in this book.

We wish to express our gratitude to the Department of Economics, The University of Queensland for the use of facilities and the congenial atmos-phere that we enjoyed during the period of writing this book.

We are grateful to Macmillan Press Ltd., especially Mr Tim Farmiloe, for accepting our manuscript and extending the deadline for its comple-tion. We also wish to thank Ms Linda Auld, Editorial Service Consultant for excellent copy-editing of our original manuscript.

We wish to express our gratitude to Professors John W. Mellor and Vernon W. Ruttan for their encouragement for our research in this area. The usual *caveat* applies.

We thank the International Labour Office and Elsevier for permission to use copyright materials.

Finally we wish to thank our families for their patience and understand-ing, without which the book could hardly have been completed.

MOHAMMAD ALAUDDIN
CLEMENT ALLAN TISDELL

1 Changing Views and Perspectives on the Environment–Development Nexus

1.1 INTRODUCTION

The period encompassing the last two to three decades has witnessed prolific growth in the literature on the relationship between economic development and the environment. It is now widely recognised that the economic development–environment relationship can be delicate and that a ruthless pursuit of growth can cause substantial irreversible damage to the environment and can threaten sustainability of development (Ahmed and Doeleman 1995; Pearce 1993). As Woodhouse (1992, p.121) succinctly puts it:

> ... the concern with 'global environment' has become one of the potent political factors shaping politics in industrialised countries, engendering a debate that concerns not only the environmental consequences of economic development through industrialisation, but also environmental degradation in non-industrialised economies... the question of environmental change has become a key element in discussion and analysis of Third World development.

This chapter provides a broad picture of the changing views and perspectives on the environment and development in LDCs. It briefly traces the historical background to the environment–development relationship and specifically asks: Why did environmental issues not feature in earlier development literature? How important is the environment in the contemporary development literature? Why this change? These questions are addressed keeping in view the problems facing the LDCs. This chapter also provides an overview of issues and the plan of this volume.

1

1.2   CHANGING VIEWS AND PERSPECTIVES ON THE
ENVIRONMENT–DEVELOPMENT NEXUS

The concern about environmental consequences of and constraints on development is fairly recent even though it is long overdue. As World Bank (1992, p.1) puts it:

> ... although the desirability of development is universally recognised, recent years have witnessed rising concern about whether environmental constraints will limit development and whether development will cause serious environmental change – in turn impairing the quality of life of this and future generations ...

World Bank (1992) also views the environment–development nexus in a two-way relationship in that:

● *environmental quality is itself part of the improvement in human welfare which is supposed to result from development; and*
● *environmental damage can undermine future productivity growth – a critical factor in economic development.*

Earlier literature on development paid very little attention to the environment–development relationship. Even though environmental economics is not new (its theoretical underpinnings lie in the main in welfare economics), it did not develop as a coherent body of literature until the 1960s. Pearce and Maler (1991, p.52) suggest its application to LDCs is more recent still and it is only in the last decade or so that significant advances in this area have been made.

The World Commission on Environment and Development (WCED 1987, also known as the Brundtland Report) played a central role in defining environmental aspects of economic development. According to this report sustainable development is defined as 'Development that meets the needs of the present without compromising the ability of future generations to meet their own needs ... ' (WCED 1987, p.43).

Since this report and earlier and subsequent concerns (Conway 1986; Tisdell 1988; Barbier 1987; Pearce *et al.* 1990; Douglass 1984; Pearce 1993; Lele 1991) the operational significance of environmentally sustainable development has assumed new dimensions. The focus has shifted significantly to considering the sustainability of ecosystems and environmental factors on which continued agricultural development in particular and economic development in general depends. There is a growing realisation that despite the non-existence of markets for many environmental goods there is little or no excuse for treating them as 'free goods'. Furthermore, there is an increasing acceptance of the view that the concept of sustainability must be integrated in project appraisal. There seems to be a growing realisation that the spectacular economic growth, especially in the developed countries, at least in part can be attributed to the 'cost' imposed on the environment through the depletion of non-renewable natural resources and damage to the physical environment. For instance it is argued 'although the GNP of Indonesia increased at 7 per cent a year between 1970 and 1984, the true growth rate would fall to 4 per cent a year' after allowing for the depreciation of natural capital resulting from environmental degradation (Repetto *et al.* 1989). This type of discrepancy between 'nominal' growth rates and growth rates adjusted for environmental degradation may be characteristic of many LDCs including Bangladesh (Bhalla 1992).

The next section discusses the issues considered and the plan of this volume. As a prelude to that let us provide a brief overview, in terms of selected indicators, of four major South Asian countries (shown in Figure 1.1): Bangladesh, India, Pakistan and Sri Lanka .

Table 1.1 sets out some basic information on the four South Asian countries. The following points are worth noting:

- *Bangladesh is the second smallest country both in terms of population and geographical area. However, Bangladesh is three times as densely populated as India and Sri Lanka and is five times as densely populated as Pakistan.*
- *Bangladesh has the lowest per capita income among the four countries while Sri Lanka's per capita income is the highest in the group.*
- *Life expectancy at birth for Sri Lanka is far ahead of the other three countries. A similar picture emerges in regard to adult literacy rate. Percentage of female labour force is the highest for Sri Lanka followed closely by India. Bangladesh has the lowest percentage of female labour force.*
- *Bangladesh is the least industrialised of the four South Asian nations as indicated by the share of their manufacturing sector.*

While problems of the environment, poverty, and low level of economic development are widespread throughout the Third World, there are few regions where they have taken a more severe toll than in the Indian subcontinent. This region is the home of more than a billion people and is characterised by a dwindling supply of arable land per capita, a very high

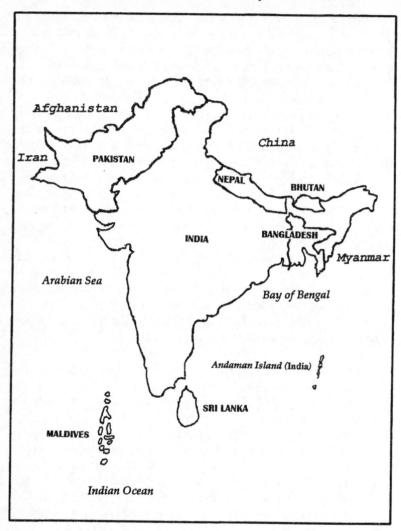

Figure 1.1   A generalised map of South Asia

rate of population growth, and a declining stock of natural resources. Simplistically one could identify a two-way causation between poverty and environmental degradation. However, a closer examination reveals that both poverty and environmental degradation have deep and complex causes. High rates of population growth complicate the problems even

Table 1.1 Four major South Asian countries: Some selected indicators of socio-economic development

South Asia	Population 'millions' mid-1994	Total Area '000' sq. km	Population density	Life expectancy at birth (years) 1994	Adult literacy rate (%) 1995	Female labour force (% of total) 1993	GNP per capita US$ 1994	Average inflation rate (%) 1984–94	Share of GDP (%) 1994			
									Agriculture	Industry	Manufacturing	Services
Bangladesh	117.9	144	819	57	38	8	220	6.6	30	18	10	52
India	913.6	3288	278	62	52	25	320	9.7	30	28	18	42
Pakistan	126.3	796	158	60	38	13	430	8.8	25	25	18	50
Sri Lanka	17.9	66	271	72	90	27	640	11.0	24	25	16	51

Source: Based on World Bank (1995a, 1996b); UNDP (1996).

further (Mahtab and Karim 1992; Myers 1992; Dasgupta 1992). Following
Lele (1991, pp.614–5) the complexity of the issues can be illustrated using
Figure 1.2.

1.3   ISSUES CONSIDERED AND THE PLAN OF THIS VOLUME

Against this background this volume examines the environment–
development–poverty nexus concentrating on the situation of Bangladesh
but also considering the comparative circumstances of South Asia
generally. Where possible examples are drawn from other LDCs.

Chapter 2 overviews environmental issues and biodiversity as well as
welfare in South Asia paying particular attention to the Bangladesh
context but providing a comparative analysis. It identifies major environmental issues, their socio-economic impact and consequences for the

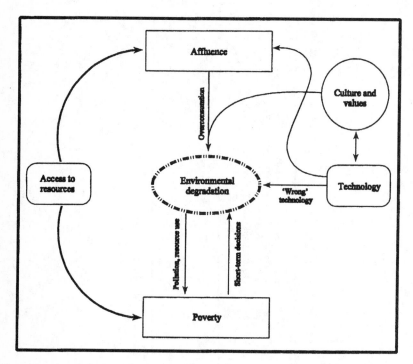

Figure 1.2   A schematic representation of the poverty–environmental degradation
problem

welfare of the population. There is a growing body of literature (for example, Ahmad *et al.* 1989, WRI 1990b, Pearce 1993) which points out that the present system of national accounting suffers from limitations in as much as it does not contain an explicit environmental dimension. The recent literature contains several approaches to natural resource accounting (El Serafy and Lutz 1989; Pearce 1993; Repetto *et al.* 1989). The present exercise attempts to apply a range of approaches to the Bangladesh context while recognising the limitations of each (see, for instance, WRI 1990a; Mahmud *et al.* 1991).

Chapter 3 identifies the relationship between natural resources and the environment with special emphasis on land and water resources in Bangladesh. Both land and water resources are under considerable strain from intensification and extension of agriculture facilitated by the Green Revolution technologies, inappropriate government policies for water use and development, deforestation and loss of natural vegetation cover. According to Hasan (1996, p.234) the important issues of Bangladesh's water sector include poor charge of aquifers, increased salinity in coastal areas, drainage schemes to modify wetlands and the major changes in the watersheds outside Bangladesh with effects on its water supplies. The major problems are essentially man-made. The close relationship between environmental, economic and other problems in Bangladesh is illustrated.

Chapter 4 provides an in-depth analysis of the process of technological change and employment generation in Bangladesh especially on farms. Earlier studies (Alauddin and Tisdell 1991b; Tisdell and Alauddin 1992; Jayasuriya and Shand 1986; Ishikawa 1978) cautioned about the ability of the agricultural sector to generate sufficient employment to absorb all new entrants into the labour market. The initial optimism surrounding the ability of the Green Revolution technologies to create a very high level of employment in agriculture and absorb surplus agricultural labour seems to have remained largely unrealised. This is despite some positive employment effects of the Green Revolution especially during the dry season. In this chapter labour intensities per cropped hectare before and after the introduction of the new agricultural technology are estimated. Constraints to further employment growth in the agricultural sector are investigated. Furthermore, this chapter considers sustainability of employment both on- and off-farm, including employment in highly urbanised areas. It also examines the extent to which the latter is dependent on the agricultural surplus being maintained. In this connection non-agricultural employment prospects are examined.

Against the background of the preceding discussion, Chapter 5 provides insights from farm-level data on the technology–environment–employment nexus in rural Bangladesh. Environmental issues are to a large extent a result of changes in technology. It must be emphasised, however, that environmental problems are not confined to rural Bangladesh. Serious environmental problems exist in urban areas as well. Nevertheless, rural environmental issues predominate, for Bangladesh is primarily a rural society. The focus of Chapter 5 is on major economic and related environmental changes which have occurred in three Bangladesh villages. These changes have been associated with, *inter alia,* the adoption of new agricultural technologies, population growth and penetration of market forces. These have impacted on employment opportunities to earn a livelihood. These effects are documented using case studies from three villages from three ecologically different areas of Bangladesh. The specific empirical evidence from the three study villages follows a brief overview of rural environmental trends and a disaggregated analysis from district level secondary data on crop sector employment. The objective is to investigate if the broad trends considered in Chapters 3 and 4 are supported by farm-level evidence.

International development agencies now stress the importance of good governance and appropriate property rights as prerequisites for sustainable development. This implies a close relationship between governance, property rights and the environment. Chapter 6 explores this relationship. The orthodox western economics favours private and state property compared to communal property. Consequently, western economics overlooks the scope for beneficial administration of resources by local communities or by co-management. Examples from Bangladesh and India are employed to analyse the close connections between governance, property rights and the state of the environment.

Chapter 7 concentrates on the income distribution consequences of recorded environmental changes in rural India and Bangladesh making use of village level data. It identifies winners and possible losers from such changes. Special attention is paid to the plight of many of the rural poor following these changes. It provides a brief critique of the existing literature (eg. Quibria 1994) which pays inadequate attention to environmental and gender matters in development in rural poverty analysis. This chapter concentrates on possible variations in the relative economic position of the rural poor compared to those who are better off. It summarises some of our previous findings from village surveys in Bangladesh and the Indian state West Bengal. The status of women and children is examined in the development process.

Chapter 8 examines environmental consequences of agricultural development in marginal upland areas in Bangladesh, concentrating on the *Barind* Tract. It is well known that the North Western part of Bangladesh, especially parts of (greater) Rajshahi district, suffers from severe shortage of ground water. Variable and low levels of annual rainfall, large scale destruction of the flora, and the construction of the Farakka barrage in the Indian part of the Ganges are believed to have aggravated the situation. Large scale irrigation projects like the IDA deep tubewell scheme have not taken adequate account of the hydrological conditions, the ecology and the environment. The extension of modern agricultural practices ('Green Revolution' technologies) to these areas seems likely to result in unsustainable agriculture. A number of these changes are also associated with the displacement or partial displacement on the land of local tribal people, the Santals, by Bengalis and this has involved the replacement of one set of land-use technology by another. Public policy is encouraging the above trends. This chapter examines the implications of such developments for the sustainability of development and of rural communities and also includes a case study on Northeast India.

Chapter 9 adds to the previous empirical analysis to provide a special case study of environmental impacts of economic change, namely of shrimp (prawn) cultivation in Bangladesh since it has significant environmental impacts. Shrimp exports of late contributed substantially to Bangladesh's export earnings and have created a significant amount of employment via backward and forward linkages. The existing literature pays scant attention to its possible adverse impact on the ecology, environment and agriculture. This study counterbalances this. It employs primary data on shrimp farm owners (known as *gher* owners), landowners and landless/near landless households (primarily wage labourers). The objective is to identify gainers and losers from prawn aquaculture. It investigates: employment gain/loss due to shrimp cultivation; effect on the environment; income distribution; possible conflicts between agriculture and aquaculture; and conflicts of interests between landowners and shrimp farm owners.

Energy is often considered to be a key factor in industrialisation and modernisation. Chapter 10 looks at energy resources in Bangladesh and South Asia generally and gives special attention to the supply and distribution of natural gas. Natural gas is Bangladesh's most abundant commercial energy resource but it is also a non-renewable resource. Institutional factors affecting the exploitation of this resource in Bangladesh are discussed, for example, pricing policies, distribution policies and so on. In several parts of Bangladesh, for example northern and southwestern districts, there is a fuel wood crisis but natural gas is not available. Although government regulations forbid the burning of timber in brick-kilns the people of these areas have no alternative and this adds to the increasing loss of the few remaining trees. The analysis focuses on the current state of play in respect of energy use and conservation and their implications for sustainable energy use.

Chapter 11 considers sectoral changes and the urbanisation process and outlines demographic trends. Urban environmental issues such as health, housing, sanitation, and garbage disposal are considered. Chapter 11 places the environmental situation in Bangladesh and South Asia in the global context. On a global scale, South Asia is environmentally significant. Its economic growth and development is important to the rest of the world in a number of ways:

- *Its economic growth, along with that of China, can be expected to result in a significant emission of greenhouse gases with consequential climatic changes and sea-level rises.*
- *The Indian subcontinent as a whole is a significant storehouse of bio–diversity and loss in bio-diversity on the subcontinent will be an international loss.*
- *Failure to achieve sustainable economic development on the Indian subcontinent, because of resource-depleting economic growth, may eventually result in economic collapse and the inability of the economies of the region to meet the basic needs of their population on a vaster and ecologically more catastrophic scale than hitherto. Resource-depletion could result in a collapse similar to that predicted for the Club of Rome on a global scale and this would pose a major humanitarian problem for the rest of the world.*
- *Failure to internalise environmental costs in business decisions could result in South Asia being involved in 'unfair and unjust' production for international trade. Now that India is adopting structural adjustment policies such possibilities may assume greater international significance.*

The rest of the world also has significant environmental impacts on the Indian subcontinent, or potentially so. Possible impacts relating to the environment include:

- *Sea level rises due mainly (but not entirely) to greenhouse gas emissions outside South Asia.*
- *Conditions imposed on foreign aid or loans, ensuring environmental impacts are taken into account but still effectively side-stepping the main environmental issues.*

- *External pressures to make economic reforms (eg. adopt structural adjustment policies), which may have environmental consequences.*
- *Influence from the rest of the world on international trade where, for example, this trade is restricted by environmental prerequisites.*
- *International conventions, such as the Convention on Biodiversity.*

Most of the issues which arise in South Asia in connection with the environment–technology–growth–employment nexus are not unique to it. There are parallels for example in Africa and other parts of Asia and such similarities are noted.

2 The Environment, Biodiversity and Development in South Asia

2.1 INTRODUCTION

Growth of production in the major South Asian economies has been relatively rapid since 1980 and has accelerated compared to the 1970s. While this growth has been less rapid than that of major low-income East Asian economies, the difference in growth rates between these areas may have been exaggerated in popular discussions describing the East Asian 'economic miracle' (Chakravarty 1990). However, faster population growth in most South Asian economies than in most East Asian economies has meant that per capita incomes in the former have grown at a much slower rate than in the latter. Some East Asian economies have completed demographic transition or are well on the way to doing so, even though there are notable exceptions such as the Philippines (Ogawa and Tsuya 1993). Table 2.1 provides some supporting comparative data on growth of production and population in selected South and East Asian economies.

Table 2.1 does not, of course, portray fully the diversity of economic experiences in both regions. If all countries in East Asia are considered, economic performances vary considerably, for example, if Laos or Mynamar are included, and the economic experience of the Philippines has been less satisfactory than that of most South Asian economies. Differences in growth rates of economic production have sometimes been attributed to whether individual economies are inward- or outward-looking in the orientation of their economic policies. Given the preference of the IMF and the World Bank for structural adjustment and free trade policies, there may have been a tendency to exaggerate any signs supporting this position and underplay other factors, such as the role of 'fortuitous' natural resource exports in the growth of some South East Asian economies, (for example, oil in the case of Indonesia, also timber exports in Indonesia's case and in a number of other cases).

Table 2.1   Rates of growth of production and population in selected South and East Asian economies

	GDP Annual percentage increase		Population Annual percentage increase	
	1970–80	1980–92	1970–80	1980–92
South Asia				
Bangladesh	2.3	4.2	2.6	2.3
India	3.4	5.2	2.3	2.1
Pakistan	4.9	6.1	3.1	3.1
Sri Lanka	4.1	4.0	1.6	1.2
East Asia				
China	–	9.1	1.8	1.4
Indonesia	7.2	5.7	2.3	1.8
The Philippines	6.0	1.2	2.5	2.4
Thailand	7.1	8.2	2.7	1.8

Source: Based on World Bank (1994, Tables 2 and 25).

Both in South and East Asia economic growth is proceeding at a sufficient pace to have substantial impacts on natural environments. Since the 1970s considerable loss has occurred of forested and woodland areas in Asia, and use of agricultural land has intensified principally as a consequence of the green revolution (Alauddin and Tisdell 1991c). Water utilisation and scarcity of water has increased, pollution of water and air has risen in many Asian areas and biological diversity has fallen. Economic production is starting to dominate most Asian economies as they increasingly become interdependent market economies (Roy *et al.* 1992). This is reflected in the pace of investment in infrastructure in Asia for such items as roads, communication systems, electricity generation, water supplies and irrigation, safe water and sanitation (World Bank 1994). While such developments often improve human welfare and man-made environments, they alter natural environments considerably and contribute to loss of biodiversity.

Asia's environmental problem is not just a matter of the volume of its wastes, but also their concentration. With rising urbanisation in Asia, concentration of wastes in metropolitan areas is rising, giving problems of disposal of sewage. While it is true that concentration of population may improve economies of treatment of wastes, the effect of 'treatment' may be localised. For example, more households may be connected to sewers but less nightsoil may be recycled in agriculture and aquaculture. This recycling has been the past Chinese practice. Thus the organic load of large water bodies such as rivers is increased and spillovers from cities may occur even at distant points from the urban areas. For example, the increasing incidence of red tides in the China Sea (which make fish poisonous to humans) is attributed by some to such factors. Furthermore, this type of organic pollution as well as industrial pollution could threaten China's very large aquaculture industry as China's economic growth proceeds.

2.2   THE IMPORTANCE OF NATURAL ENVIRONMENTAL RESOURCE STOCK AND SUSTAINABLE DEVELOPMENT: A DIGRESSION

Classical economists emphasized the importance of capital accumulation (man-made capital) as a vehicle of economic growth and development. For example, Marx (1956) stressed its importance and this led Paul Samuelson to suggest that for Marx capital accumulation as a means to economic growth was equivalent to most of the wisdom bequeathed by Moses and all the prophets. In addition, Engels (1959) stressed the significance of scientific and technological progress for economic growth in a trenchant attack on Malthusian economic theory.

Most economic growth and development models favoured in the mid-20th century saw capital and labour (population) as the main determinants of production, for example, the Solow–Swan model (Solow 1956; Swan 1956). Solow (1957) subsequently extended the model to include techno-logical change as an autonomous or exogenous variable in the economy's production function. This growth model was nevertheless not constrained by environmental or natural resource factors (Tisdell 1990, Ch. 3). It seemed that capital accumulation via savings and continued technological progress held the key to long-term sustainable growth and economic development. In relation to economic development, approaches such as those of Meier (1976) stressed that physical capital accumulation was essential and gave little or no attention to the role of natural resources and the environment in economic development.

It is true that in the 1970s neoclassical economic growth gave increas-ing attention to natural resources, especially depletable non-renewable resources. In general, it was believed that such resources were unlikely to pose limits or significant barriers to economic growth (Solow 1974, 1986). Neoclassical economists generally remained optimistic about the prospects for economic growth and for continuing economic development and rejected views unfavourable to this outlook such as those associated with the Club of Rome (Meadows *et al. 1972*, 1992).

The empirical studies of Denison (1962) pointed strongly (at least, in developed countries) to the significance of qualitative factors, such as education and technological progress, as sources of economic growth and suggested that they might be an even more important source of economic growth than increases in the quantity of physical capital and of labour. Furthermore, it was recognized that economies of scale in use of infrastructure could be important.

'New' endogenous economic growth theories (e.g. Romer 1986, 1994) have incorporated human capital (such as the production and transmission of knowledge) into their models and have allowed for possible external economies in economic growth. However, these theories, like their predecessors, have tended to ignore possible environmental and natural resource constraints on economic growth. In this respect, they contrast with those of writers such as Mäler (1974), Pearce *et al.* (1990, 1993), Perrings (1987) and Turner *et al.* (1993). These writers stress the importance of conserving natural environmental capital stock in order to achieve sustainable development. Diminution or destruction of this stock either by its depletion for its economic use or by pollution (the environment is used as a sink for wastes from human activity including economic activity) can threaten sustainable development.

Traditional economic discussions of economic activity have usually ignored the interdependence of such activity with the natural environment. For example, circular flow diagrams of the operation of the market economy have done this. However, the economic system cannot or does not function independently of the natural environment. The natural environment is a sink for wastes from households and productive activities such as those engaged in by business firms. It also provides inputs or resources for production as well as goods and services directly consumed by individuals and households: fresh air, recreational possibilities, etc. If natural environments are destroyed or depleted this can limit economic activity and the welfare obtained from environmental services by individuals and households. The links are emphasized in Figure 2.1 which extends the traditional circular economic flow diagram to include the natural environment. Note that the natural environment may be adversely affected by pollution from wastes arising from economic activity or by economic activity which uses natural environmental resources and thereby depletes or damages these.

In relation to Figure 2.1, note that with rapid economic growth in Asia, the scale of demands on the natural environment in Asia are increasing rapidly.

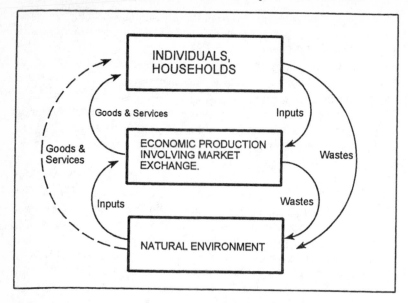

Figure 2.1 Economic links with the natural environment

Consequently, both the demand to use natural resources for economic production is rising and so too is the demand to use the natural environment as a sink for pollution and wastes from human activity. Thus, concern has arisen about the sustainability of Asia's projected economic growth.

Most environmental economists (Pearce 1993, Ch. 2) stress that in considering economic growth and development, particularly its sustainability, three types of capital stock play a significant role:

- *man-made capital, mostly physical capital*
- *human capital, including technical and scientific knowledge and education*
- *natural environmental capital.*

Possible relationships between these forms of capital and labour as an input into the production of man-made capital are indicated in Figure 2.2. Social and cultural capital might, in addition, be considered as a part of human capital and includes the stock and nature of institutions in society. Production of physical capital (and in some cases, human capital) is often at the expense of the stock of natural environmental capital.

The question has arisen of the extent to which it is possible to safely substitute other forms of capital for the stock of natural environmental

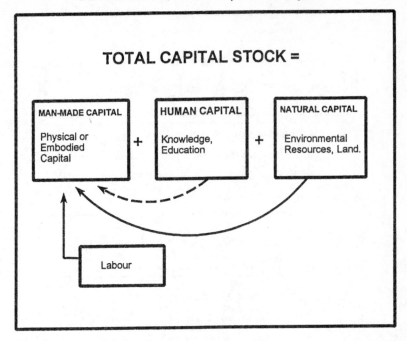

Figure 2.2   Production of man-made capital usually draws on natural capital and makes use of human capital and labour. Man-made capital is subject to depreciation, but natural capital is not usually and the same is true for human capital

resources and still sustain economic development. Two different stand-points have been identified in the literature (Pearce 1993, Ch. 2):

- *Substitution of physical and human capital for natural environmental capital is likely to be compatible with sustainable development (this is identified as weak sustainability since it proposes weak conditions for sustainable development).*
- *The view that such substitution is incompatible with sustainable development is described as strong sustainability since it proposes a strong condition for sustainable development, namely that the stock of natural environmental resources be fully preserved.*

The conditions for sustainable development as classified by Pearce (1993) apply to sustainable development in the sense commonly used by economists, namely that the incomes of future generations be no less than those

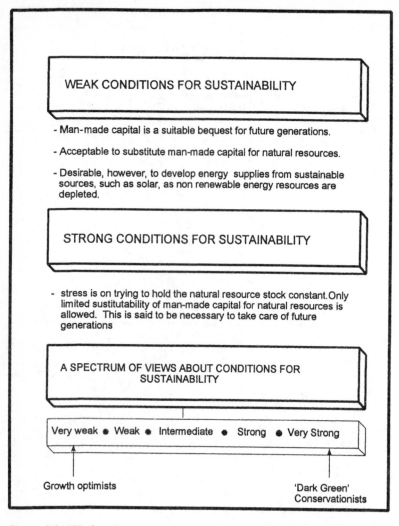

Figure 2.3 Weak and strong conditions for sustainable development and spectrum of views about those conditions according to Pearce (1993, Ch 2.)

of present generations. There are a spectrum of views about the extent to which natural environmental resources can be forgone and development can be sustained in the above sense. These are summarised in Figure 2.3 along the lines suggested by Pearce (1993). In Asia, it appears that weak conditions for sustainability have been accepted, at least in the past, and that growth optimism is the dominant political force.

Note that Pearce's classification, given his accepted definition of sustainable development, is anthropocentric. However, ecocentric values should also be considered. Some individuals argue that positive weight should be put on preserving or not extinguishing other species, independently of the wishes of individual humans. Given this point of view, some 'dark green' conservationists may in fact favour conserving natural environments even when this is at the expense of the income of present and future generations. Whether or not Asian countries are likely to put much weight on ecocentrism or the preservation of other species for their own sake can be debated. However, features of Buddhism and Hinduism support such ethics and the Chinese traditional view of the importance of balance of mankind with nature can also support wider conservation ethics than purely man-centred ones.

An intermediate position on conservation (not captured in Figure 2.3) has been proposed by Turner *et al.* (1993), namely that substitution of other forms of capital for natural environmental capital is consistent with sustainability except for substitution from a *core* of the natural resource stock. Once the stock of natural environmental capital is reduced to the core, strong sustainability conditions apply. Note that as a result of global economic growth we may be rapidly approaching the core of the natural environmental stock for the world as a whole or possibly could have reached it. It is even possible that some individual Asian countries such as Bangladesh and China, are already approaching a similar situation. If so, they would need to be wary of increasing their physical capital stocks at the expense of their natural environmental stocks. In any case, all countries, including those in Asia, should attempt to preserve their environmental core if they want to achieve sustainable development. Unfortunately, however, Turner *et al.* have not provided us with a simple means to identify the core of the natural environmental resource stock.

The above may indicate that while the early economic ascent of mankind obtained by substituting other forms of capital for natural capital was appropriate, this process is less appropriate now because natural resource stocks have become reduced. This constraint (if it is a real one) may be especially unfortunate for less developed countries, such as those in Asia, because much of the reduction of the globe's natural resources has not been of their own making but brought about by more developed countries. Nevertheless, despite this, it would be pointless to ignore the question of whether economic growth in Asian countries is sustainable in view of its likely impacts on their natural environments.

2.3   DEMOGRAPHIC FEATURES

Most neo-Malthusians (e.g. Daly 1980; Ehrlich 1970, Meadows *et al.* 1992) see rising populations and increasing levels of per capita economic production as the main threats to natural environments. While appropriate advances in technology can reduce the adverse impact of these factors, they are unlikely to offset these completely in the longer term as for example suggested by Georgescu-Roegen (1971, 1976). Because Asia contains more than half the world's population, the growth in its population level is of particular interest from an environmental viewpoint.

In most Asian countries, the rate of population growth is declining. However, this is not the case for all as can be seen from Table 2.1 and rates of population growth are still high for most low income countries in the region, although Sri Lanka and China have relatively low rates of population growth. On the whole, the rate of population increase in South Asia is higher than in East Asia.

Despite encouraging signs from an environmental point of view of decreases in the rate of population growth of most countries in Asia, the population levels of the majority of these countries are predicted to rise considerably in coming decades. For example, on the basis of the World Bank's 'intermediate' predictions Bangladesh's population is expected to more than double (compared to its 1992 level) before it stabilises. The same is true for India and Pakistan and the Philippines but not for China, Sri Lanka, Indonesia and Thailand although the population of the latter two is expected to almost double. Estimates and projections of the World Bank for these countries are set out in Table 2.2.

Given these estimates and given the plans of Asian countries to increase their levels of per capita income, it is apparent that natural environments in Asia will remain under continuing and increasing threat for several decades. In addition, growth in these countries can be expected to have significant global environmental impacts, for example in adding to greenhouse gas emissions (Tisdell 1995).

As can be seen from Table 2.3, the major South Asian economies have recorded a positive average annual growth rate in per capita GNP since 1982, but their rates of growth have not been as high as in China and Thailand nor that in most East Asian countries. Nevertheless, all East Asian countries have not been high economic performers. For example, in the case of the Philippines, per capita GNP has actually declined.

It is apparent from Table 2.3 that GNP per capita in high-income countries (as classified by the World Bank) exceeds that in the low Asian income countries by several fold. For example, average per capita income in high income countries exceeds that in Bangladesh one-hundred fold, in

Table 2.2   Estimates and predictions of population levels for selected Asian countries: Totals in millions

	1992	2000	2025	Hypothetical stationary level
South Asia				
Bangladesh	114	132	182	263
India	884	1016	1370	1888
Pakistan	119	148	243	400
Sri Lanka	17	19	24	29
East Asia				
China	1162	1255	1471	1680
Indonesia	184	206	265	355
The Philippines	64	77	115	172
Thailand	58	65	81	104

Source: Based on World Bank (1994, Table 25).

Table 2.3   GNP per capita in 1992 U.S. dollars for selected Asian economies, its growth rate 1980–92 and the number of times by which GDP per capita would need to be multiplied to equal that of high-income countries

	GNP per capita	Average annual growth (%) 1980–92	Necessary multiple to equal per capita income in high income economies
South Asia			
Bangladesh	220	1.8	110.8
India	310	3.1	71.5
Pakistan	420	3.1	52.75
Sri Lanka	540	2.6	41.0
East Asia			
China	470	7.6	47.1
Indonesia	670	4.0	33.0
The Philippines	770	−1.0	28.8
Thailand	1840	6.0	12.0

Source: Based on World Bank (1994, Table 1).

the case of India by more than seventy fold, and in the case of China by 47 times. The income gap between less developed Asian countries and high income ones remains very large, despite the limitations of such comparative statistics. There is little doubt that if by some 'miracle' Asian countries were able to achieve the same level of income as in high-income countries, the environmental consequences could be catastrophic because Asia's production would increase more than fifty fold. The magnitude of this environmental effect would be further increased by the predicted doubling of Asian's population before it stabilizes.

2.4   UTILISATION OF NATURAL RESOURCES AND ENVIRONMENTAL QUALITY

With increasing population and economic production throughout Asia, utilisation of its natural resources has risen considerably. As can be seen from Table 2.4, this has been manifested in Asia by an increase in the area of cropland, a rise in the area allocated to permanent pasture and a decline in the area of forest and woodland. On the whole since 1979 the extent of deforestation in East Asia has been much greater than in South

Table 2.4   Land use in selected Asian countries, for Asia, Europe and the world as a whole – percentage change in area, 1979–91

	% change				
	Cropland	Permanent pasture	Forest and woodland	Other	Forest as % of total area
South Asia					
Bangladesh	2.1	0.0	−13.4	9.7	14.6
India	0.7	−2.0	−0.7	−1.0	22.5
Pakistan	4.0	0.0	19.7	−2.8	4.4
Sri Lanka	1.5	0.0	17.9	−14.3	32.1
East Asia					
China	−4.0	19.9	−6.5	−14.7	13.6
Indonesia	12.3	−1.5	−6.6	17.4	60.6
The Philippines	2.5	24.0	−16.9	19.5	34.7
Thailand	25.5	29.7	−14.3	−16.1	27.8
Asia	1.3	9.5	−4.9	−4.6	
Europe	−1.8	−3.7	1.1	6.2	
World	1.8	2.4	−7.8	5.5	

Source: Based on WRI *et al.* (1994, Table 17.1).

Asia, even though Bangladesh is an exception: deforestation in Bangladesh has been severe.

In addition, intensification of cropping has increased in Asia with multiple cropping rising substantially. Areas irrigated have expanded rapidly and so too has the use of artificial fertilizers and pesticides. This intensification process has had adverse impacts on natural environments.

Freshwater utilisation has risen with economic growth in Asia. It is estimated that in 1987 annual withdrawals of freshwater in Asia amounted to 15 per cent of available resources, the same percentage as for Europe (WRI *et al.* 1994, Table 22.1). However, the percentage withdrawal differs considerably between countries. In the case of Pakistan it exceeds 33 per cent. Furthermore, these annual figures disguise the fact that in many Asian countries freshwater is in especially short supply during the dry season. Most of Asia, in contrast to Europe, is subject to monsoonal influences. The extension of green revolution agricultural technologies (combined with population and income growth) have added markedly to the demand for water throughout the dry season in Asia. In some cases, this demand has been compounded by subsidisation of reticulated water supplies and open-access to water supplies.

Furthermore, water bodies have had to carry increasing loads of wastes and emissions from rising economic production and population growth. Consequently the quality of many water bodies in Asia, especially in the dry season, is well below internationally accepted standards. For example, their oxygen content is low and *E. coli* counts, for example, are high. Air quality has declined in many parts of Asia and is well below world standards in several major cities. This is mainly a consequence of increased use of fossil fuels for energy production but petrochemical and industrial plants contribute as does the increasing use of motor vehicles. Further economic growth combined with increased urbanisation can be expected to compound these problems.

2.5   URBANISATION, WASTES AND ENVIRONMENTAL PROBLEMS

Urbanisation is proceeding at a rapid pace in Asia as can be seen from Table 2.5. Between 1965 and 1995 the average annual percentage increase in urban population in Asia was 3.5 per cent. From Table 2.5, it can be seen that Bangladesh has experienced a particularly rapid rate of urbanisation but most Asian countries have experienced high rates. This has created a need for a significant expansion of economic infrastructure and has added to environmental problems.

Table 2.5   Urbanisation in Asia

	Urban population as % of total		Average annual urban population change % 1965–95
	1965	1995	
South Asia			
Bangladesh	6.2	19.5	6.7
India	18.8	26.8	3.3
Pakistan	23.5	34.7	4.2
Sri Lanka	19.9	22.4	2.1
East Asia			
China	18.2	30.3	3.5
Indonesia	15.8	32.5	4.6
The Philippines	31.6	45.7	3.9
Thailand	12.9	25.4	4.5
Asia	22.2	34.0	3.5
Europe	63.8	75.0	1.0
World	35.5	45.2	2.7

Source: Based on WRI *et al*. (1994, Table 17.2).

Despite this, all major South Asian countries have managed to increase the proportion of their urban population served by safe drinking water and sanitation (as indicated in Table 2.6) except Sri Lanka. Sri Lanka's proportionate sanitation coverage has declined. In Indonesia, in the period 1980–90 no rise occurred in the proportion of its urban population with access to safe water, while in the Philippines the proportion of its urban population having access to sanitation declined. Thus the absolute number of urban residents without safe water has risen in Indonesia as has the number without access to sanitation in the Philippines. Because of the general deterioration in water quality in Asia, the importance of having access to safe water supplies has increased (cf. Brandon and Ramankutty 1993, p.48).

In general, air quality has deteriorated to unacceptable levels in many Asian cities and disposal of wastes has become a major problem (see, for example, Brandon and Ramankutty 1993, Ch. 3). While urbanisation in Asia is growing rapidly and urban areas account for 34 per cent of Asia's population, Asia still has a considerable way to go to reach Europe's 75 per cent urbanisation figure. Further urbanisation can be expected in Asia

Table 2.6   Access of urban population to safe drinking water and sanitation in Asia, 1980 and 1990

	percentage of urban population			
	Safe drinking water		Sanitation	
	1980	1990	1980	1990
South Asia				
Bangladesh	26	39	21	40
India	73	77	27	44
Pakistan	72	82	42	53
Sri Lanka	65	80	80	68
East Asia				
China	..	72	..	100
Indonesia	35	35	29	79
The Philippines	65	93	81 .	79

Source: Based on World Bank (1994, Table A.2).

as its economic growth proceeds. Already Asia contains more than half of the world's 21 megacities.

2.6   PROTECTION OF BIODIVERSITY

Biological diversity continues to decline throughout the world as economic growth occurs, and this is apparent in Asia. In most of South Asia the percentage of land area in which nature is protected is low compared to that in Europe and the USA (see Table 2.7). As can be seen from Table 2.7, only a very small proportion of Bangladesh is protected and then only partially. Most of the protected areas in India and Pakistan are only partially protected. The situation in Sri Lanka, as far as the area afforded nature protection is concerned, is the most favourable for all of the major South Asian economies.

In the case of China, a smaller proportion of its land area than in India is protected and nearly all of its protected area is only partially protected. The situation in the Philippines, while not as unfavourable to nature conservation as in Bangladesh, is nevertheless dismal. In relative terms, the position in Indonesia and Thailand is much better. Nevertheless, one needs

Table 2.7   Protected areas as a percentage of total land area and percentages of protected area totally and partially protected, 1993, for selected Asian countries

	All protected areas IUCN categories I–V	Totally protected IUCN categories I–III	Partially protected IUCN categories IV–V
South Asia			
Bangladesh	0.7	0	100.0
India	4.0	28.3	71.7
Pakistan	4.6	24.1	75.9
Sri Lanka	11.9	62.8	37.2
East Asia			
China	3.2	0.3	99.7
Indonesia	10.2	71.9	28.1
The Philippines	1.9	39.4	60.6
Thailand	12.6	52.9	47.1
Asia	4.4	29.1	70.1
Europe	9.3	18.8	81.2
USA	10.5	39.3	60.7

Source: Based on WRI *et al.* (1994, Table 20.1).

to exercise caution in drawing conclusions from these data because the legal and *de facto* position as far as nature protection is concerned can differ significantly between countries and these data are based on official figures of the countries concerned.

Many mammals, birds and higher plants are threatened with extinction in Asian countries. The numbers threatened in selected Asian countries are shown in Table 2.8. The number of plants threatened is very large. Indonesia has the greatest number of threatened species in all categories but the numbers are substantial in all countries, being especially high for China, Thailand, India and the Philippines. In relation to its land use, however, the nature conservation situation for Bangladesh is particularly adverse. It will be a major challenge to save Asia's threatened species in the face of economic growth in Asia.

Note that the number of species threatened by extinction in Asia is large compared to the number in developed countries. However, comparison of absolute numbers may overstate the comparative position for Asia, particularly for Asian countries located in tropical areas. This is because tropical

Table 2.8   Number of species of threatened mammals, birds and higher plants in the 1990s in selected Asian countries

	Mammals	Birds	Higher plants
South Asia			
Bangladesh	15	27	2074
India	39	72	2363
Pakistan	15	25	1168
Sri Lanka	7	8	1781
East Asia			
China	40	83	3340
Indonesia	49	135	4311
The Philippines	12	39	2907
Thailand	26	34	3442

Source: Based on WRI *et al.* (1994, Table 20.4).

countries usually have a greater number of species per unit area than temperate countries, and most high-income countries are located in temperate areas.

2.7   THE HUMAN DEVELOPMENT INDEX AND A HUMAN DEVELOPMENT/CONSERVATION (OR BIODIVERSITY) INDEX APPLIED IN ASIA

As is well known, GDP per capita is an inadequate indicator of economic development and economic welfare. In order to rectify this partially, UNDP has suggested a Human Development Index (HDI). This involves a weighting of life expectancy, adult literacy and mean years of schooling, and GDP per capita. It has a maximum value of unity (UNDP 1994, p.91). As noted for example by Pearce (1993), this implies that the indifference curves of the social welfare function depicted by HDI are linear and that components of the function are perfect substitutes. For instance, an increase in the education variable or in GDP per capita would provide perfect substitutes for reduced life expectancy if HDI applies. One is likely to have doubts about this substitution especially if the degree of substitution involved is large.

It is interesting to see how Asian countries compare in terms of HDI even though one must be cautious about its welfare implications (see for example, McGillvray 1991). HDI values for selected Asian countries are

Table 2.9   Human Development Index (HDI) 1992 for selected Asian countries

Country	Index
Thailand	0.798
Sri Lanka	0.665
China	0.644
The Philippines	0.621
Indonesia	0.586
Pakistan	0.393
India	0.382
Bangladesh	0.309

Source: Based on UNDP (1994, Table 1).

set out in Table 2.9. It can be seen that except for Sri Lanka, HDI values for major South Asian countries are well below those of the selected East Asian countries listed.

Nevertheless, HDI has, apart from the above reservation, further limitations as an indicator of development and of human welfare. For example, it provides only a partial indication of the quality of life and it does not measure the extent to which development is sustainable. Natural resource accounting (Ahmad *et al.* 1989, Repetto *et al.* 1989) has been proposed as a way to provide more information about the sustainability of development. While it does this, it still has a number of limitations.

Natural resource accounting provides an anthropocentric assessment of sustainability but it is ill equipped to take account of the value of preserving biodiversity even from a man-centred viewpoint because its valuations are based on relatively simple natural resource asset models covering such resource categories as forests, fisheries and minerals. No allowance as such is made for valuing biodiversity as an asset in itself or for the preservation of biodiversity as an ethically desirable goal in itself. The latter goal reflects the growing belief that social value orderings should not be solely dependent on the utilities of individual human beings, but should be based on wider ethical perspectives. Examples of such an approach include Blackorby and Donaldson (1992) and Ng (1986) who take into account animal welfare by means of extended utility approaches. The desirability of preserving biodiversity is, however, not necessarily based on the principle of extended utility maximisation, although 'justifications' are possible on this basis. For many, it is based upon mankind's stewardship or moral responsibility role for the preservation of nature (Leopold 1966; Passmore

1974; Tisdell 1991, Ch. 1). If this point of view is accepted, it is unsatisfactory to have a valuation index for development, such as HDI, which is solely man-centred and ignores the biodiversity element.

One way to allow for this shortcoming is to construct a value of development index which combines anthropocentric and non-anthropocentric elements, for example, one that combines HDI and a conservation of nature index (CI) or a biodiversity index (BI). This development valuation function, V, might be similar in nature to the Bergson (1938) social welfare function. There are basically two problems to be solved:

- *how to estimate CI or BI and*
- *how to combine this index with HDI.*
  Available information limits approaches to estimating CI.

A simple way to estimate CI is to take a similar approach to that for estimating HDI. For most countries, data are available on the percentage of their land area afforded nature protection. Few countries have more than 20 per cent of their land area protected in this way so this may be used to provide the upper value of CI and is set equal to unity for scaling purposes. Any country with 20 per cent or more of its area protected would have a CI of unity and any country with no protected area a CI of zero, with those in-between having a CI in proportion to their protected area in relation to the upper value, 20 per cent. Table 2.10 sets out the conservation indices for selected Asian countries estimated on this basis. Incidentally, the upper limit for the index may either be a desired *standard*

Table 2.10   Conservation Index (CI), HDI, and value ordering,
$V = 2/3$ HDI $+ 1/3$ CI, for selected Asian countries

Country	CI	HDI	V
Thailand	0.63	0.798	0.742
Sri Lanka	0.595	0.665	0.643
Indonesia	0.51	0.586	0.561
Pakistan	0.23	0.393	0.339
India	0.20	0.382	0.321
China	0.16	0.644	0.496
The Philippines	0.095	0.621	0.446
Bangladesh	0.035	0.309	0.218

Source: Based on Tables 2.7 and 2.9.

or could be based upon observed upper limits; the latter approach is used in estimating HDI.

In constructing V, one has to determine the relative weight to place on HDI and CI since this will significantly affect the ordering of development in most cases. Also, one needs to consider the functional way in which these influences should be combined to obtain V. For simplicity, the following linear form is postulated:

$$V = \alpha\text{HDI} + (1 - \alpha)\,\text{CI} \tag{2.1}$$

where $0<\alpha<1$. The value α reflects the relative weight placed on human development and the conservation of nature, using the protected areas variable as a proxy for the conservation of biodiversity. Although this value-ordering implies perfect substitutability between HDI and CI, in practice this may only be so over a limited range.

The 'social' preference or valuation function V can be represented by a series of parallel straight-line indifference curves (iso-value lines) like those shown in Figure 2.4. Rearranging equation (2.1), it can be seen that these lines can be specified using the relationship

$$\text{HDI} = \frac{1}{\alpha} V - \left(\frac{1-\alpha}{\alpha}\right) \text{CI} \tag{2.2}$$

If for example $\alpha = {}^{2}/_{3}$,

$$\text{HDI} = 1.5V - 0.5\text{CI} \tag{2.3}$$

Suppose that there happens to be a trade-off possibility frontier between the human welfare element of development as measured by HDI and biodiversity conservation as indicated by the conservation index, CI. Then given the relevant value ordering function based on (2.1), an optimal combination could be determined in principle. For example, if the trade-off possibility frontier happened to be as indicated by curve ABCD in Figure 2.4, the optimal combination would correspond to point C.

Note that if only human welfare were to count, the optimal combination would correspond to point B. In this case, the valuation indifference curves are horizontal straight-lines. In the illustration (Figure 2.4) observe that some nature conservation is necessary to maximise HDI. On the other hand, extreme ecocentrism would result in combination D as being optimal because the valuation indifference curves would be vertical lines. Other forms of the trade-off frontier can also be considered.

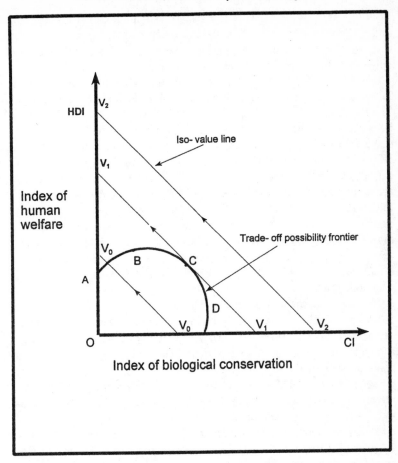

Figure 2.4 Representation of valuation frontier incorporating human welfare and biodiversity conservation as considerations, trade-off possibilities and optimisation

For the purpose of this exercise, *suppose* that $\alpha = 2/3$. This means that more weight is given to human welfare than to species conservation using this crude approach, but that the preservation of biodiversity is also ethically important. The values of V for selected Asian countries using this weighting are shown in the last column of Table 2.10. Different weightings on HDI and CI will of course give different results.

It can be seen from Table 2.10 that the conservation indices for these countries are substantially below unity. A very unsatisfactory situation from this perspective exists in Bangladesh, The Philippines, China, India and Pakistan with a much better situation prevailing in Indonesia, Sri Lanka and the Philippines. Nevertheless, all countries fall considerably below the 20 per cent protected area standard.

The main consequence of taking into account CI is that Indonesia rises in the valuation rank order of Asian countries considered and China and The Philippines slide down the scale. Furthermore, the degree of disparity between CI and the estimated V-values is considerably higher than for the disparity in HDI-values. A positive association or correlation between HDI and CI values can also be observed. This might suggest a positive causal relationship between HDI and CI and appears to give credence to the Brundtland Committee's view (WCED 1987) that human poverty is the main source of environmental degradation. However, it would be unwise to draw this conclusion. The situation is much more complicated (Tisdell 1992) and the evidence insufficient to reject neo-Malthusian concerns and the worries of some conservationists about the likely threat to biodiversity (Wilson 1992) of rising human populations and of substantial economic growth.

Note that the method used above to estimate the nature conservation index CI is subject to several limitations. It takes no account of whether the natural areas involved are totally or partially protected. In principle, account could be taken of such variations in the degree of protection by using information of the type given in Table 2.7 even though the appropriate relative weight to place on the different categories of protection would remain contentious. In addition, these categories are based upon the legal rather than the actual situation. It is well known that in some less developed countries areas that are legally totally protected are not so in practice, for example, illegal human settlement and improper use of protected areas occurs. A further problem in that no account is taken of the quality or productivity of the protected areas in relation to conservation of biodiversity. While these are serious limitations, they are less serious than failing to take any account of nature conservation in the evaluation of alternative states of the world.

One might imagine that indicators of the number of species saved from extinction by protective measures might provide an improved measure of biodiversity conservation. The other side of the coin here is the number of species lost as a result of not taking 'adequate' defensive action to save them. A problem, however, of concentrating on the latter is that most developing countries will appear to be 'especially bad' when it comes to nature conservation. This is because most developing countries are located in the tropics or the sub-tropics where biodiversity in relation to land area tends to be much higher than elsewhere on the globe (Wilson 1992). The same absolute loss of protected land area in these less developed countries can be expected to lead to loss of more numerous species than in countries located in temperate zones, mostly the more developed countries. Given that humankind's stewardship of nature is a global responsibility, this is one reason why protection of biodiversity in less developed countries requires aid from more developed countries, namely more species tend naturally to occur in developing countries.

2.8   CONCLUDING COMMENTS

Economic development appears to have been mostly defined in relation to man-centred attributes as is, for example, apparent from the components of HDI. Conservation of natural environments and of biological diversity have no weight *per se* in most indicators of economic development. In practice, measures of the sustainability of economic development are not widely used.

Considerable economic growth has occurred in Asia, both in South Asia and East Asia with substantial loss of natural environments. Given strong aspirations for higher incomes in Asia and unavoidable further rises in Asia's population, further loss and damage of natural environments is inevitable. Therefore, there is a need for realistic and well thought out environmental policies throughout Asia. This is particularly so in the Indian subcontinent which still continues to experience a high rate of population growth. A danger exists in some less developed Asian countries, such as Bangladesh, of unsustainable development (cf. Barbier and Markandya 1993; Tisdell 1994b) due to the gradual depletion of their natural resource-base and a reduction in the quality of their natural resource-stock. This process may also exact a considerable toll in terms of further losses of biological diversity.

3 Natural Resources: Water and Land-use in Bangladesh

3.1 INTRODUCTION

The water resources of Bangladesh are under considerable environmental strain from intensification and extension of agriculture facilitated by the 'Green Revolution' technologies, and deforestation and loss of natural vegetation cover. Population increase (combined with attempts to at least maintain the already low per capita income) is the main underlying cause of such pressure. Industry and urbanisation put added environmental pressures on water resources. There are adverse spillovers not only for agriculture itself but also for fisheries and navigation. Fish is an important part of the Bangladeshi diet and is the main source of animal protein. Fish supplies have been substantially reduced by changes in the quality and quantity of water resources. Water transport in Bangladesh is important particularly in rural areas – up to one third of all goods transported in Bangladesh are transported by water. Again environmental change is adversely affecting this mode of transport.

A guiding principle of Bangladesh in pursuing economic development has been to attain self-sufficiency in grain supplies. But the 'one-eyed' pursuit of this policy has been economically detrimental to Bangladesh because adequate account had not been taken of spillovers or opportunity costs from water management/development projects and from other methods to increase grain production. Furthermore, while some of the poor benefited from increased exploitation of natural resources and the environment in Bangladesh, it is hard to escape the conclusion that on the whole the poor (mostly the landless and the near landless) have been the main losers from such 'developments' (see Chapter 7). The close relationship among environmental, economic and other crises in Bangladesh is illustrated by this research and the findings have parallels in other Asian developing countries.

Bangladesh is a country which as a whole is well endowed with water resources (Dalal-Clayton 1990). The land area of Bangladesh is 14.5 million hectares and includes 1.4 million hectares of inland water bodies, that is, approximately 10 per cent of its land area (Bangladesh Agricultural Sector Review, *Main Report* 1989, p.30). In addition, Bangladesh has an exclusive economic marine zone in the Bay of Bengal which is roughly equal to its land area. But, despite Bangladesh's apparent abundance of inland water resources, their sustainable use is threatened, especially by demands on them in the dry season and by environmental changes such as loss of forests and natural vegetation cover.

The purpose of this chapter is to point out ways in which economic development programmes and patterns in Bangladesh have failed to take account of important environmental spillovers. These spillovers are adversely affecting water quality and its availability, contributing to poverty and economic deprivation and are impediments to sustainable aggregate production. The water problems occurring in Bangladesh are not unique: they also occur in other less developed countries as, for example, is emphasised in *Caring for the Earth: A Strategy for Sustainable Living* (IUCN – UNEP – WWF 1991).

During the wet-season Bangladesh has excess water but during the dry season water is in very short supply. Demand for using water during the dry season has increased considerably in agriculture as a result of the introduction of Green Revolution technologies. These seed-fertiliser technologies rely heavily on irrigation. They have reduced the length of the growing season and have increased the incidence of multiple cropping (Alauddin and Tisdell 1991b). In addition, the growing population of Bangladesh has increased the demand for water for direct human use.

Increased demand for water for irrigation and direct human use has adversely affected the inland fisheries in Bangladesh and has made inland waters less navigable. Since inland water navigation plays an important role in Bangladesh's transport system, any loss in this facility involves a significant economic cost. Furthermore, loss of forest cover and of natural vegetation has added to water problems in Bangladesh – siltation of waterways, reduction in water quality and so on.

The water management problems of Bangladesh are complex. The main problems are how to:

- *provide sufficient water to satisfy competing demands in the dry season, and*
- *decide on and implement appropriate flood control measures for the wet season as well as appropriate drainage schemes.*

However, an additional important problem is how adequately to maintain water quality and the value of water bodies for non-agricultural purposes such as fisheries and transport.

We proceed first of all with an overview of the water resource problem in Bangladesh. This is followed by a discussion of water use for agriculture and navigation. Aspects involving fisheries, including acquaculture, are then detailed. Interrelationships among access to water and income distribution and poverty are outlined and implications for forests and natural vegetation loss are identified.

3.2   AN OVERVIEW OF WATER RESOURCE PROBLEMS IN BANGLADESH

In order to reconcile conflicting interests in relation to use of water resources, Bangladesh has developed the National Water Plan (1985–2005). Its objectives in relation to the development of water resources are to:

- *maximise the net value added in agriculture and fisheries and contribute to economic growth;*
- *provide adequate water supplies in time and quantity for domestic and industrial use, navigation, salinity control and environmental management. (Nishat 1989, p.85)*

In pursuance of these objectives, the waters of minor rivers and static waters are treated as a regional resource and the policy is to reserve 40 per cent of these waters for other than irrigation use – fisheries, navigation and potable water. However, waters in the Brahamaputra and the Ganges (Padma) rivers are treated as non-regional resources.

Within the National Water Plan period (1985–2005) Bangladesh plans to irrigate an additional 1.2 million hectares using surface water and an additional 2.3 million hectares using groundwater. It is believed that by the end of the plan period (2005) most of the potential for agricultural growth in Bangladesh based on development of water resources will be exhausted. However a number of environmental problems and issues are emerging.

Project evaluation for water development projects appears to be weak in Bangladesh (Lindquist 1989, pp.6, 36–37). For example, spillover effects on fisheries and economic use of water other than for agriculture are not always taken fully into account in project evaluation. Increases in *food-grain* production are emphasised as the main benefit of extension of irrigation because the government of Bangladesh has had foodgrain self-sufficiency as a basic policy aim. Consequently opportunity costs in terms of such considerations as catch of fish forgone are not fully taken into account. Thus significant environmental spillovers are being ignored. Furthermore, doubts have been expressed about the reliability of National Water Plan estimates of available groundwater resources, its estimates of water requirements for stream-flow, salinity controls and for navigation (Cf. Siddiqui and Nishat 1990). Competition between donors to fund water development projects often results in less attention being given to economic evaluation and to consideration of the environmental effects of such projects than is desirable (Lindquist 1989, p.36). The prime aim of the donor agencies is frequently to get their donated funds allocated.

Considerable loss in fish production has occurred as a result of flood control and drainage in Bangladesh. During the National Water Plan period almost 3 million hectares of land will be drained or excluded from flooding. It has been estimated that this loss of water area will result in a reduction in the inland fish harvest of approximately 100 000 to 150 000 tonnes (Ali 1990, p.155). This amounts to approximately 13–20 per cent of the total 1983–84 fish harvest for Bangladesh or 15–23 per cent of the inland fish harvest and therefore is a substantial loss which will lead to concomitant reductions in employment in fisheries. The loss can be regarded as an adverse externality or spillover from agricultural development. Given that the net value of fish in Bangladesh is equivalent to US\$ 2–3 per kilogramme this amounts to an annual economic loss of US\$ 200–450 millions – a very large loss by any standard.

Doubts have been raised about whether demands on underground water can be sustained. There is a trend in a number of districts for the level of ground water during the dry season to become lower (see Khan 1990, esp p.143). This means that only deeper tubewells can reach it in the critical dry season. Lack of moisture has affected agricultural crops. "In addition to agricultural crops, many fruit and deep rooted trees within this Northern region (Rajshahi) have been affected due to decline in groundwater level. Forest and mango cultivation within Rajshahi division has dropped down to about 50 per cent. The most important issue in this region is the possible effect of reducing the amount of soil-moisture available to vegetation, particularly to crops and trees, which has focused attention on the possibility of groundwater development projects upsetting the natural ecological balance" (Khan 1990, p.142). The loss in tree-crops and trees is an adverse economic spillover not taken into account by private users of water. This leads to a significant divergence between private costs and social costs of water use.

In Bangladesh, underground water is a common property resource to which there is open access (Bromley and Cernea 1989). This results in non-optimal economic use of these resources (Tisdell 1991a). It may be possible to improve management of those resources by the introduction of a suitable pricing system. However, politically this may be difficult and agency costs have to be taken into account. Alternative means of improved economic management of use of underground water resources should be explored taking account of local *institutional* realities.

A further problem is that surface water and underground water supplies tend to be interconnected. Consequently, underground water levels can be reduced by greater abstraction of surface water as well as by direct pumping from underground supplies.

Pollution of both surface and underground water is also a problem for sustaining production and employment. Some of this pollution comes from industry. Factories tend to be located on waterways and they discharge their untreated wastes directly into such waterways. Although Bangladesh has a low level of industrialisation, there are areas where effluent from industry adversely affects fisheries and sometimes farmland. Sugar mills are sometimes offenders. Serious harm occurs on the Chandana-Barasia river and the Chandraghona (Bangladesh Agricultural Sector Review, *Main Report* 1989, p.39). Moreover, use of agro-chemicals such as pesticides and nitrogenous fertilisers are a source of water pollution. Leaching of salts from soils as a result of irrigation is a further problem. This can cause salt to seep into underground water supplies and add to salt loads in surface waters. Thus at the same time as irrigation reduces stream flows, it tends to increase salt loads in streams. This places limits on the extent to which irrigation can be expanded and still add to agricultural production and employment.

Appropriate water management in Bangladesh is a most serious problem because to a large extent water is the 'life-blood' of Bangladesh. Although water is an important asset for Bangladesh, its quality is being adversely affected by environmental pollution and increasing use of it, particularly in the dry season. Furthermore, the allocation of water among alternative uses appears not to be optimal from an economic point of view because environmental spillovers have not been internalised and inadequate account has been taken of spillovers in evaluation of water projects. Thus problems for sustaining production and employment have arisen, and economic benefits from Bangladesh's water resources are not maximised at present.

Water pumped or taken from natural sources such as rivers, baors, ponds and underground aquifers is not priced in Bangladesh and while that taken from irrigation canals is priced, its price does not reflect environmental costs of water-use (cf. World Bank 1992, p.69). Furthermore, a pricing system does not apply to the use of water-bodies as waste-disposal sinks. Pricing systems can be used effectively to correct for environmental spillovers and for external costs associated with water use (Tisdell 1991a). The scope for improvement in water pricing in Bangladesh should be explored.

3.3   AGRICULTURAL WATER USE

The introduction of the new agricultural technology in Bangladesh has led to considerable increase in water use for production of agricultural crops. Bangladesh's strategy of expanding irrigation coverage was adopted in the early 1960s. But it was not until the later part of the 1960s, when the new high-yielding varieties (HYVs) of rice and wheat were introduced, that the use of irrigation assumed any real significance.

Table 3.1 sets out information on trends in irrigation in Bangladesh since 1969–70. Total area irrigated (**TOTAL**) has more than trebled. Its two components, surface water and ground water use, have also increased. While the use of surface water (**SURFACE**) for irrigation has increased only slowly over the years (albeit with fluctuations) and recently shows a

Table 3.1   Agricultural water use in Bangladesh, 1969–70 to 1992–93

YEAR	TOTAL	GROUND	SURFACE	MODERN	TRADITIONAL
1969	1057.89	32.58	1025.31	366.28	691.61
1970	1169.14	48.06	1121.08	569.40	599.74
1971	1050.87	38.02	1012.85	461.26	589.62
1972	1210.97	37.46	1173.50	604.53	606.43
1973	1295.93	53.11	1242.82	741.79	554.14
1974	1467.30	94.62	1372.68	814.58	652.72
1975	1432.40	106.83	1325.57	784.10	648.30
1976	1252.27	94.58	1157.69	737.59	514.68
1977	1501.01	127.13	1373.88	850.10	650.91
1978	1494.80	257.30	1237.50	937.50	557.30
1979	1569.10	235.60	1333.50	979.20	589.90
1980	1639.00	358.70	1280.30	1174.80	464.20
1981	1725.70	525.50	1200.20	1392.90	332.80
1982	1848.00	688.80	1159.20	1595.60	252.40
1983	1920.00	718.90	1201.10	1519.60	400.40
1984	2072.60	741.60	1331.00	1569.50	503.10
1985	2097.60	893.00	1204.60	1664.70	432.90
1986	2199.00	908.70	1290.30	1723.80	475.20
1987	2347.30	1300.80	1046.50	1943.10	404.20
1988	2737.40	1401.00	1336.40	2228.40	509.00
1989	2936.10	1473.20	1462.90	2306.80	629.30
1990	3026.80	1746.50	1280.30	2594.10	432.70
1991	3228.80	1949.40	1279.40	2804.70	424.10
1992	3252.20	1981.40	1270.80	2826.40	425.80

Contd...

Table 3.1   (Continued)

YEAR	ITOTAL	IGROUND	ISURFACE	MODTRAD	GROUNDSURF
1969	100.00	100.00	100.00	52.96	3.18
1970	110.53	147.52	109.34	94.94	4.29
1971	99.35	116.70	98.79	78.23	3.75
1972	114.48	114.99	114.45	99.69	3.19
1973	122.51	163.01	121.21	133.86	4.27
1974	138.71	290.43	133.88	124.80	6.89
1975	135.41	327.91	129.28	120.95	8.06
1976	118.38	290.29	112.91	143.31	8.17
1977	141.90	390.20	134.00	130.60	9.25
1978	141.31	789.75	120.70	168.22	20.79
1979	148.34	723.14	130.06	165.99	17.67
1980	154.94	1100.98	124.87	253.08	28.02
1981	163.14	1612.95	117.06	418.54	43.78
1982	174.70	2114.18	113.06	632.17	59.42
1983	181.51	2206.57	117.15	379.52	59.85
1984	195.93	2276.24	129.81	311.97	55.72
1985	198.30	2740.95	117.49	384.55	74.13
1986	207.88	2789.13	125.84	362.75	70.43
1987	221.90	3992.63	102.07	480.73	124.30
1988	258.78	4300.18	130.34	437.80	104.83
1989	277.57	4521.79	142.68	366.57	100.70
1990	286.14	5360.65	124.87	599.51	136.41
1991	305.24	5983.43	124.78	661.33	152.37
1992	307.45	6081.65	123.94	663.79	155.92

Notes: 1969 means financial year beginning July 1969 etc. Figures in the top panel are in millions of hectares while those in the bottom panel are indices and percentages. **TOTAL** means total area irrigated, **SURFACE** and **GROUND** mean area irrigated using surface and ground water. **MODERN** and **TRADITIONAL** respectively represent area irrigated by modern and traditional methods. **ITOTAL, ISURFACE** and **IGROUND** respectively represent indices of total irrigated area, and those irrigated using surface and ground water with 1969–70 as the base. **MODTRADR** means percentage of area irrigated by modern methods to that by traditional methods. **GROUNDSURF** represents the percentage of area irrigated using ground water to that using surface water.

Source: Based on data from BBS (1985b; 1990a); BMOA (1995); World Bank (1982).

declining tendency, a spectacular (more than 60-fold) increase in the area under ground water irrigation has occurred. The ratio of ground water to surface water use (**GROUNDSURF**) increased dramatically from only 3 per cent in 1969–70 to 156 per cent in 1992–93. Area irrigated by modern methods (shallow and deep tubewells, lowlift pumps and large-scale canal, **MODERN**) has increased by a factor of four during the same period. On the other hand, the size of irrigated area using traditional methods (**TRADITIONAL**) is continuously declining. The ratio of area irrigated by modern methods to the area irrigated by traditional methods (**MODTRADR**) has shown a spectacular increase from about 53 per cent in 1969–70 to nearly 660 per cent in 1992–93. As already mentioned, increased use of ground water is causing serious environmental problems in Bangladesh. Water tables have dropped in a number of areas in Bangladesh adversely affecting trees in the dry season and making access to water more difficult. The latter has affected those dependent on shallow wells for water supplies for drinking and other purposes who very often are the poorer members of the community.

Not all underground aquifers are being fully recharged even during the wet season. Furthermore, as mentioned by Dalal-Clayton (1990), several flood mitigation works in Bangladesh may impede the recharging of ground water. For example, flood control levy banks, by preventing the spread of floods, may reduce the supply of water to underground water bodies. The lowered level of streams in the dry season also reduces inflows of water to underground water bodies.

3.4 NAVIGATION

In Bangladesh, communication by internal waterways is of great impor-tance. During the months of May to November (the wet season) water-ways are busier than all the other forms of communication taken together (Rashid 1991, p.368). Bangladesh Inland Water Transport Authority (BIWTA) estimates the length of the waterways during the rainy season to be 8000 kilometres that shrink to about half, 4000 kilometres, in other seasons. But according to Rashid (1991) the waterways may be more extensive than that. Table 3.2 shows the lengths of waterways by season and by type of navigability. Table 3.2 clearly shows that there is a great variation in the length of waterways and navigability during the monsoon and non-monsoon months.

Waterways are also important as a means of transportation of goods. About a third of all goods transported are carried by water transport. Table 3.3 shows the movement of goods since the early 1980s. The steady growth of transportation by road and waterways can be clearly seen with their respective shares remaining much the same. By contrast

Table 3.2   Waterways by season and type of navigability in Bangladesh

Length of waterways (kms) suitable for		
Vessels 4 tonnes or more	Small boats	Total length
6500* Pre-monsoon (around March) 4800	18 000	24 500

* Length navigable by big boats is about half and large paddle steamers can
  operate only on routes totalling about 3200 kms.

Source: Adapted from Rashid (1991, p.368).

Table 3.3   Movement of goods by means of transportation: Bangladesh
1980–81 to 1991–92

			Quantity of Goods (000 metric ton)		
Year	Bangladesh railway	Road	Water	Air	Total
1980–81	2984	69230	27970	2	100186
1981–82	3280	63440	29277	2	100949
1982–83	2998	74158	30286	2	107444
1983–84	2986	73569	31049	2	107606
1984–85	3057	75078	32376	2	110513
1985–86	2341	74580	33898	2	110821
1986–87	1984	75735	35127	2	112848
1987–88	2518	75259	36958	2	114737
1988–89	2493	79359	39442	2	121296
1989–90	2410	81045	41441	2	124898
1990–91	2517	81102	43562	2	127183
1991–92	2506	80857	47670	2	131035

Source: BBS (1990a, 1994a).

the quantity of goods carried by rail has declined both relatively and
absolutely.

Waterways remain an extremely important means of transport in
Bangladesh. Bangladesh is particularly dependent on water transport
during the wet season when many of its roads become impassable. Despite

increasing environmental barriers to water transport in Bangladesh and increasing competition from road transport due to extension of the road network, water transport has managed to maintain its relative position as a mode of transport in Bangladesh.

3.5   FISHERIES INCLUDING AQUACULTURE

Fish is the main source of animal protein for Bangladeshis, but average per capita consumption of it has fallen in recent years because supplies have not kept up with human population increases. Severe protein deficiency exists in Bangladesh, and intake of protein of animal origin is only about 25 per cent of the recommended level (Islam 1989, p.110). Fisheries appear to provide the greatest potential for increasing animal protein intake in Bangladesh. Fish accounts for nearly four-fifths of animal protein in the average Bangladeshi diet. Fisheries are also important in general economic terms, contributing about 4 per cent of Bangladesh's GDP and 12 per cent of its exports. They are important sources of employment. They employ 1.2 million Bangladeshis full-time and provide substantial part-time employment to a further 10 million fishermen (DOF 1995; see also Chapter 9). However, domestic availability has declined due to rising exports and per capita fish intake has declined by more than a third between 1962 and 1988 (Karim and Ahsan 1989, p.5).

Inland water bodies account for more than three-fifths of the total catch. In recent years however, this share has been steadily declining and the total catch today is no higher than the level two decades ago (BBS 1994). Because fish production in Bangladesh is so dependent on inland waters, this production faces a number of environmental threats detailed below. Table 3.4 provides some details about the source of Bangladesh's fish supply by weight for 1983–84 and 1990–91. While the major portion of fish is supplied by capture fisheries, the share of aquaculture in the total supply increased (from about 16 per cent of the volume of fish in 1983–84 to about 24 per cent in 1990–91). The production of fish from open-waters (shared or open-access waters) in Bangladesh is declining and the catch is falling. Let us consider the specific reasons for this.

Overfishing due to open-access and lack of effective regulation on fish harvesting is reducing both the standing and breeding stocks of fish. Fish stocks have been reduced below the maximum sustainable yield level and most likely below the maximum economic yield level. There are also no effective size limits on fish caught. This means that fish are caught which would enhance productivity if left (for example, very young fish, and spawning fish).

Table 3.4   Sources of fish supply in Bangladesh: Percentage contribution in terms of weight, 1983–84 and 1990–91

Source	Percentage	
	1983–84[*]	1990–91[**]
Inland Fisheries		
Capture	61.4	49.5
Culture	15.7	23.6
Inland Total	77.1	73.0
Marine Fisheries		
Artisanal	20.3	26.0
Industrial	2.6	1.0
Marine Total	22.9	27.0
Total	100	100

[*] Total weight 754 710 tonnes.
[**] Total weight 895 395 tonnes.
Source: Based on Aminul Islam (1989, Table 5, p.116) and BBS (1994a, p.217).

Some species of fish are now not able to breed as effectively as in the past because their access to their usual breeding grounds is impeded due to obstructions such as dams. Also some of the breeding grounds have changed environmentally, for example due to the building of dams and/or reduced water quality. In many cases the areas of suitable breeding grounds for fish have declined (Minkin 1988). Furthermore, capital works for flood control and drainage have reduced the area of water available for fish production thereby reducing the fish population.

In dry seasons, a reduced water area is available to fish because of reduced stream flows through deforestation in the headwaters of streams and impoundment of streams. Water off-take for irrigation has increased with the adoption of high-yielding crop varieties. The introduction of these varieties has led to multiple cropping and to considerable demands on water in the dry season for irrigation purposes. This, apart from lowering the levels of running streams, lowers the levels of closed water areas used for irrigation purposes, for example water in ox-bow lakes and river cut-offs. Sometimes, as a result, the level of water in these is reduced below that critical for the survival of fish stocks.

Water quality has also become less satisfactory for fish production due to the increased use of agro-chemicals and the release of industrial effluents. For example, 40 per cent of urea fertiliser used in agriculture is leached from the soil into water bodies where it encourages the growth of plants, especially weeds such as water hyacinth. The decaying of this increased volume of organic matter reduces the available oxygen in the water with detrimental impact on populations of fish. Another serious problem for fish populations in Bangladesh is the use of pesticides, especially insecticides injurious to fish such as organochlorines including DDT. Organochlorides are the most widely used pesticides in Bangladesh and are particularly toxic to fish. Although the use of organochlorides has been restricted in developed countries, their indiscriminate use in Bangladesh continues unabated (Islam 1989, pp.150–51). Releases of acids, heavy metals and poisonous substances from mining and manufacturing works also constitutes a threat to fish populations (Ali 1990; Ahmed and Reazuddin 1990). There are virtually no effective controls on these releases.

Moreover, institutional problems add to environmental problems in fisheries management for example in aquaculture. Production of fish from some closed water-bodies could be substantially increased as a result of a small investment in stock supplementation with suitable fingerlings and low intensity fertiliser-use. This has not occurred in many cases because the water-bodies are shared amongst a number of people, finance is not readily available, the owner of the water-body is absent or because local people lack knowledge of more productive techniques of aquaculture.

A particularly contentious issue in Bangladesh has been shrimp or prawn farming in the coastal areas where tidal forests occur. Expansion in these activities has caused environmental conflicts. Although shrimps account for about 80 per cent of the value of Bangladesh's fish exports or 4 per cent of its total exports, this is not in itself an indicator of the economic value or worth of the industry.

Over 100 000 hectares of brackish water aquaculture ponds exist in Bangladesh (for further details see Chapter 9). This area exceeds 15 per cent of the estimated area of tidal forests in Bangladesh. Most involve very simple (primitive) aquaculture techniques – basically impoundment of natural stock and reliance on natural food supplies transported by tidal variations. Several environmental problems are associated with brackish water culture of shrimp in Bangladesh (See Chapter 9).

Clearing of mangrove forests for shrimp culture is a problem, in the Chittagong region in particular. Apart from reducing forest resources, this may reduce the recruitment of natural stocks of fish by lowering nutrient availability and destroying nursery habitat. Also mangroves provide some coastal protection against the effects of cyclones and erosion.

Rice farmers in areas near aquaculture ponds may suffer from seepage of saline water from shrimp ponds, or from deliberate release of such water. This may reduce rice yields or make the land unsuitable for rice altogether. Very often owners or holders of shrimp farms come from higher income groups. It is reported that some, in order to increase the size of their holding, deliberately release saltwater to nearby farms in order to make these unsuitable for rice and to enable the aquaculturalist to lease these areas paying low levels of rent.

Different claims have been made about the impact of shrimp farms on employment. Rahman *et al.* (1984) claim that the labour requirements for shrimp culture activities on a one hectare farm are greater than for rice cultivation in areas where these are alternatives. They estimated 201.6 person-days for the former and 175.5 person-days for the latter. While their estimates make an allowance for shrimp seed collection and transportation, they make no allowance for employment on account of rice seed production, storage and/or transportation. The labour requirement factor needs further investigation. Furthermore, shrimp farming in some areas may prove to be less sustainable than rice-growing. Rashid (1989, p.146) claims that present extensive culture of shrimp reduces employment compared to rice cultivation but that intensive culture could increase employment. Thus the issue remains unresolved.

Landless individuals collecting food and fishing are excluded from some areas because of impoundment of water for aquaculture purposes. Thus there is an opportunity cost as a result of exclusion. Furthermore, because of impoundment of natural stocks, natural stock in nearby areas may be reduced. This is an adverse production externality from this aquaculture. These impoundments may add little to the total production of shrimps but serve to privatise them (confer property rights on the owners of the impoundments – often the richer members of society) to the detriment of poor fishermen. Conceivably, in the absence of such ponds, production of shrimps might not be lowered substantially and income might be less unequally distributed.

The collection of seed prawns from nature (as is done in Bangladesh) may encounter constraints due to over-harvesting of shrimp due to open-access and a reduction in natural free-ranging stocks of prawns because their natural areas are enclosed for prawn farms. This happened for example in Ecuador (Meltzoff and LiPuma 1986). Therefore continued expansion of shrimp aquaculture as now practised in Bangladesh can be expected to be ecologically unsustainable.

Thus serious environmental problems exist in Bangladesh in relation to its fisheries sector. Fisheries production and fish stocks are not being maintained in the capture fishery, and aquaculture, especially shrimp farming, involves a number of unresolved environmental issues.

Bangladesh's prime desire for foodgrain self-sufficiency has had serious adverse effects on its fisheries. As pointed out in the Bangladesh Agriculture Sector Review *Main Report* (1989, p.40)

The pursuit of foodgrain self-sufficiency through drainage, poldering and irrigation projects, has destroyed many perennial and seasonal water bodies. Social cost-benefit analysis of public sector interventions must be more rigorously applied to make sure that the changes being brought about lead to sustainable increment in production capacity; linkages and externalities must not be ignored.

3.6 SOME OTHER CONSIDERATIONS, ESPECIALLY INCOME DISTRIBUTION AND POVERTY

Two other dimensions of access to water can be identified:

- *health and other household problems related to water*
- *income distribution and poverty aspects.*

3.6.1 Health and other household problems related to water

Increased use of agrochemicals pollutes water in that they are carried into various water bodies from which rural people use water for bathing and to some extent drinking. This has long-term implications for health.

Poor drainage from rural roads in many parts of Bangladesh leads to stagnant water that creates environmental pollution. Furthermore, it becomes a breeding ground for mosquitoes with adverse effects on health. There is a resurgence of malaria and hepatitis B in many parts of Bangladesh.

Dwindling access to surface water creates problems for raw jute processing (retting, that is the process of separating jute pulp from its fibre, Alauddin *et al.* 1995). While this may be a general problem it is more acute for smaller farmers. In many cases retting is done in the standing water of bigger ditches within the village. It presents significant environmental pollution and health risks.

3.6.2   Income distribution and poverty aspects

The rural poor, consisting of the landless and the near landless, increasingly face problems of gaining access to water. Water is the most important resource, after land, influencing the income of the poor who usually work as wage labourers. The income of the rural poor consists of two components: exchange income – primarily wage determined in the main through the market system – and non-exchange income – determined in the main by institutional/sociological systems in the rural community and usually obtained directly from nature without exchange (Alauddin and Tisdell 1989; Lipton 1985; Conway 1985; Jodha 1985, 1986). Even though the exchange component is important to the rural poor, during slack periods of employment non-exchange sources of income become critically important. Water is an important ingredient in determining the size of the non-exchange component of the income of the rural poor because with access to water from ponds and tanks they can grow vegetables both to supplement their diet and to earn some exchange income. With the average Bangladeshi diet, following the Green Revolution, declining in quality and becoming less varied (Alauddin and Tisdell 1991a), supplements to the standard diet are extremely important. Thus declining free or low-cost access to water resources has both a qualitative (dietary) and quantitative (exchange income) dimension. Access of Bangladesh's rural poor to water is becoming more difficult (Alauddin and Tisdell 1989 1991c; Alauddin *et al.* 1995).

Both quality and quantity of water affect the welfare of the rural poor. The former *directly* affects health while the latter *directly* affects income. However, farm-level evidence (Alauddin and Tisdell 1989; Alauddin *et al.* 1995) indicates that many members at the lower income end of the rural community are forced to sell their land and other belongings to meet health and medical expenses. Thus while the problem of reduced access to water affects smaller farmers adversely it affects the rural poor comparatively the most. Especially during the dry season, the distance travelled to collect water has increased and the role of women and to some extent children in supplementing income from formal sources has been undermined, because they traditionally help grow fruits and vegetables which require watering in the dry season in their backyards.

Basically the rural poor are to be found for the most part amongst the landless and near landless. This group has increased in relative size since the Green Revolution (see Bangladesh Agriculture Sector Review 1989, *Main Report*, p.84). This group has been increasingly denied open or free access to natural resources, most of which have increased in price (for example, fuel).

On balance, the type of environmental changes which have occurred in Bangladesh seem to have disadvantaged the rural poor. Even though it might be thought that the poor encroaching on forests in hill areas have benefited, the position is not clear-cut. Often the encroachment is under the protection of a local power-broker who thereby obtains *de facto* property rights in the area and a payment for protection from the poor peasant settling illegally in the forest. Furthermore, the relatively poor people already in the forest or dependent upon it, such as hill tribes or other local people, are made worse off by being denied access to their traditional resource.

Adverse spillovers from large scale water development projects usually adversely affect the poor and the underprivileged most. The building of the huge Kaptai Lake reservoir displaced many poor local hill tribes from their traditional homeland without compensating them.

As pointed out above, actual and planned water projects are expected to significantly reduce Bangladeshi's supply of fish. A loss in net value of fish production of up to US$450 million per year is anticipated. This will adversely affect the livelihood of fishermen, one of the poorest social groups in Bangladesh.

Irrigation can of course only *directly* benefit those with land, and the number without land in Bangladesh has risen greatly. Furthermore, relatively speaking it is the large farmers who have benefited most from irrigation. In 1977, 29 per cent of small farms had irrigation compared to 33 per cent of large farms. In 1983–84, 60 per cent of large farms had irrigation as against 40 per cent of smaller farms. The Bangladesh Agriculture Sector Review (1989) *Main Report* pointed out that income distribution within the rural sector is likely to worsen if these trends continue.

3.7   FORESTS AND NATURAL VEGETATION LOSS

Forests and natural vegetation have several important functions in relation to water resources. They tend to act as slow-release reservoirs for rainfall. This results in less variable stream flows and maintenance of stream flows over a longer period than is otherwise likely to occur, and less soil erosion. In turn this may mean less flooding, increased availability of water in streams during dry seasons and less turbidity and siltation of water ways. Turbidity and siltation can adversely affect fish populations, as can very low water levels during the dry season. Siltation of waterways, apart from adding to navigation problems, increases the likelihood of flooding. According to Hasan (1996, p.233) the total amount of sediment carried to the Bay of Bengal by the Bangladesh river system is 2.4 billion tons annually and the Ganges alone carries 1.5 billion tons. A large proportion of this sediment comes from the erosion of the river banks. Unplanned canal digging programmes, undertaken during 1978–81 and reinitiated in the early 1990s, contribute to siltation of the river beds. As Hasan (1996, p.233) succinctly puts it:

> Only in one project, Ulashi-Jadunathpur (UJ) 1.7 million cubic metres of canal digging was undertaken. Trees were to be planted on both sides of the canal but in most cases it was not done. Further, general maintenance was slack. For these two reasons dug out earth was washed back to the newly dug or excavated channels. These projects were abandoned only after one monsoon rain

Natural vegetation can also supply nutrients and organic matter of value to fish populations. Thus forest and natural vegetation cover has important positive spillovers on waterways and the removal of such cover has negative external effects. Forests and natural vegetation cover in Bangladesh are under pressure from several sources. The main pressures are for the supply of fuel needs and for expansion of agriculture. These pressures are causing particular environmental damage in the hill areas of Bangladesh which cover approximately one-eighth of its surface area.

Availability of traditional fuels has fallen alarmingly in Bangladesh. The per capita supply of such fuels declined by 9 per cent in the ten-year period beginning 1976–77 (Bangladesh Agriculture Sector Review, *Main Report* 1989, p.40). A fuel famine has developed which is driving up fuel prices and causing encroachment on forests for fuel-gathering. While the widespread adoption of social forestry and agroforestry could relieve this pressure, an end to Bangladesh's present fuel crisis is unfortunately not in sight, and the problem affects most parts of rural Bangladesh.

Acute environmental problems as a result of unsustainable land-use practices are occurring in the hill areas of Bangladesh especially in the Chittagong Hill Tracts and in Sylhet. These areas are being rapidly eroded and degraded due to deforestation, extension and intensification of agriculture and the use of environmentally inappropriate agricultural practices and crops. There are several reasons for this.

Substantial population pressures exist in these areas due to:

- *high rates of population increase (higher than the Bangladeshi average);*
- *immigration of lowlanders (Bengalis) to these areas; and*
- *displacement of hill tribes from a part of their former range due to incursions by Bengalis (which mean that tribes are crowded onto a*

smaller area) and displacement of many local people by the building of the Kaptai Lake water reservoir.

Considerable conflict has been generated between hill tribes and Bengalis. Lowland migrants have deforested large areas at the headwaters of rivers in the Chittagong Hill Tracts. Immigrants often grow pineapples and *kankrol* on the steep slopes of hill areas so encouraging erosion.

The Bangladesh Agriculture Sector Review (*Main Report* 1989, p.41) points out

> The Chittagong Hill Tracts Regulation of 1900 severely restricted migration to the Chittagong Hill Tracts districts until the 1970s. Since the area was opened to lowlanders in that decade, the damage to soil resources has been alarming. The lowlanders brought with them no traditional skills or experience for the proper management of hill soils; they grow whatever seems to provide an immediate opportunity for eking out a living. In the process, the fertility of large areas has been undermined. Indeed, some may become unfit for anything but scrub vegetation.

At the same time, local hill tribes have been reducing the length of their slash and burn (*jhum*) cycle because of population pressures and their confinement to smaller areas of land. This also reduces soil fertility. Similar problems involving hill people and lowlanders are occurring throughout much of Asia.

Erosion problems are occurring in hilly areas other than the Hill Tracts as a result of land clearing. In most cases, this land degradation occurs following the illegal clearing of protected forests. Pineapple and betel leaf growers are causing damage to forests and loss of top soil in the hills of south Sylhet. Similar losses are being caused by pineapple growers in the Garo foothills and by arum growers in the Lalmai Hills of Comilla (Bangladesh Agriculture Sector Review, *Main Report* 1989, p.41). When poverty is widespread, it is difficult to prevent the illegal extension of agriculture and to convince farmers of the need to take account of the adverse environmental spillovers from their activities. Poverty itself can be a serious obstacle to sound environmental management.

The forest land resource of Bangladesh is very limited with only 0.02 hectare (ha) of forest land per person. An estimated 2.45 million ha (17 per cent of the total land area of Bangladesh) is either forest or potential forest land and of this 2.18 million hectare is government owned. The rest is privately controlled homestead forest scattered over the country. Of the total government forest land, 1.46 million ha is the national forests under the control of the Forest Department and the rest is virtually barren under the control of Local Government Councils in Chittagong Hill Districts. More than 90 per cent of the area of state-owned forests is concentrated in 12 districts in the east and south-eastern regions of the country. Out of 64 districts of the country, 28 districts have no public forest at all. At present, only about 61 per cent of the Forest Department controlled forest is productive and the rest is either encroached, barren, scrub or grass land. It is estimated that the crown cover of the existing forests varies from only 30 to 70 per cent (BPC 1990). This low crown cover is partially a result of illegal human intrusion into official state forests.

Forests, along with other renewable natural resources, help to maintain the environment. Extensive tree planting in combination with appropriate nature conservation programmes minimize soil erosion and stabilize newly accreted charlands and sloping land. Trees provide biomass for fuel and industries in addition to fruits, fodder, timber, wood and other raw materials. Moreover, trees create a protective cover against the eroding power of rain and wind, reduce evaporation of soil moisture and absorb atmospheric carbon dioxide and release oxygen enhancing the life-supporting biosphere. Efforts are necessary, therefore, to preserve and enhance the tree cover in volume, diversity and quality through comprehensive development of the forest resources in the country. The preservation and expansion of the biodiversity of forests and protection of their wildlife is an essential element of the efforts to improve the environment for ensuring sustainable development in Bangladesh.

3.8   CONCLUDING COMMENTS

From the above discussion it can be seen that many of Bangladesh's environmental problems are interdependent and closely related to its water resources. The nature of this environmental relationship is schematically summarised in Figure 3.1. Intensification and extension of agriculture has been the major source of damage to the natural environment of Bangladesh. Bangladesh's water problems are by no means unique amongst developing countries. They have been exacerbated by the introduction of Green Revolution technologies (and other technologies), population growth, and inadequate management of resource-utilization. In rural areas the bias has been in favour of agricultural development with fisheries (and water transport) relatively most neglected. Possibly this is because the landowning groups form a stronger electoral or political group than

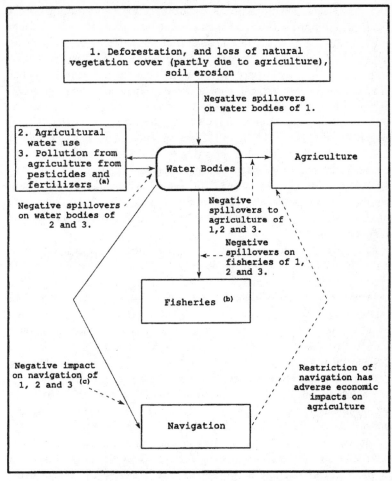

Notes:
(a) Industrial and urban uses also add to water demand and add pollutants to water bodies with adverse consequences for industry generally, agriculture, fisheries and navigation.
(b) As a consequence diets and income distribution are adversely affected.
(c) Leaching of artificial fertilizers such as nitrates promotes growth of water weeds e.g. growth of water hyacinth so impeding navigation.

Figure 3.1 Schematic representation of important environmental interdependencies in Bangladesh linked to water bodies and effected by economic change

those involved in fisheries and water transport. Similar prejudice exists in favour of lowlanders compared to hill tribes.

To a certain extent, Bangladesh's water problems are transboundary ones. The Brahmaputra rises in Tibet and flows through Northeast India, and the Ganges (Padma) flows for most of its length through India. Intensification of land-use in the catchment areas of these rivers in India and China and greater off take of water from these rivers in India have had adverse spillovers on Bangladesh. Due to greater off take of water in India from the Ganges, mainly for irrigation, the volume and quality of water entering Bangladesh in the dry season have fallen. Due to the extension of agriculture and the clearing of forests, sediment loads in the Brahmaputra may have increased and its flow rate has become more variable even though Dalal-Clayton (1990, p.17) expresses doubt about this, and quoting Ives and Mosserlie (1989), claims that there is little evidence of recent increases in sediment load or in magnitude of floods on the Ganges-Brahmaputra floodplains. In any case, Bangladesh's neighbours and near-neighbours cannot be blamed entirely for Bangladesh's environmental predicament. Its own circumstances and policies have been the major influence.

While Bangladesh's goal of foodgrain self-sufficiency seems admirable, a one-eyed pursuance of this goal has had unfortunate environmental and dietary consequences. Mainly as a result of fish losses due to water projects intended to increase grain output, pursuance of this goal has reduced the intake of animal protein, chiefly fish, by Bangladeshis. It has resulted in reduced production of many non-grain food crops, especially horticultural crops. Consequently the diet of the average Bangladeshi has deteriorated. To boot, it has brought about environmental changes that appear principally to have disadvantaged the poor and the already underprivileged.

The above study underlines the point made by the WCED (1987) that we do not have separate environmental and socio-economic crises; they are interdependent and interacting. Thus Bangladesh's water problem, its economic poverty, its fuel crisis, its population problem, the occurrence of environmental degradation in Bangladesh, and its difficulty of securing employment are not separate problems. They are part of one general economic and ecological problem facing Bangladesh. Bangladesh's environmental and socio-economic predicament is not unique among the less developed countries.

4 Rural Employment, Technological Change and the Environment

4.1 INTRODUCTION

The agricultural sector of most Asian LDCs, including Bangladesh, is characterised by an abundant and rapidly expanding supply of labour, and by a steadily declining supply of scarce arable land per capita. Limited growth of non-farm agricultural production in several Asian countries places the main burden of employing the increasing labour force on agriculture. This is consistent with Ishikawa's (1978, p.3) view that the 'solution to the employment and rural poverty problems in Asia has to be found in the direction of a significant increase in labour absorption in agricultural land .... ' or at least in a significant increase in employment in rural areas.

The introduction of Green Revolution technologies to many LDCs in the mid-1960s generated optimism that these technologies would be both land-augmenting and labour-using (see, for instance, Ruttan and Binswanger 1978; Johnston and Cownie 1969). Early studies (for example, Barker and Cordova 1978) indicated that significant increases in demand for both family and hired labour were occurring as a result of the adoption of these technologies.

Recent evidence, however, is that simultaneous adoption of labour-saving and labour-using technologies associated with the Green Revolution has neutralised or more than counterbalanced the employment-augmenting impact of the new agricultural technology in much of contemporary Asia (Jayasuriya and Shand 1986). Earlier Ishikawa (1978, p.35) predicted this as a possible outcome.

This chapter is concerned with the growth in overall labour absorption in Bangladeshi crop production since the late 1960s when Green Revolution technologies were introduced to Bangladesh. In Bangladesh about 60 per cent of the (employed) labour force is engaged in agriculture. The rate of unemployment and underemployment is very high in this sector perhaps of the order of over 30 per cent (BPC 1985, p.V-14). Even though the share of total work force engaged in agriculture has fallen from

85 per cent in 1961 to 73.8 per cent (BBS 1992a) in recent years, this sector is still the largest source of employment for the civilian labour force.

Variations in agricultural productivity, labour intensity and overall employment are discussed and explanatory factors are identified. These are considered on an annual basis as well as for the two crop seasons: *kharif* (wet) and *rabi* (dry). As far as we are aware, this is the first in-depth investigation of these relationships for Bangladesh.

This chapter provides an in-depth analysis of the process of technological change and employment generation in Bangladesh especially on farms. Earlier studies (Alauddin and Tisdell 1991b, Tisdell and Alauddin 1992, Jayasuriya and Shand 1986; Ishikawa 1978) cautioned about the ability of the agricultural sector to generate sufficient employment to absorb all new entrants in the labour market. The initial optimism surrounding the ability of the Green Revolution technologies to create a very high level of employment in agriculture and absorb surplus agricultural labour seems to have remained largely unrealised. This is despite some positive employment effects of the Green Revolution especially during the dry season. In this chapter labour intensities per cropped hectare before and after the introduction of the new agricultural technology are estimated. Constraints to further employment growth in the agricultural sector are investigated. Furthermore, this chapter considers sustainability of employment both on- and off-farm, including employment in highly urbanised areas. It also examines the extent to which the latter is dependent on the agricultural surplus being maintained. In this connection non-agricultural employment prospects are examined.

4.2   THE DATA

The basic data used in the empirical analysis are reported in Alauddin and Tisdell (1995) but have been updated to include more recent information as well as that prior to the Green Revolution. The basic information on overall labour utilisation and intensities of labour use (persondays per hectare) and on other relevant variables is taken from BBS (1976; 1979; 1980; 1984a; 1984b; 1985a; 1985b; 1985c; 1986a; 1986b; 1990; 1992b; 1992c) and BPC (undated). The labour absorption data are based on 50 crops comprising seven broad commodity groups[1] for the period 1960–61 to 1990–91. The total land area allocated to these crops constitutes more than 98 per cent of the gross cropped area. The estimates have been derived taking into account irrigated and non-irrigated cropped areas as well as traditional and modern techniques of irrigation.

4.3   PRODUCTIVITY, EMPLOYMENT AND LABOUR INTENSITY

Let us analyse the trends over time of overall crop sector employment, different variants of labour intensity per cropped hectare as well as various measures of land productivity. Figure 4.1 depicts trends in yield per gross cropped hectare (including area under multiple cropping, **IGYFDT**), crop sector employment (**ITOTAL**) and labour intensity per gross cropped hectare (**IMDPHA**) for the period 1960–61 to 1990–91. It can be clearly seen that while foodgrain yield per gross cropped hectare has increased quite steadily, overall crop sector employment as well as labour intensity per gross cropped hectare have increased at a much slower pace. During the period of nearly 25 years since the Green Revolution, overall employment in the crop sector has increased by only 14 per cent. If one considers

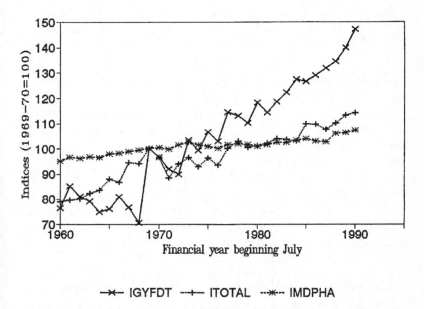

Figure 4.1   Trends in foodgrain yield per gross cropped hectare (**IGYFDT**), crop sector employment (**ITOTAL**) and labour intensity per gross cropped hectare (**IMDPHA**): Bangladesh 1960–61 to 1990–91

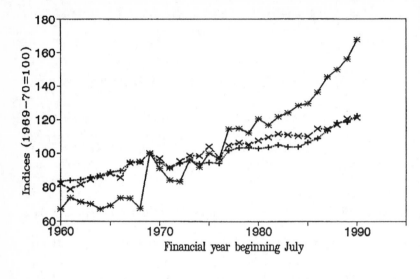

Figure 4.2   Trends in foodgrain yield per net cropped hectare (**INYFDT**), food-grain sector employment (**IMDFG**) and labour intensity per net cropped hectare of foodgrain (**IMDNHA**): Bangladesh 1960–61 to 1990–91

the labour intensity per gross cropped hectare, the difference between the pre- and post-Green Revolution periods is even less striking.

Figure 4.2 shows trends in foodgrain yield per net cropped hectare (**INYFDT**), labour intensity per net cropped hectare (**IMDNHA**) and total employment in foodgrain production (**IMDFG**) as functions of time. As can be seen, yield has increased at a much faster rate than the other two variables. Since the late 1960s, foodgrain yield per net cropped hectare increased by nearly 68 per cent whereas total labour employment and labour intensity in foodgrains increased by only 21 and 14 per cent respectively (see Figure 4.2). However, if one looks at the scenario for the early 1960s the changes are much more striking even for employment and labour intensity (nearly 48 and 20 per cent respectively).

Average labour productivity (kilogrammes per person-day) for food-grain (**LPPHFG**), as well as for *kharif* and *rabi* foodgrains (**LPPHKF** and **LPPHRF**) show considerable fluctuations over time. However, labour productivity for the *rabi* season is on the whole higher than for the *kharif* season and in comparison to annual average productivity. Note that this is true broadly for the period of the new technology (1968–69 to 1990–91). Such a scenario is not unexpected because non-labour purchased inputs per cropped hectare would be higher in the dry season compared to the wet season necessitating higher yields to cover extra costs and/or cultivation of only the most productive arable land. One might also note that it is in *rabi* season that the Green Revolution has had the biggest impact on crop yields. This is because it has made it economic to grow crops under controlled environmental conditions involving irrigation to a considerable extent (Oldfield 1989; Shand 1973; Tisdell 1991a). However, in the last 2–3 years labour productivity for the *rabi* season seems to be declining slightly compared to the two other indicators of labour productivity.

If one considers the association between total employment in foodgrain production (**MDFG**) and land productivity per net cropped hectare of foodgrain (**NYFDT**), two clusters can be observed. Up until 1968–69 (that is, before the Green Revolution) the total employment generated from foodgrain production seems to be invariant with or may even be inversely related to yield per net cropped hectare. Since 1969–70 (that is, after the introduction of the Green Revolution) the two variables appear to show a strong positive association. Equation (4.1) specified in Table 4.1 captures

Table 4.1   Relationship between total employment in foodgrain production (IMDFG) and yield per net cropped hectare (INYFDT): Bangladesh, 1960–61 to 1990–91

	Equations (dependent variable IMDFG)		
	4.1 (1960–90)[+]	4.1A (1960–68, D = 0)[+]	4.1B (1969–90, D = 1)[+]
INTERCEPT DUMMY	–54.204		
t-value	–2.951[*]		
SLOPE DUMMY	0.756		
t-value	2.924[*]		
INYFDT	–0.403	–0.381	0.338
t-value	–1.588[**]	–1.196	19.063[*]
CONSTANT	116.870	113.430	66.906
t-value	6.647[*]	5.082[*]	31.572[*]
R^2	0.952	0.595	0.948
DW	1.932[≠]	1.61[*]	1.620

[*]   Significant at least at the 5 per cent level.
[**] Significant at least at the 10 per cent level.
[+]   1960–90 means 1960–61 to 1990–91 etc. Dummy variables are used for sub-periods based on visual observation of the plottings (not reported here).
[≠]   After adjusting for first-order positive autocorrelation using Cochrane–Orcutt method.

these two phases of this changing relationship between the two variables. Table 4.1 presents the estimated equations for the entire period as well as the one for the corresponding clusters (Equation 4.1A and 4.1B respectively). In estimating the regression lines index numbers (**IMDFG** and **INYFDT**) of the above two variables have been used taking 1969–70 as the base.

Using a dummy variable (based on visual observation of plotting not reported here, D = 0 for 1960–61 to 1968–69 and D = 1 for the remainder of the time series), it can be clearly seen that there is significant negative relation between food yield per net cropped hectare and total employment in the foodgrain sector prior to the Green Revolution, while the period of the new technology is characterised by a significantly positive relationship. This underscores the contribution of the new technology in raising land productivity and labour usage in the crop sector.

4.4   CAPITAL INTENSITY, LABOUR INTENSITY AND EMPLOYMENT

From the preceding discussion it is possible that increased production of foodgrains has resulted more from an increase in the usage of capital, rather than labour, in Bangladesh. The question that arises is: Has Bangladeshi agriculture become more capital-intensive over the years? Have labour intensity and overall labour-use increased commensurate with increased capital intensity? Let us consider this possibility. Even though time-series data for capital-use in agricultural production are not readily available let us use two proxies, namely fertiliser and irrigation, for it. One must also bear in mind that it is extremely difficult to measure capital as controversies surrounding its definition and measurement indicate (see, for example, Robinson 1969; Harcourt 1972).

First consider fertiliser applied per hectare of gross cropped area (**FERT**) as a proxy for capital intensity. Fertiliser application increased in Bangladesh dramatically from less than 2 kilogrammes per gross cropped hectare to over 70-kilogrammes per gross cropped hectare over a period of 30 years. Consider the association between overall labour-intensity values (index of person days per gross hectare, **IMDPHA**) against capital intensity (kilogrammes of fertiliser in nutrient terms per gross cropped hectare, **IFERT**). Overall a positive association can be observed between these two variables. A closer examination of the observations reveals two distinct patterns in the association. The values until approximately the first half of the period seem more closely associated compared to the second phase.

Using a dummy variable (based on visual observation of plottings not reported here) corresponding to the two phases, regression lines were fitted to the data. The first cluster corresponds to the period 1960–61 to 1974–75, for which the dummy variable assumes a zero-value while the second corresponds to the 1975–76 to 1990–91 period when the dummy variable assumes a value of unity. Table 4.2 presents Equation 4.2, the regression line for the entire period, and Equation 4.2A and Equation 4.2B which relate to the first and second clusters respectively. Equation 4.2 is employed as an aid to understanding the changing nature of this relationship. The slopes of the two lines differ significantly at 1-per cent level. The slope of the fitted line relating to the first period is appreciably steeper than the one for the second cluster. This implies that employment-augmenting effect of capital is becoming weaker and that capital intensity has increased markedly in Bangladesh agriculture.

Now consider irrigation as a proxy for capital stock. Over the years, the area under irrigation has increased significantly in Bangladesh. Furthermore, a gradual shift from traditional methods of irrigation (*doon, swing basket, dugwell etc*) to modern methods of irrigation (large-scale canal, shallow and deep tube-wells, low lift pumps) has occurred. In other words there has been a switch from less capital-intensive (more labour-intensive) to more capital intensive (less labour-intensive) techniques of irrigation over time. For instance, area irrigated with modern methods, as a percentage of total irrigated area (**PCIMODIR**), increased from a very low base in 1960–61 to over 85 per cent in 1990–91. Considering indices of total labour use in crop production (**ITOTAL**) and indices of total labour ratio as measured by area irrigated by modern methods per person day (**IMODRMD**), one can identify two distinct patterns similar to those for fertiliser. One relates to the 1960–61 to 1969–70 period while the other corresponds to the 1970–71 to 1990–91 period. Equation 4.3 (presented in Table 4.2) using a dummy variable (D = 0 for the first period and 1 for the second period) identifies differential impact of **IMODRMD**. The slopes of the two lines differ substantially as indicated by the statistical significance of the slope dummy. The decline in the value of the coefficient of **IMODRMD** from 0.242 in the first period to 0.102 in the second period implies that the employment effect of the irrigation technology has decreased quite considerably.

Let us consider the time series data on overall *rabi* season employment (**IMDR,** index of **MDTOTRAB**) against the proxy for capital intensity (**IMODRMD**). The relationship is depicted in Figure 4.3. Several phases can be identified:

Phase 1 (1960–68, pre-Green Revolution): Rising capital intensity with increase in overall *rabi* season employment.

Table 4.2 Relationship between overall labour intensity per hectare (IMDPHA), overall and rabi season labour use (ITOTAL and IMDR) and capital intensity (FERT and IMODRMD)

	Equations (Dependent variable IMDPHA)			Equations (Dependent variable ITOTAL)		
	4.2 (1960–90)+	4.2A (1960–74, D = 0)+	4.2B (1975–90, D = 1)+	4.3 (1960–90)+	4.3A (1960–68, D = 0)+	4.3B (1969–90, D = 1)+
INTERCEPT DUMMY	3.284			10.839		
t-value	3.787*			1.857*		
SLOPE DUMMY	-0.349			-0.113		
t-value	-5.890*			-1.579**		
FERT	0.469	0.469	0.120			
t-value	8.254*	11.403*	5.956*			
IMODRMD				0.174	0.229	0.062
				2.735*	8.723*	3.048*
CONSTANT	94.995	94.995	98.279	76.841	74.439	87.800
t-value	181.970*	251.390*	118.230*	21.643*	58.106	17.181*
R²	0.905	0.909	0.717	0.908	0.911	0.751
DW	2.149	1.770	2.238	1.902#	1.803#	1.862#

* Significant at least at the 5 per cent level.
** Significant at least at the 10 per cent level.
+ 1960–90 means 1960–61 to 1990–91 etc. Dummy variables are used for sub-periods based on visual observation of plottings (not reported here).
# After adjusting for first-order positive autocorrelation using Cochrane–Orcutt method.

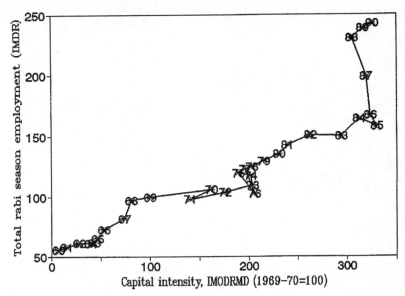

Figure 4.3 Relationship between capital intensity (indices of irrigated hectare per man-day of employment generated in the production of *rabi* crops, **(IMODRMD)** and total *rabi* season employment **(IMDR)**: Bangladesh 1960–61 to 1990–91

Phase 2 (1969–76, early Green Revolution): Rapidly rising capital intensity with slower increase in overall *rabi* season employment.

Phase 3 (1977–83, advancing established phase): Rapidly rising capital intensity with a relatively faster increase in overall *rabi* season employment.

Phase 4 (1984–90, stagnating established phase): Stagnating capital intensity with significant increase in overall *rabi* season employment.

Consider now the *rabi* season labour intensity. Figure 4.4 provides a scatter plot of the behaviour of labour intensity per hectare of *rabi* food-grains **(IMDHFR)** against the proxy for capital intensity **(IMODRMD)**. Figure 4.4 suggests division into four phases broadly similar to the above for overall employment during the *rabi* season.

Phase 1 (1960–68): Labour intensity rising at a fast rate with increases in capital intensity, even though capital intensity did not rise markedly.

Phase 2 (1969–74): Capital intensity rose markedly during this period. Even though labour intensity and capital intensity tended to rise together, labour intensity rose at a slower rate with capital intensity than in the pre-Green Revolution period.

Phase 3 (1975–83): Labour intensity is declining as capital intensity rises, but capital intensity is rising markedly.

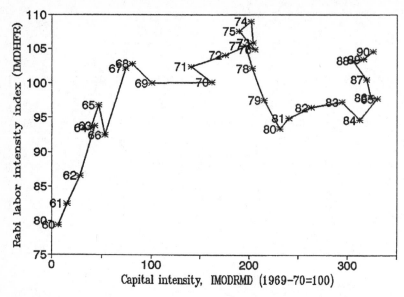

Figure 4.4   Relationship between capital intensity (indices of irrigated hectare per man-day of employment generated in the production of *rabi* crops, **(IMODRD)** and labour intensity per hectare of *rabi* foodgrains **(IMDHFR)**: Bangladesh 1960–61 to 1990–91

Phase 4 (1984–90): Capital intensity is stagnating in this period but labour intensity is rising. This may indicate that labour is being absorbed in agriculture because it has few opportunities elsewhere.

Employment per hectare continued to rise in the early phase of the Green Revolution in the dry season but at a slower rate in relation to rising capital intensity than before the Green Revolution. After the mid-1970s labour intensity slowed down for about a decade as capital intensity rose. From 1984–85 to 1990–91, capital intensity was basically stationary and accompanied by rising labour intensity. If employment in the *kharif* (wet) season is more or less stagnant, the dynamics of employment in the *rabi* (dry) season is of crucial importance for agricultural employment.

The foregoing discussion has analysed the impact of increased use of capital on crop sector employment using fertiliser and irrigation as proxies with both being given equal weights. However, the two inputs differ in practice. Fertiliser is a highly divisible input while irrigation is much less so. Rather than treating the two capital intensive inputs separately and giving them equal weights, a better alternative might be to use their interaction as a proxy for capital. This, in our view, is a better representative of capital intensity than their separate treatment might indicate.[2] Hence the remainder of this discussion examines the relationship between use of capital and labour absorption in the Bangladeshi crops sector. To that end, we define capital intensity as a product of fertiliser applied per gross cropped hectare (**FERT**) and percentage of gross cropped area irrigated (**IRRI**). Thus the new variable is defined as the index of the product of **FERT** and **IRRI** with 1969–70 as the base and is designated as **INDFIRRI**.

Now consider the behaviour of overall labour intensity per hectare (**IMDPHA**), total *rabi* season employment (**IMDR**) and total crop sector employment (**ITOTAL**) in relation to capital intensity (**INDFIRRI**). A casual observation suggests that there might be a structural shift in these relationships around the later half of the 1970s. In each of the three cases, two distinct patterns seem noticeable – one prior to 1974 and one after 1974. In the pre-1974 phase the process of labour absorption have proceeded at a much faster pace than during the past-1974 phase.

In order to fully appreciate the quantitative significance of this apparent structural shift in the behaviour of various indicators of labour absorption in relation to the use of capital, regression lines employing appropriate dummy variables were fitted to the relevant data. These are presented as Equations 4–7 in Table 4.3. The period 1960–74 can be identified as the prior to and early Green Revolution period whereas 1975–90 is a phase in which the Green Revolution is well established. Judged by the usual criteria of explanatory power and statistical quality of the parameters, all the estimated regressions give excellent fits. Both the differential intercepts and slopes are highly significant statistically suggesting that there was a clear shift of the underlying structural relationship between capital intensity and various proxies of labour intensity. This further indicates that the impact of labour absorption in earlier years of the Green Revolution may now be tapering off.

Thus regardless of whether one uses fertiliser and irrigation as separate variables or their interaction as surrogates for capital intensity the following pattern seems to emerge: *Despite faster rate of crop sector labour absorption accompanying greater capital intensity in the initial stages of the Green Revolution, there is an appreciable slow down of the process in later years. This structural shift in the pattern and extent of labour absorption seems to be confirmed by the statistical analysis.*

4.5 LABOUR ABSORPTION IN BANGLADESH AGRICULTURE: SOME FURTHER CONSIDERATIONS

Against the background of the preceding discussion the objective of this section is to shed some further light on the process of labour absorption in Bangladeshi agriculture. The striking feature of this process is that crop

Table 4.3 Relationship between overall labour intensity per hectare (IMDPHA), overall and rabi season labour use (ITOTAL and IMDR), and fertiliser irrigation interaction (INDFIRRI)

	Equations (Dependent variable IMDPHA)			Equations (Dependent variable IMDR)			Equations (Dependent variable ITOTAL)		
	4.4 (1960–90)+	4.4A (1960–74, D=0)+	4.4B (1975–90, D=1)+	4.5 (1960–90)+	4.5A (1960–75, D=0)+	4.5B (1976–90, D=1)+	4.6 (1960–90)+	4.6A (1960–76, D=0)+	4.6B (1977–90, D=1)+
INTERCEPT DUMMY	3.362			−6.014			19.579		
t-value	5.957*			−0.706			4.408*		
SLOPE DUMMY	−0.025			−0.067			−0.057		
t-value	−7.591*			−2.185*			−3.264*		
INDFIRRI	0.030	0.030	0.004	0.133	0.165	0.084	0.061	0.056	0.009
t-value	8.946*	9.181*	6.869*	4.122*	3.958*	8.539*	3.720*	2.935*	4.420*
CONSTANT	96.469	96.396	99.831	94.955	69.507	97.551	83.193	83.178	98.820
t-value	277.870*	272.100*	191.830*	4.076*	8.928*	9.952*	31.218*	27.260*	54.500*
R²	0.919	0.920	0.771	0.979	0.934	0.950	0.911	0.754	0.710
DW	1.899	1.972*	2.220	1.289*	1.349*	1.574*	1.974*	1.927*	1.869*

* Significant at least at the 5 per cent level.
+ 1960–90 means 1960–61 to 1990–91 etc. Dummy variables are used for sub-periods based on visual observation of the plottings (not reported here).
* After adjusting for first-order positive autocorrelation using Cochrane–Orcutt method.

sector employment in the *rabi* season (**MDTOTRAB**) has more than quadrupled over a period of three decades since the beginning of the 1960s. This is despite a slowdown in the trend of labour intensity for *rabi* crops (**MDPHAR**) as well as that for *rabi* foodgrains (**MDHFR**). The area under cultivation during the *rabi* season (**RABIA**) has more than trebled while *rabi* foodgrain (*boro* rice and wheat) area (**RABIAF**) has had a six-fold increase. Land which remained fallow during the dry season has been brought under cultivation and this has led to an increase in the incidence of multiple cropping. On an annual basis increased frequency of cultivation (cropping) has resulted in the increase of effective (gross) area under cultivation annually, despite a decline in the net cropped hectareage (that is, the total area of land cropped at least once a year) from 8.5 to 8.2 million hectares between the early 1960s and the late 1980s. These changes have led to a significant increase in the intensity of cropping from an average of 133 per cent in the early 1960s to an average of about 167 per cent in the late 1980s. Area triple cropped has nearly doubled from around 480 to around 936 thousand hectares between 1965/66–1969/70 and 1986/87–1990/91.

The increase in the incidence of multiple cropping typified by greater frequency of cropping and the resulting rise in the intensity of cropping has increased the demand for labour during the *rabi* season. Furthermore, a relatively faster rate of growth in overall employment in this season has reduced inter-seasonal differences in employment. The difference in labour requirements between the two seasons (**SEASDIFF**) has declined from over 1.3 billion persondays in the early 1960s to less than half a billion persondays in-recent years. In proportionate terms (**PROPSEAS**) this implies a decline of from over 84 per cent to around 30 per cent. This comes into sharper focus if we consider the trend of the difference between employment between the *kharif* and *rabi* seasons as a percentage of overall *kharif* season employment (**PROPSEAS = [SEASDIFF/MDTOTKHA]** × 100). The regression line postulating **PROPSEAS** as a function of time (*T*) is presented as Equation (7) set out in Table 4.4. It can be clearly seen that the statistical quality of the estimates and the explanatory power are very good. This lends support for the hypothesis that seasonal differences in employment have indeed narrowed down quite considerably with the advent of the Green Revolution technologies. This indicates a more stable (or less variable) pattern of employment throughout the year which may, of course, have positive welfare implications.[3]

What factors determine overall employment both annually as well as seasonally? Given the earlier discussion it seems possible that employment is significantly influenced by increase in the effective area under cultiva-

Table 4.4   Trend in difference in employment during the kharif and rabi seasons:
Bangladesh 1960–61 to 1990–91

	Equation 4.7 (Dependent variable PROPSEAS)
T	−1.704
t-value	−5.421*
CONSTANT	89.831
t-value	14.88*
R²	0.939
DW	1.518*

* Significant at least at the 5 per cent level.
* Adjusted for first order autocorrelation using Cochrane–Orcutt method.

tion. Let us explore that possibility in terms of overall (annual) and seasonal employment figures for all crops as well as for foodgrains. The results are set out as Equations 8A–8F in Table 4.5. The dependent variables **ITOTAL**, **ITOTKHA**, and **ITOTRAB** respectively represent indices (1969–70 = 100) of total annual employment generated in the crop sector, during the *kharif* and during the *rabi* seasons while **IMDFG**, **IMDFK** and **IMDFR** represent total corresponding employment generated in the food sectors. The independent variables **TOTALA**, **KHARIA** and **RABIA** are respective areas under all crops, *kharif* and *rabi* crops while **AFOOD**, **KHARIAF** and **RABIAF** respectively represent areas under all foodgrains, *kharif* and *rabi* foodgrains. **JUTEA** is area under jute.

One can clearly see the statistical quality of the estimated parameters and explanatory powers of the regressions reported in Equations 8A–8F. Our results confirm that the respective areas under cultivation of various crops or in various seasons or over the year are predominant determinants of employment in the Bangladeshi crop sector. It is interesting to note that the coefficient of area under jute (**JUTEA**) is highly significant. Given that it depends on jute-paddy price relatives and that it competes with *aus* paddy, it is not surprising that **JUTEA** is a significant determinant of *kharif* season employment (Equation 8B).

To what extent do areas under cultivation emerge as significant determinants of labour intensities? This possibility is explored in terms of labour intensities per hectare of all *kharif* (**MDPHAK**), all *rabi* (**MDPHAR**) and all crops (**MDPHA**) as well as *kharif*, *rabi* and all foodgrains (**MDHFK**, **MDHFR** and **MDPHFG**) and the relevant independent variables. The results are set out as Equations 9A-9F in Table 4.6.

Table 4.5 Relationship between area under various crops and seasons, and (total) labour use: Bangladesh, 1960–61 to 1990–91

	Equation 4.8A (Dependent variable ITOTAL)	Equation 4.8B (Dependent variable ITOTKHA)	Equation 4.8C (Dependent variable ITOTRAB)	Equation 4.8D (Dependent variable IMDFG)	Equation 4.8E (Dependent variable IMDFK)	Equation 4.8F (Dependent variable IMDFR)
TOTALA	8.672					
t-value	20.49*					
KHARIA		8.735				
t-value		27.540*				
JUTEA		8.323				
t-value		9.672*				
RABIA			51.567			
t-value			23.230*			
AFOOD				9.933		
t-value				15.86*		
KHARIAF					10.654	
t-value					91.39*	
RABIAF						104.28
t-value						36.91*
CONSTANT	−9.820	−0.461	−12.333	2.015	0.660	−6.564
t-value	−1.68*	−0.164	−1.83*	0.203	0.492	−1.187
R²	0.991	0.986	0.993	0.990	0.998	0.998
DW	1.781*	1.597*	1.603*	1.168*	1.354*	1.677*

* Significant at least at the 5 per cent level.
* Adjusted for first order autocorrelation using Cochrane–Orcutt procedure.

Table 4.6   Relationship between labour intensity per hectare for different crops and relevant land areas under cultivation: Bangladesh 1960–61 to 1990–91

	Equation 4.9A (Dependent variable MDPHAK)	Equation 4.9B (Dependent variable MDPHAR)	Equation 4.9C (Dependent variable MDPHA)	Equation 4.9D (Dependent variable MDPHFG)	Equation 4.9E (Dependent variable MDHFK)	Equation 4.9F (Dependent variable MDHFR)
JUTEA	15.728					
t-value	9.969*					
RABIA		40.872				
t-value		3.249*				
NCA					0.463	
t-value					0.758	
KHARIAF					-0.338	
t-value					-1.177	
JUTRICE					-0.195	
t-value					1.090	
KHARIA	-1.074					
t-value	-1.790**					
TOTALA			2.411			
t-value			2.762*			
IMODRMD				0.020		0.922
t-value				1.106		6.370*
SLOPE DUMMY+		-40.625				-0.942
t-value		-3.034*				-5.731*
CONSTANT	171.960	120.720	150.800	175.39	162.320	197.030
t-value	32.825*	5.484*	13.560*	16.881*	37.204*	21.104*

Table 4.6 (Continued)

	Equation 4.9A (Dependent variable MDPHAK)	Equation 4.9B (Dependent variable MDPHAR)	Equation 4.9C (Dependent variable MDPHA)	Equation 4.9D (Dependent variable MDPHFG)	Equation 4.9E (Dependent variable MDHFK)	Equation 4.9F (Dependent variable MDHFR)
INTERCEPT DUMMY[+]	0.007	94.757				69.056
t-value	0.006	3.708*				4.875*
R^2	0.806	0.849	0.859	0.942	0.927	0.889
DW	1.576[l]	1.641[l]	1.966[l]	1.245[l]	1.078[l]	1.567[l]

* Significant at least at the 5 per cent level.

[+] Dummy variable D = 0 for 1960–68 and D = 1 for 1969–90. Dummy variables are used for sub-periods based on visual observation of plottings (not reported here).

[l] After adjusting for first-order positive autocorrelation using Cochrane–Orcutt method.

** Significant at least at the 10 per cent level.

In terms of overall explanatory power and statistical significance of the coefficients, all of the estimated regression lines (except the one for *kharif* foodgrains, Equation 9E) provide reasonably good fits. All the coefficients except those in Equation 9E are highly significant and the explanatory power ranges between 0.56 and 0.82. In general the explanatory powers of the equations incorporating *kharif* season labour intensities (**MDPHAK** and **MDHFK**) are lower than those of labour intensities for *rabi* or overall crop or foodgrains.

Overall labour intensity (**MDPHA**, Equation 9C) is significantly influenced by total area under cultivation (**TOTALA**), while that for all foodgrains is significantly influenced by the proxy for modern irrigation (**IMODRMD**). Jute area (**JUTEA**) is a significant positive determinant of *kharif* season labour intensity (**MDPHAK**) as is its total area (**KHARIA**). Note that the intercept dummy is statistically significant (D = 0 for 1960–61 to 1968–69 and D = 1 for the remainder of the time series). Regressions using slope dummy were run but did not turn out to be significant so are not reported here. Note also that the negative sign of the coefficient implies that despite fall in the *kharif* area (**KHARIA**) labour intensity has increased slowly but with fluctuations due to year to year variations in jute area. If one looks at Equation 9E the jute-rice interaction variable (**JUTRICE**) seems to have a significant (even though only at 10 per cent level) negative influence on *kharif* season foodgrain labour intensity (**MDHFK**).

Overall *rabi* season labour intensity (**MDPHAR**) is significantly positively influenced by *rabi* area (**RABIA**). However, there has been a structural shift in this relationship as can be seen from the statistical significance of the slope and intercept dummies (D = 0 for up to and including 1968–69 and D = 1 otherwise). The relationship seems to have changed from one of being significantly positive to being significantly negative in the period of new technology. One should note however, that labour intensity for *rabi* crops (**MDPHAR**) shows a declining tendency after reaching a higher level during the period of the new technology compared to the pre-Green Revolution period. One might also note that increase in area under *rabi* crops is partly due to increase in area under less labour intensive crops (for example, pulses) since the later half of the 1980s and partly due to the expansion of the area irrigated by modern methods which are relatively less labour-intensive compared to traditional techniques of irrigation. This seems to be supported by the statistical significance of the slope and intercept dummies for the variable proxying for modern irrigation (**IMODRMD**) (see Equation 9F). There is clear structural shift in the relation between *rabi* foodgrain labour intensity (**MDHFR**) and modern irrigation (**IMODRMD**).

4.6   GROWTH OF NON-AGRICULTURAL EMPLOYMENT

Now consider some indicators of changes in the structure of the Bangladeshi labour force at the macro-level. The relative share of agriculture in total employment fell from 78.5 per cent in 1973–74 to 64.9 per cent in 1989–90 (BBS 1992a, p.25). If one considers the sectoral distribution of labour force and labour productivity, one gets a clearer picture of the dynamics of the labour market. The 1989 *Labour Force Survey* (BBS 1992a, p.25) findings identified construction, manufacturing, trade and transportation as the fastest growing employment sectors in the Bangladesh economy. Information presented in Table 4.7 sets out the pattern of non-agricultural employment and productivity growth. While the growth in non-agricultural employment seems impressive, the decline in labour productivity in all sectors except transportation casts doubt about the real significance of the structural change in the labour market. This

Table 4.7   Non-agricultural employment and productivity growth: Bangladesh, 1974–1989

Year	Manufacturing	Construction	Trade	Transport
Employment (million)				
1974 Census	1.026	0.036	0.841	0.351
1983 LFS	2.483	0.487	3.255	1.088
1984 LFS	2.700	0.600	3.600	1.200
1985 LFS	3.000	0.600	3.800	1.300
1989 LFS	7.000	0.600	4.100	1.300
Value added per labourer (in 1972–73 Taka)				
1973	3315.789	47583.333	6114.150	6387.464
1983	3196.536	6156.057	2026.421	5175.551
1984	2971.259	7506.000	2156.444	7609.167
1985	2904.200	8686.000	2184.474	8400.769
1989	1407.314	9916.333	2193.415	9080.615
Index of value added per labourer (1973 = 100)				
1973	100.000	100.000	100.000	100.000
1983	96.403	12.937	33.143	81.027
1984	89.609	15.774	35.270	119.127
1985	87.587	18.254	35.728	131.520
1989	42.443	20.840	35.874	142.163

Note: LFS means labour force survey. The years in the middle and bottom panels refer to the corresponding financial years beginning July.

Source: Based on data from BBS (1979; 1984b; 1990a; 1990b; 1992b; 1992c).

seems to support the view of Khan and Hossain (1989, p.19) who argue that '... as agricultural growth absorbed less labour at the margin, more and more people found themselves with agriculture as the secondary, rather than primary source of employment ... It is very likely that a good deal of increase in non-agricultural employment was in activities with very low productivity (e.g. rudimentary trading in rural areas)'.

An important facet of the dynamics of the labour market is the significant employment contribution of the ready made garment industry through a series of backward and forward linkages. As of 1991–92 this sector employed 0.690 million members of the labour force. Of the total number of those employed in this sector more than three-quarters are women, about 75 per cent of whom were from the rural areas. The growth of this industry has added a new dimension to the pattern of rural–urban migration, industrial relations and occupational structure. The labour force employed outside of the garment industry and in the public sector are highly unionised compared to those that are employed in it. Hussain (1993, p.50) claims that cultural reasons are responsible for women workers being less union prone, more disciplined and more vulnerable. They provide a fertile ground for wage discrimination (cf. Quasem 1992, pp.133–134). Anecdotal evidence suggests low labour productivity in the garment industry by international standards (Hossain 1993, p.52). The price advantage of Bangladeshi products is not based on high productivity but on low wage rate (DCCI, nd).[4] This seems to support the view that non-agricultural employment growth has not necessarily resulted in high growth in productivity.

Let us now look at the growth in agricultural and non-agricultural real wages. The information on real wages is set out in Table 4.8. **RWINDEX1** and **RWINDEX2** are real agricultural wages deflated by industrial and food CPIs respectively, while **INDWAGE** represent real industrial wages. Very little growth in real wages can be observed. What seems to be more disturbing is the instability of the wages series especially agricultural wages. This is clearly illustrated by Figure 4.5. On the whole however, the average in the later years is higher than that in the early phase of the Green Revolution.

We have been concerned so far with the employment generated within agriculture by the Green Revolution. However, the adoption of Green Revolution technologies and growth in agricultural production has also led to considerable growth in employment outside the agricultural sector. It is necessary to take account of both the direct and indirect employment effects of new technologies in agriculture. There are a number of different ways in which the intersectoral linkages of agriculture can be classified. We can for example divide these into interdependencies in supply and interdependence due to demand factors.

Table 4.8 Trends in agricultural and industrial real wages: Bangladesh, 1969–70 to 1988–89

Year	RWINDEX1	RWINDEX2	INDWAGE
1969	100	100	100
1970	102	101	104
1971	106	94	102
1972	83	85	67
1973	84	88	66
1974	71	60	46
1975	82	87	58
1976	85	93	63
1977	76	85	76
1978	80	85	90
1979	80	80	85
1980	83	87	88
1981	80	84	82
1982	84	91	83
1983	87	91	81
1984	97	101	85
1985	106	110	95
1986	113	108	93
1987	102	91	106
1988	99	97	107
1989	90	100	95
1990	90	104	95
1991	93	106	98
1992	91	98	106
1993	86	96	109

Note: 1969 means financial year beginning July 1969 etc.; **RWINDEX1** and **RWINDEX2** are indices of are real wages (taka/day) and are derived by deflating nominal wages by consumer price indices of industrial and food commodities respectively. **INDWAGE** are indices of real industrial wages. All indices are constructed with 1969–70 = 100.

Sources: Based on data from BBS (1979; 1984b; 1990a; 1992c); BMOA (1994); World Bank (1995b).

The following supply-side interdependencies can be noted:

- *Green Revolution production depends much more heavily on inputs from the non-agricultural technologies than prior technologies. Backward linkages exist on account of increased demand for fertiliser use, pesticides, certified seed, machinery and fuel and the supply of irrigation water, just to mention a few factors. These have been found to be high in the case of rice and jute, for example (Alauddin 1986).*

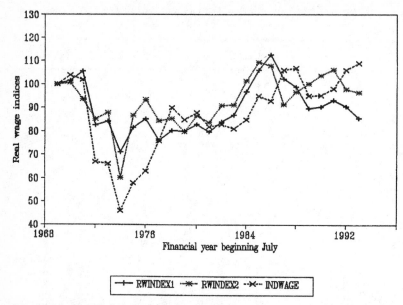

Figure 4.5 Trends in indices (1969–70 = 100) of real agricultural (**RWINDEX1** and **RWINDEX2**) and industrial wages (**INDWAGE**): Bangladesh 1969–70 to 1993–94. **RWINDEX1** and **RWINDEX2** are indices of real wages derived by deflating nominal wages and food commodities respectively. **INDWAGE** are indices of real industrial wages

- *Furthermore, increased agricultural production has a number of forward linkages. We would expect increased agricultural production as a rule to lead to greater demand for transport services; for distribution services and downstream processing. In the case of Green Revolution technologies, this linkage is enhanced because greater specialisation in production can be expected to occur as the market system becomes more widely established. Such specialisation results in greater exchange and demand for transport services. Trade and transport services have significant employment linkages (Alauddin 1986; Hossain 1987). There is little doubt that the Green Revolution has substantially increased the volume of agricultural output entering internal trade in Bangladesh.*

Consider now the impact of the Green Revolution from the point of view of the disposal of net farm incomes. The following may be noted:

- *Even though the demand of poor agricultural households for non-agricultural goods tends to be proportionately low in relation to their income, most have some demand for such goods. Since the total number of households directly supported by agriculture has increased, some rise in demand for non-agricultural goods could be expected as a result of this scale factor. Indonesia has experienced considerable economic growth in recent years. Agricultural growth has contributed strongly to this. It has been estimated that in the 1980s about one-third of total income growth was used to expand the market for non-agricultural goods and services (Tabor 1992, p.162).*
- *Income in agriculture appears to have become more unequal since the onset of the Green Revolution. Higher income earners have a proportionately higher demand for non-agricultural goods. A recent study (Mujeri et al. 1993) finds very little difference between consumption patterns of the rural rich and the urban rich in Bangladesh.*
- *Some agricultural households have achieved a higher net income as a result of the Green Revolution. To the extent that this leads to increased investment by these households in the non-agricultural sector, it also leads to greater off-farm employment.*

Taking all of the above factors into account, there is strong evidence (Hossain 1984; 1987) that the Green Revolution has generated substantial indirect employment in rural and urban areas in Bangladesh. However, its prospects for increasing direct and indirect employment further seem to be diminishing. The growth rate of agricultural production is diminishing and this will slow down the growth of its indirect impacts on employment. Prospects for increasing employment within the agricultural sector do not seem good. When this is combined with Bangladesh's rate of growth of population, its prospects for eliminating underemployment and unemployment seem poor.

It is possible that Bangladesh has lost the opportunity to generate continually expanding employment through the development of rural and urban industries by using the surplus generated by the Green Revolution. By contrast, China appears to have harnessed a surplus from agriculture to industrialise, and in particular to build up rural industries. China has been following rural employment generation by encouraging the growth of non-agricultural industries (Tisdell 1993, Ch. 8). This was one of the policies considered by Ishikawa (1978) for absorbing the agricultural labour surplus, and was also recommended by Chayanov (Thorner *et al.* 1966) in the Russian context.

The above discussion lends support to two hypotheses:

- *The employment-generating impact of the Green Revolution technologies in agriculture is slowing down. That us, agricultural output growth at the margin has become relatively less labour-intensive in recent years than was the case at the onset of the Green Revolution.*
- *Apparent changes in the occupational structure of the Bangladeshi labour force may merely reflect a relocation of surplus labour from agriculture to the non-agricultural sector where much of it may be still surplus. It would be misleading to term this phenomenon a real turning point.*[5]

4.7   CONCLUDING OBSERVATIONS AND POLICY IMPLICATIONS

This chapter highlights the contribution of the Green Revolution technologies in employment generation in Bangladesh agriculture. Important changes have taken place in Bangladesh agriculture since the introduction of the new agricultural technology. This has led to significant employment gains compared to the pre-Green Revolution situation. While the *kharif* (wet season) employment has remained stagnant or may even have declined slightly, there has been a four-fold increase in employment during the *rabi* (dry) season. Thus the overall increase in employment in the crop sector is of the order of around 30 per cent between the 1960s and the late 1980s. Due to a dramatic decline in the interseasonal differences in employment, employment is more evenly spread throughout the year. Herein lies the real significance of the employment contribution of the Green Revolution in Bangladesh.

Increased incidence of multiple cropping, permitted by increased irrigation, has led to an increase in the effective area under cultivation which has resulted in significant employment gains during the *rabi* season. During the initial years labour intensity per hectare of cultivated land grew at a reasonable pace but in recent years it seems to be declining, albeit slightly, but is still higher than that of the pre-Green Revolution period. Thus at the margin agriculture absorbs labour at a slower rate than previously because the marginal contribution of extra labour is quite low.

The growth in employment has resulted primarily from the increase in gross area under cultivation and to a lesser extent from increased labour usage per hectare. Thus the employment increase is more area-based than intensity-based which contrasts with the pattern of output growth which is more productivity-based than area-based (Alauddin and Tisdell 1991a). There are signs that greater reliance on increasing the effective area cropped via irrigation may not be ecologically sustainable. In some cases underground water supplies are being unsustainably utilised (Ahmed 1986; Sinha 1984). This, combined with the risks for yields of further intensification of agriculture, make it unlikely that the foodgrain sector of Bangladesh will continue to add substantially to agricultural employment.

It is interesting to note the pattern of labour transfer from agriculture to non-agricultural sectors. Non-agricultural employment has increased significantly but has been accompanied by declining productivity and little or no consistent or steady increase in agricultural or non-agricultural real wages. Thus while more and more people are able to find employment as a result of the Green Revolution, there has been very little change in the real income for the masses. This pattern of labour transfer contrasts with that of the contemporary developed countries of the West or of East Asia (Alauddin and Tisdell 1991b; Tisdell and Alauddin 1992).

Notes

1. The 50 crops considered in this chapter are as follows:

    CEREALS: Six crops of rice viz., *aus* local, *aus* HYV, *aman* local, *aman* HYV, *boro* local and *boro* HYV; two crops of wheat, viz. wheat local and wheat HYV (8).

    CASH CROPS: Jute, sugarcane, tobacco, tea and cotton (5).

    OILSEEDS: Rape and mustard, *kharif* sesame seeds, *rabi* sesame seeds, linseed, *kharif* groundnut, *rabi* groundnut, and coconut (7).

    PULSES: Lentil, gram, *mashkalai*, *moong*, *khesari* and pea (6).

    FRUITS: Mango, banana, pineapple, jackfruit, watermelon (5).

    VEGETABLES: Potato, sweet potato, tomato, cabbage, cauliflower, *jhinga, karala, kharif* egg plant, *rabi* egg plant, *kharif* pumpkin, *rabi* pumpkin, radish, bean, aram (14).

    SPICES: *Kharif* chilli, *rabi* chilli, onion, garlic, turmeric (5).

2. There is a fair degree of interaction between fertiliser and irrigation. In fact, as is well known, HYVs respond better to fertiliser under irrigated conditions than otherwise.

3. For an elaborate and insightful analysis of this aspect see Gill (1991).

4. This and related issues are addressed in a separate paper (Alauddin 1996).

5. For an excellent discussion of this point see Osmani (1990).

5 Village Perspectives on Technology, Employment and the Environment

5.1 INTRODUCTION

The relationship encompassing technology, employment and the environment is very complex. This is illustrated in Figure 5.1 (adapted from Markandya 1995). The preceding chapter provided an aggregate-level analysis of the relationship between employment and technological change following the Green Revolution. The primary focus was on the prospects for the crop sector providing employment to the growing labour force and labour transfer from agricultural to non-agricultural sectors and trends in agricultural and non-agricultural wages.

This chapter provides insights from farm-level data on the technology–environment–employment nexus in rural Bangladesh. Environmental issues are to a large extent a result of changes in technology. It must be emphasised, however, that environmental problems are not confined to rural Bangladesh. Serious environmental problems exist in urban areas as well. Nevertheless, rural environmental issues predominate, for Bangladesh is primarily a rural society.

The focus of this chapter is on major economic and related environmental changes which have occurred in three Bangladesh villages. These changes have been associated with *inter alia* the adoption of new agricultural technologies, population growth and penetration of market forces. These have impacted on employment opportunities to earn a livelihood. These effects are documented using case studies from three villages from three ecologically different areas of Bangladesh. The specific empirical evidence from the three study villages follows a brief overview of rural environmental trends and a disaggregated analysis from district level secondary data on crop sector employment.

5.2 STATE OF THE RURAL ENVIRONMENT: A BRIEF OVERVIEW

The state of the environment in rural Bangladesh has been discussed in somewhat greater detail elsewhere (Alauddin *et al.* 1995, pp.222–4). We do

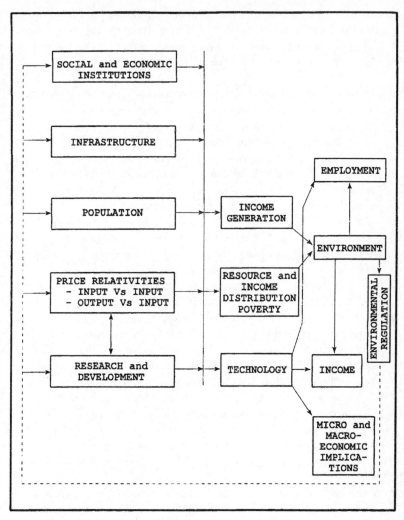

Figure 5.1 Schematic diagram representing inter-relationships among technology, the environment and employment

not wish to repeat them here. A large number of natural environmental problems such as floods, droughts and cyclones befall Bangladesh with monotonous regularity. To a considerable extent economic growth has magnified the effect of such natural disasters and has exacerbated environmental problems in rural Bangladesh. This can in the main be attributed both to economic developments and population growth in Bangladesh. It is also due to externalities or spillovers from economic developments and change in neighbouring countries such as India and Nepal. These have resulted in intensification of land- and water-use. This phenomenon in its turn has entailed adverse environmental effects. However, one must note the following:

- *Increased uncertainty in flows of rivers and streams, resulting both in greater severity of flooding and reduced availability of water during the dry season with adverse consequences for navigation, fish stocks, siltation, water quality and so on.*
- *Reduced availability of water and reduced water quality, for example salinisation due to reduced inflows of freshwater into rivers and streams, or the leaching of nitrates into groundwater from artificial fertiliser use in the growing of crops.*
- *Decline in soil quality due, for example, to the increasing incidence of multiple cropping. The humus content, structure and nutrient content of the soil can suffer from such practices. The use of artificial fertilisers can also increase soil acidity and destroy useful flora and fauna in the soil (Islam 1990). Increased pesticide use, especially of insecticides, has had adverse environmental externalities.*
- *Increased deforestation due to logging, extension of agriculture in some areas and intensification of slash-and-burn agriculture which has reduced the length of the rotation cycle in jhum cultivation. Deforestation has a number of serious environmental consequences such as greater fluctuations in river flows, more rapid soil erosion and loss of wildlife with implications for reduced genetic diversity.*
- *Comparative crowding out of traditional varieties of crops, usually well adapted to natural local conditions, since the advent of the new agricultural technology resulting in narrowing of the genetic base of agricultural production (see for example Alauddin and Tisdell 1991).*
- *Substantial reductions in stock of inland fish as a result of environmental changes such as reduced water availability and quality in streams and rivers, draining and filling of water bodies, and to some extent as a result of greater chemical use in agriculture associated with the adoption of Green Revolution technologies.*
- *Continued disappearance of indigenous wildlife, mainly as a result of over-harvesting and habitat alteration. Habitat alteration is brought about by expansion and intensification of economic activity and by rising levels of human population in Bangladesh.*

The incidence of environmentally related disease is high in Bangladesh and is to a large extent linked to faecal pollution of surface water. In

Bangladesh, 80 per cent of illness has in fact been attributed to water-borne diseases (Haque and Hoque 1990). This incidence remains high in rural areas and, apart from the suffering which it causes, it is a serious economic impediment. In some parts of Bangladesh extension of the area under irrigation has added to the incidence of malaria by providing a more hospitable environment for mosquito-breeding.

5.3 SOME EVIDENCE AT THE DISAGGREGATED LEVEL

Against the background of the aggregate analysis in the preceding chapter and as a prelude to village level analysis let us consider some evidence at a relatively disaggregated (district) level. Bangladesh Bureau of Statistics (BBS) has published data on the input-use in the production of major agricultural crops for the 1989–90 crop year (BBS 1991a; 1991b; 1992b). The BBS data are collected at the farm level and then published in aggregated form at the districts level. Using such data for 22 districts and the Cobb-Douglas functional form the BBS estimates the impact of several inputs on the yield per acre of three rice varieties (HYVs of *boro*, *aman* and *aus* rice). The inputs included physical quantities per acre of labour hours, kilograms of chemical fertilisers and bundles of seedlings, and per acre expenditures on irrigation and pesticides. The estimated yield functions gave elasticity of yield with respect to labour of 0.003, –0.03 and –0.02 respectively for HYVs of *boro*, *aman* and *aus* rice. Table 5.1 sets out some relevant information on these. One must exercise caution in placing too much confidence in the results in view of the quality of the estimates of Cobb-Douglas production functions.

It can be seen from Table 5.1 that the value of marginal product (VMP) of labour is substantially lower than its marginal cost as measured by the going wage rate. If this is true, it indicates that there is an agricultural surplus taking Marglin's definition (Marglin 1976) and one may even exist in Lewis' sense (Lewis 1954) because of the negative values of marginal yields (cf. Cao and Tisdell 1991). In reality, however, the going wage rate may not measure the opportunity cost of family labour because wage-employment may not be easy to obtain or may not be available with appropriate duration and at an appropriate time for all members of the family. A similar situation has been observed for China during the Republican period. Rural women in Wuxi worked at home in sericulture even though cash earnings in factories were higher than when working at home. Factory work meant prolonged absence of women and families were deprived of other benefits from women being able to work at home (Bell 1992, p.240). Nevertheless, after taking this into account, it seems

Table 5.1   Marginal revenues and costs of HYV paddy farmers in Bangladesh, by district, season and labour input: District level data 1989–90

Technology, season and input	Elasticity of yield[a]	Average Yield[b] (kgs)	Marginal Yield (kgs)	Output price/unit (taka)	VMP (taka)	MC (taka)	VMP/ MC
HYV of Paddy							
Boro season							
Labour[c]	0.003	2.63	0.00789	4.99	0.039	5.16	0.0076
Aman season							
Labour	−0.03	4.84	−0.1452	4.98	−0.723	3.56	−0.2031
Aus season							
Labour	−0.02	4.10	−0.082	4.75	−0.390	4.82	−0.0809

Notes: [a] Coefficients in Cobb–Douglas production functions.
     [b] Per hour of labour input.
     [c] In hours.
The Cobb–Douglas production function for yields of different HYVs of paddies are as follows:
BORO YIELD = 1.57 LABOR$^{0.003}$ SEED$^{0.043}$ FERT$^{0.088}$ IRRIGATION$^{0.390}$ PEST$^{0.049}$
   ($R^2 = 0.55$, F = 3.94) The contribution of labour, seedling and fertilizer are not significantly different from zero at the 5% level while irrigation and pesticide variables are significant at 6 and 1 per cent level respectively (BBS, 1992, pp.28–9).

AMAN YIELD = 4.78 LABOR$^{-0.03}$ SEED$^{0.115}$ FERT$^{0.140}$ IRRIGATION$^{0.071}$ PEST$^{0.166}$
   ($R^2 = 0.63$, F = 4.056) None of the regression coefficients is statistically significant at the 5% level (BBS, 1991b, pp.28–33).

AUS YIELD = 9.52 LABOR$^{-0.02}$ SEED$^{-0.27}$ FERT^{019} IRRIGATION$^{0.05}$ PEST$^{-0.09}$
   ($R^2 = 0.54$, F = 2.65) Fertilizer coefficients are statistically significant at the 5% level. Labour coefficient is significant at 6% level (BBS, 1991a, pp.58–9).

highly probable that surplus labour is being employed in Bangladesh agriculture at least in the Marglin sense. Possibly more worrying from an employment point of view is that substantial increases in labour employment in agriculture do not appear to be feasible without large concomitant rises in capital formation in agriculture. Using modern technology during the *Boro* season, for example, an increase of 10 per cent in labour *ceteris paribus* can be expected to result only in 0.03 per cent rise in paddy production. Without a substantial increase in capital inputs, little increase in rice supplies can be expected using modern rice technology and could be even less using traditional technology. BBS (1991b, p.28) reports negative marginal physical product of labour for local transplant *aman* which is the major traditional variety of paddy.

Cost-return surveys indicate that the return to capital is much higher than that of labour. Depending on the region, return on capital for modern varieties exceeds that of labour by between 50 per cent and nearly 200 per cent (Alauddin and Tisdell 1986, p.13) and thus capital bias may be present. One needs to point out, however, that the price of labour input relative to capital input has gone up in recent years. This is despite withdrawal of subsidies on agricultural inputs. This may have encouraged the use of relatively more capital-intensive inputs such as chemical fertilisers and modern irrigation methods (Alauddin and Tisdell 1995).

5.4 FARM-LEVEL ANALYSIS AND AN OVERVIEW OF THE SURVEY VILLAGES

Let us now consider some farm-level evidence relating to agricultural employment. The basic data for this survey were derived from primary surveys in three Bangladesh villages. The farm-level data relate to 1992–93. In all, 359 households were interviewed on the basis of pre-designed questionnaires. Of the 359 respondents, 209 were paddy growers. More than 90 per cent of the paddy farmers in each of the three villages were interviewed.

The survey villages are located in ecologically different regions of Bangladesh. There are significant inter-village variations in topography, soil, precipitation and other geo-physical conditions.

Rajmangalpur, a village in the greater Comilla district in Northeastern Bangladesh, belongs to the Surma-Kushiara floodplain, receives very high annual rainfall and is susceptible to floods. This village has a very high incidence of landlessness. Nearly 48 per cent of the households are functionally landless. Rajmangalpur has a less diversified cropping pattern. Rice is the dominant crop even though many farmers produce betel leaves. *Boro* (dry season) HYV paddy is planted to about 50 per cent of the land area operated. Roughly about the same percentage of the operated area is allocated to *aman* (wet season) HYV paddy. Percentage of total paddy cropped area (including multiple cropping) allocated to HYVs is more than 70 per cent. Forty one per cent of the operated area is under modern irrigation. About 63 per cent of the paddy farming households owned land areas below an average size of 0.40 hectare.

Durgapur is a village located in the greater Kushtia district in Southwestern Bangladesh. It is on a shallow floodplain area, with distinct dry and wet seasons owing to the monsoon. While the Kushtia district has low rainfall occasional flooding does occur during the monsoon. Durgapur has a very diversified cropping pattern with the main crops grown being rice, jute, sugarcane, oilseeds and pulses. About a third of the household are functionally landless. The incidence of landlessness is lower than in the other two survey villages. HYV *boro* paddy is planted to less than a quarter of the operated area while about 28 per cent of the total operated area is allocated to HYV *aman* paddy. Thus the percentage of area under HYV paddy (including multiple cropping) is more than 50 per cent. The average size of holding is about 0.90 hectare with more than 46 per cent of the households having an area of less than 0.40 hectare. Just over a third of the total operated area is irrigated by modern techniques.

Rangamati is a village located in the greater Dinajpur district of northwestern Bangladesh. Topographically land in this village is relatively dry. In terms of cropping pattern the village is less diversified, with rice being the principal crop even though some farmers grow jute and betel leaves. More than 50 per cent of the households are functionally landless. More than 30 per cent of the paddy farming households owned less than 0.40 hectare of arable land. The average size of hold is 1.75 hectares. *Boro* HYV is planted to 37 per cent of the total paddy area (multiple cropping), while 34 per cent is allocated to *aman* HYV. Thus the total HYV paddy area is more than 70 per cent.

5.5   EMPLOYMENT CREATION IN RICE FARMING: PATTERNS AND DETERMINANTS

This section focuses on employment creation in rice farming in three survey villages.

5.5.1   Overall employment: Family labour versus hired labour, labour intensity

Table 5.2 sets out relevant information on employment generation in rice farming in three villages. The following points are worth noting:

● *The introduction of the new agricultural technology has made a significant contribution to employment creation. On a seasonal basis the dry season HYV (**BOROH**) cultivation is particularly noteworthy. The contribution of **BOROH** to total rice employment ranges between 25 per cent in the case of Durgapur and just above 40 per cent in the other two villages. Without the introduction of the seed–fertiliser– irrigation technology this would hardly have been possible. This has made the distribution of employment opportunities more even throughout the year. This is consistent with the overall pattern of crop sector employment for Bangladesh as a whole.*

● *A transition from traditional to modern varieties leads to an increase in the relative share of hired labour in total employment. This suggests greater opportunities for wage employment.*

Table 5.2   Employment in rice production: Three Bangladesh villages

CROP	FAMLAB	HIRELAB	TOTAL	PCFMLAB	PCHRLAB	CROPAREA	LINTN
Rajmangalpur							
AUSL	142	189	331	42.90	57.10	1.93	172
AMANL	460	649	1109	41.48	58.52	6.54	170
AMANH	755	1213	1968	38.36	61.64	9.35	210
BOROH	929	1593	2522	36.84	63.16	11.69	216
TOTAL	2286	3644	5930	38.55	61.45	29.51	201
Durgapur							
AUSL	2820	4411	7231	39.00	61.00	36.65	197
AMANL	494	497	991	49.85	50.15	6.14	161
AMANH	1743	3287	5030	34.65	65.35	25.31	199
BOROH	1757	2640	4397	39.96	60.04	21.01	209
TOTAL	6814	10835	17649	38.61	61.39	89.11	198
Rangamati							
AUSL	1079	1491	2570	41.98	58.02	14.54	177
AMANL	599	807	1406	42.60	57.40	9.62	146
AMANH	1593	3839	5432	29.33	70.67	27.78	196
BOROH	2024	4326	6350	31.87	68.13	30.58	208
TOTAL	5295	10463	15758	33.60	66.40	82.52	191

Notes: **AUSL** is local variety of *aus* (early monsoon) rice. **AMANL** and **AMANH** are respectively local and high yielding varieties of of aman (wet season) rice. **BOROH** is high yielding varieties of *boro* (dry sason) rice. **FAMLAB** and **HIRELAB** are persondays of family labour and hired labour respectively. **PCFMLAB** and **PCHRLAB** respectively represent percentages of family and hired labour. **CROPAREA** is land area in hectares cropped with a variety of rice crop. **LINTN** is labor intensity per hectare of cropped land.

● *There seem to be few little inter-village differences in labour intensities per hectare of cropped land. As expected, labour intensities for HYVs seem to be higher than for traditional varieties.*

Now consider in greater detail labour intensities and their determinants. To start with we shall look at the distribution of labour intensities across farms and across regions. The following aspects need to be noted:

● *For aus local variety of rice nearly two-thirds of the Rajmangalpur farms use 150–176 person days of labour per hectare while the remaining farms use between 176 and 200 person days of labour. The bulk of Durgapur farms use 176–225 person days per hectare. Rangamati farms are more or less equally divided between the 150–175 and 176–200 person days per hectare categories.*

● *For aman local variety of rice the heaviest concentration of Rajmangalpur farms is in the below 200 person days category. In*

Rangamati more than 90 per cent of the farms use less than 176 person days per hectare. The distribution is more even among the first three categories of farms in Durgapur.

● *For* aman *high yielding variety of rice most Rajmangalpur farms use in excess of 200 person days per hectare. This is very similar to the pattern of labour use by Rangmati farms. For Durgapur about a third of the farms use up to 200 person days of labour per hectare while nearly two thirds use labour in excess of 200 person days per hectare, the heaviest concentration being in the 200–225 person days category. For* boro *HYV rice the pattern of per hectare labour use seems to be broadly similar in all the three villages.*

Table 5.3   Labour intensity per hectare of land cropped with rice: Three Banglaesh villages

LINTN	AUSL	AMANL	AMANH	BOROH
		(Percentage of farms)		
Rajmangalpur				
Below 150	–	5.3	–	–
150–175	63.6	36.8	–	–
176–200	36.3	36.8	6.7	2.7
200–225	–	21.1	80.0	81.1
Above 226	–	–	13.3	16.2
Durgapur				
Below 150	–	28.1	1.2	–
150–175	2.1	34.4	1.2	–
176–200	59.0	21.9	30.5	11.8
200–225	34.7	9.4	52.5	50.6
Above 226	4.2	6.2	14.6	37.6
Rangamati				
Below 150	–	31.3	2.6	–
150–175	41.4	62.5	–	–
176–200	44.8	6.2	5.3	14.7
200–225	13.8	–	89.7	79.4
Above 226	–	–	2.6	5.9

Notes: **AUSL** is local variety of *aus* (early monsoon) rice. **AMANL** and **AMANH** are respectively local and high yielding varieties of of aman (wet season) rice. **BOROH** is high yielding varieties of *boro* (dry sason) rice. **FAMLAB** and **HIRELAB** are persondays of family labour and hired labour respectively. **PCFMLAB** and **PCHRLAB** respectively represent percentages of family and hired labour. **CROPAREA** is land area in hectares cropped with a variety of rice crop. **LINTN** is labor intensity per hectare of cropped land.

5.5.2 Patterns and determinants of labour intensity

Let us now consider the factors that determine the pattern of labour use. Let us investigate the extent to which yield per hectare influences the intensity of labour use per hectare. Table 5.4 sets out the relevant regression equations.

Table 5.4 Impact of yield per hectare on intensity of labour use per hectare for different rice varieties: Three Bangladesh villages

Crop	Regression equation		*t*-value	R^2
	Constant	Coefficient		
All Samples				
AUSL	172.33	0.0117	2.06*	0.03
AMANL	202.63	−0.0164	−1.56	0.04
AMANH	229.16	−0.0055	−1.30	0.01
BOROH	181.26	0.0098	3.38*	0.07
Rajmangalpur				
AUSL	235	−0.0357	−1.09	0.11
AMANL	201.56	−0.0099	−0.32	0.006
AMANH	204.79	0.0033	0.31	0.004
BOROH	193.66	0.0069	0.86	0.02
Durgapur				
AUSL	204.31	−0.0017	−0.36	0.002
AMANL	202.19	−0.0171	0.70	0.02
AMANH	235.96	−0.0075	−1.26	0.02
BOROH	199.83	0.0058	1.25	0.02
Rangamati				
AUSL	131.01	0.0281	1.54	0.08
AMANL	134.79	0.0067	0.81	0.04
AMANH	159.59	0.0120	1.09	0.03
BOROH	170.84	0.0101	2.33*	0.14

* Significant at least at 5 per cent level.

Notes: **AUSL** is local variety of *aus* (early monsoon) rice. **AMANL** and **AMANH** are respectively local and high yielding varieties of of aman (wet season) rice. **BOROH** is high yielding varieties of *boro* (dry sason) rice. **FAMLAB** and **HIRELAB** are persondays of family labour and hired labour respectively. **PCFMLAB** and **PCHRLAB** respectively represent percentages of family and hired labour. **CROPAREA** is land area in hectares cropped with a variety of Xrice crop. **LINTN** is labor intensity per hectare of cropped land.

For all samples taken together, labour use per hectare seems to vary directly with increase in yield per hectare in the case of the local variety of *aus* rice. A similar result seems to hold for HYV *boro* rice. Both local and high yielding varieties of *aman* rice seem to show that intensity of labour use per hectare tends to decline with increase in yield. However, the coefficients are not statistically significant and the explanatory powers of the estimated equations are poor.

In the case of Rangamati, the estimated equations portray a positive association between yield per hectare and intensity of labour use per hectare. However, only in the case of *boro* HYV rice is the relationship statistically significant. For Durgapur and Rajmangalpur none of the coefficients are statistically significant, and none of the estimated equations has high explanatory power. For Rajmangalpur, the per hectare yields of HYVs of both *aman* and *boro* rice are positively associated with labour intensities. For Durgapur, on the other hand, labour intensity is negatively associated with yield per hectare. *It seems clear that yield per hectare is not a good predictor of intensity of labour use. Even though yield might be regarded as a proxy for technology, a more direct surrogate for technological change might a better predictor of labour intensity per hectare.*

To investigate the relationship between technology and labour use, three proxies were used separately to *explain* variations in overall labour intensity (**LIOVERAL**). The three proxies were: irrigated area as a proportion of total area cropped with all varieties of rice (**PCIRRI**), HYV area as a proportion of total area cropped with all varieties of rice (**PCHYV**) and kilograms of chemical fertilisers used per hectare (**KGFHEC**). The estimated equations were poor both in terms of the statistical significance of the coefficients as well as their explanatory powers. Therefore they are not reported here. Instead two alternative proxies are used. These are derived as composite variables and used as surrogates for technological change. The two such composite variables are:

$$\textbf{INTERACT} = (\textbf{PCHYV}) \times (\textbf{PCIRRI}) \times (\textbf{KGFHEC})$$
$$\textbf{INTERACT1} = (\textbf{PCHYV}) \times (\textbf{PCIRRI})$$

Regression equations with **LIOVERAL** as the dependent variable and **INTERACT** (or **INTERACT1**) as independent variable are estimated. The results are set out in Table 5.5. Eight equations using each of the two alternative technological proxy variables are estimated. The equations relate to the entire sample as well as to the three villages. It can be clearly seen that all the equations are satisfactory from the point of view of statistical significance of the coefficients. The explanatory powers, while not

Table 5.5 Impact of technology on overall intensity of labour use per hectare:
Three Bangladesh villages

| | Estimated equation | | | |
Sample	Constant	Coefficient	*t*-value	R^2
A: Dependent Variable: LIOVERALL				
Independent Variable: INTERACT				
All farms	196.76	0.0409	5.71*	0.16
Rajmangalpur	186.72	0.1158	5.87*	0.46
Durgapur	190.01	0.0775	5.90*	0.27
Rangamati	190.46	0.0235	2.88*	0.17
B: Dependent Variable: LIOVERALL				
Independent Variable: INTERACT1				
All farms	190.38	37.43	7.22*	0.23
Rajmangalpur	180.14	71.82	5.77*	0.47
Durgapur	196.07	29.49	4.56*	0.18
Rangamati	175.10	60.12	5.67*	0.43

* Significant at least at 5 per cent level.

Note: LIOVERALL is OVERALL labour intensity per hectare of total area
cropped with all varieties of rice. INTERACT is interaction of kilograms of
chemical fertiliser per hectare (KgfHec) irrigated area as a percentage of
total cropped area (PCIRRI) and HYV area as a percentage of total cropped
area (PCHYV). Thus INTERACT = KGFHEC × PCIRRI × PCHYV.
INTERACT1 = PCIRRI × PCHYV.

very high, may not be all that unsatisfactory for a set of cross-sectional
data. Thus the results seem to confirm the dominant influence of the new
agricultural technology on the intensity of labour use. This is consistent
with the picture for Bangladesh as a whole presented in Chapter 4.

5.6 ENVIRONMENTAL TRENDS AND THE STATE OF THE RURAL ENVIRONMENT

Rural environments in many parts of the developing world have experienced the impact of increased population and a greater degree of commercialisation following penetration of market and technological forces.
Declining soil quality and fertility, depleting natural resource base, intense
pressure on surface and ground water, loss of *flora* and *fauna* (hence loss

of biological and genetic diversities) epitomise some of the major environmental implications (Conway 1985, Biggs and Clay 1981). Similar changes in the rural environment seem to have taken place in Bangladesh. Previous studies on the subject (for example, M. Ahmed 1986; M.F. Ahmed 1986; Hamid *et al.* 1978; Jones 1984; Tisdell and Alauddin 1989; Alauddin and Tisdell 1991) shed light on environmental changes in rural Bangladesh. Such changes include, *inter alia* , lowering of ground water level beyond the suction limit, loss of fish output in paddy fields and other water bodies, loss of natural soil fertility, increasing dependence on a narrow range of genetic materials (Alauddin *et al.* 1995).

This section investigates whether our primary data from three villages support such trends. It should be noted however that the three survey villages do not typify the environment and changing environmental conditions of the whole of rural Bangladesh. A larger number of villages would need to be surveyed to make the findings more representative and generalisations more meaningful. Nonetheless, all the three villages have been affected by the seed–fertilizer–irrigation technology. Technological change, and the resulting economic growth, often leads to variation in the relative mix of exchange and non-exchange incomes (Alauddin and Tisdell 1991). This could disadvantage the poor and the underprivileged, including the landless, the women and the children who form the most vulnerable group in rural Bangladesh.

5.6.1   Environmental changes in survey villages

Over the years growth in population has led to extension of human habitation to cultivable or cultivated areas. Marginal land area has been brought under cultivation by clearing jungles and bushes, destroying or at least disturbing habitats of wildlife in the survey villages. During the last 2–3 decades, especially in the last 20 years, a number of fruit trees like mango and jackfruit, *khejur* palm (*Phoenix sylvestris*), *jam* (*Syzygium jambolana*), *tal* palm (*Boro ssus flabellifer*) have been cut down for fuel wood for use in the urban centres as well as for commercial brick kilns in some cases. Today one notices few fruit-yielding trees compared to a multitude some twenty years ago. In the last few years, however, the relatively wealthy farmers in Durgapur have begun to plant *shisham* (*Dalbergia sissoo*). This has a high value for timber and is quite profitable to grow.

Livestock populations, including those of sheep, goats and poultry, have remained stationary or have even declined slightly. This is primarily due to:

- *a significant decline in area under fodder crops;*
- *the virtual disappearance of pasture and grazing land; and*
- *a shift from long-stem to short varieties of rice cultivation (e.g. aman local to aman HYV).*

Furthermore, the rapid depletion of trees such as *banyan (Ficus bengalansis)* and *Oshot (Ficus religiosa)* and acacia has led to a decline in the supply of green leaves and fruit which are used as livestock fodder. It was found during the course of fieldwork in Durgapur that fish production in the paddy fields has declined by about two-thirds over the last ten years due to increased use of agro-chemicals. Similar observations can be made about other survey villages. In the study villages, some farmers engage in commercial culture of exotic fishes. Even though these are high-yielding, they are susceptible to diseases and are inferior in taste. The supply of indigenous species of fish has declined. The use of agro-chemicals interrupts natural breeding and causes discontinuity in the life-cycle of fish. Furthermore, reclamation of *beels* and low lying areas for rice production has contributed to a reduction of habitat for local fish.

The new agricultural technology has had several other environmental spillovers. These include:

- *Decline in natural soil fertility due to inappropriate application of chemical fertilisers which are required in greater quantities to maintain crop yields. Due to a stagnation (if not a reduction) in livestock populations, the supply of cow dung for use as an organic manure has not increased. As a result of declining availability of fuel wood, cow dung is increasingly used as a cooking fuel. Furthermore, loss of trees has resulted in the drastic reduction of tree leaves that could be used as green manure.*
- *Comparative crowding out of several indigenous rice varieties due to the introduction of new rice varieties.*
- *Continued application of pesticides has met with the development of resistance. Moreover, insecticides have affected non-target populations, such as predators and parasites that might prove beneficial to human beings. For instance, increased use of chemical agents has much depleted the frog/toad population.*

In the light of the preceding discussion: What implications do these changes have for the rural poor? Are the increased employment opportunities adequate to compensate for the loss in environmental quality?

It has been argued elsewhere (see for example Alauddin and Tisdell 1989; Alauddin *et al.* 1995) that the income of the rural poor, consisting of the landless and the near-landless, has two components:

- *Exchange income: primarily wage income determined in the main through the market mechanism.*
- *Non-exchange income: determined in the main by institutional/ sociological systems in the rural community and usually obtained directly from nature without exchange. It includes, inter alia, wild fruits, firewood, building and thatching materials, water from tanks and ponds for growing vegetables, free-ranging of poultry and some grazing land for sheep, goats and cattle.*

The sources of the exchange component depend on the general level of economic activity (both agricultural and non-agricultural) while the extent of non-exchange income depends primarily on common access or low-cost access to natural resources. It is claimed that the non-exchange component of income could be important in the off-peak periods and is even more significant in abnormal years when both the period of employment is shortened and real income falls, resulting in reduced exchange entitlement (Sen 1981). In other words, the exchange and non-exchange components complement each other and in adverse circumstances the latter component acts as a buffer.

Our empirical evidence from the survey indicates that following the Green Revolution the scope and opportunity for exchange income has increased quite significantly. On the other hand, it seems probable that the scope for non-exchange component income has declined. Available resources for supply of non-exchange income appear to be becoming scarcer in Durgapur. Population pressure and technological forces have depleted them and greater penetration of technological and market forces may have led to some resources being priced which were previously free or freely accessible. Although our data base is limited and quantification must await further research, the evidence in Durgapur indicates reduced availability of non-exchange income.

Fish stocks in the paddy fields have fallen or disappeared. Depletion of fish stocks in the paddy fields implies that an important source of supplementary employment, especially in the leaner months, has disappeared. Thus an important source of supplementary income for many wage labourers or low-income earners has disappeared (Alauddin and Hamid 1996) while also reducing the opportunity to supplement the diet with animal protein.

The role of women, and to some extent children, in supplementing income from formal and informal sources seems to have been undermined by:

● *Restrictions on animal husbandry and free-ranging of poultry.*
● *Loss of opportunities to collect wild fruits and firewood due to the dwindling supply of these resources. It now takes 2–3 times as long to collect fuel as in the past.*
● *Loss of opportunities for rice processing (from paddy to rice) by traditional methods (for instance, Dheki). These have been replaced by labour-saving modern methods. The traditional labour-intensive method of oil milling has also gone out of existence.*

Loss of genetic diversity raises doubts about sustainability of production. Dependence on a narrow range of genetic resources could be disastrous if there is a sudden widespread outbreak of any plant disease or pest or insect attack. Furthermore, reduction in the availability of organic/green manure is likely to lead to a decline in soil quality. While wealthier farmers may be able to replenish soil nutrients using purchased inputs, the smaller farmers may find it difficult to do so because of their limited resource base. This may result in the soil of smaller farmers declining more rapidly in fertility. Constant effort is therefore required to sustain production and employment opportunities in modern agriculture (cf. Johnston and Cownie 1969; Dhikawa 1978; Ahmed 1995) and there is always the possibility of the whole system collapsing.

5.6.2   Environmental change: Implications for sustainability of employment and development

Under normal circumstances increased crop production tends to generate greater employment. Agricultural employment has increased due to agricultural activity during the dry season. Non-agricultural employment has increased somewhat as a result of infrastructural development. Improvement of the main road linking the villages to the nearest urban centres has given some villagers the opportunity to engage in small businesses and provide transportation services. Precise quantification of non-agricultural employment is not possible. However, during the course of the field survey it was gathered that on average a labourer is currently employed for around 250 person days a year. Per capita agricultural employment ranges between 200–220 person days per year (Alauddin *et al.* 1995). Thus a total of 30–50 person days of non-agricultural employment per head seems to have resulted from the changes that followed the Green Revolution and infrastructural development. The respondents indicated that annual employment opportunities per labourer on average has increased from 150 person days to 250 person days during the period. About 30–50 per cent of this increase has resulted from expanded non-agricultural employment opportunities. However this gain seems to have been achieved at the cost of a decline in environmental quality.

5.7   CONCLUDING COMMENTS

In the three villages studied, the adoption of high-yielding varieties of crops and associated technology has increased the amount of labour used in crop production at least marginally and has increased yields substantially. Therefore, the amount of income available through market exchange of commodities seems to have risen. Intensification of agricultural production has occurred in all three villages. One consequence has been a fall in income available from non-exchange sources, such as food obtained by gathering, fishing, collecting of thatching materials and fuel and the availability of free fodder and sustenance for livestock. This has particularly affected the ability of the poor to earn extra income. Notably, the ability of women and children from poor households to supplement family income from such non-exchange sources has been affected. However, there is no conclusive evidence that overall income (from exchange plus non-exchange sources) of the poor and their welfare have declined following the adoption of new agricultural technologies. Further research is warranted.

Despite substantial increase in yields, available evidence from all the three villages suggests that maintaining these yields requires increased rates of application of artificial fertilisers. This indicates problems in sustaining yields as a result of declining soil fertility. Furthermore, local varieties of crops are disappearing as farmers come to concentrate on growing just a few high yielding varieties. While this does not have immediate negative consequences for agricultural yield and employment, in the long term widely used high-yielding varieties may fail ecologically as a result of susceptibility to a particular pest, exposing a risk of serious eventual consequences for production and employment. Preservation of genetic diversity, especially of hardy local varieties of such crops, could help guard against such a disaster. It is also clear that as a result of the introduction of modern agricultural technologies, Bangladesh is becoming dependent on the use of non-renewable resources, such as oil, natural gas and fertiliser, to maintain its agricultural production.

Although there has been a substantial increase in agricultural yields in Bangladesh, these have been at the expense of production in other sectors of the economy. In Durgapur, for example, large reductions in the availability of fish were reported. Soil erosion problems and water problems occurred in the three study villages. All such spillovers and opportunity costs need to be taken into account in quantifying the impact of environmental changes on income and employment.

Crop yields in Bangladesh are still well below those of similar crops in more developed countries and Bangladesh's rate of application of agrochemicals has, for instance, not nearly reached the levels prevailing in Japan. Possibly Bangladesh will increase its application of agro-chemicals and intensify its agriculture further along lines common in more developed countries. But further intensification of its agriculture will undoubtedly add to its environmental problems. It may be that methods of modern agriculture developed for temperate areas are not environmentally well-suited to countries located in the tropics such as Bangladesh. It seems that greater efforts should be made to adapt overseas technologies and develop new technologies which are more appropriate to the environmental and social conditions prevailing in less developed tropical countries such as Bangladesh. Much more research needs to be done to resolve these issues and to take account of environmental spillovers and their employment effects.

Environmental–employment linkages arising from technological change and production variations in agriculture in Bangladesh have been identified for the particular villages studied but, to the extent that quantification has been possible, it is mostly for on-farm or on-site effects. There is a need, apart from strengthening on-farm or on-site estimates of environmental–employment linkages and associated sustainability characteristics, to go beyond this and identify and quantify off-site effects. Such effects include production spillovers or externalities, backward and forward economic linkages and their environmental–employment effects, sustainability of production and employment taking into account all such linkages and capacities for labour absorption both in rural and urban areas. Both the overall impact of production-induced environmental change on employment and distribution require further study (Markandya 1995), including the marginalisation of women and children, and the migration from rural to urban areas.

6 Property Rights, Governance and the Environment

6.1 INTRODUCTION

Governance and property rights are closely linked and sustainable (natural) resource use and management is critically influenced by both. International agencies emphasise this close interrelationship. In fact in the 1990s the World Bank and other UN agencies, as well as individual country aid agencies, have been directing their programmes in the developing world toward improvement in governance – the process of sharing and exercising authority in the management of a country's economic, social and natural resources (Hasan 1996, p.227). In exploring the interrelationship one needs to take explicit account of the legal position (*de jure*) and the actual position (*de facto*). In many instances, especially in LDCs, there is a significant divergence between the legal and the actual positions because of costs and problems associated with the enforcement of property rights.

In the past, Western economists seemed to have concentrated on two contrasting forms of property rights as far as resource management is concerned, namely, private property and open-access property. This dichotomy has tended to result in their support for the establishment of private property or, where this is impractical, state property. The effect has been to dispossess the owners of communal or village property and this has had many adverse consequences, examples of which are available from India. Where state property or control over natural resources, such as forests and fish, has been established, this has tended to be top-down. The economic and social wisdom of this is being increasingly questioned and there are calls for greater community control over natural resources or their co-management. This chapter explores the inter-linkage involving property rights, governance and the environment. The orthodox western view favours private and state property to communal property either because of ignorance or by design or by a combination of both (Tisdell and Roy 1997). It overlooks the scope for beneficial administration of natural resources by local communities or by co-management. Examples from Bangladesh and India are employed to analyse the inextricable linkage among governance, property rights and the environment.

6.2 PROPERTY RIGHTS ISSUES IN A HISTORICAL PERSPECTIVE: A BRIEF OVERVIEW

Historically speaking, economists have been aware of the importance of good governance and property rights for the sustainability of resource use and economic welfare for a considerable time. There is little doubt that many scholars since Adam Smith, and all the great classical economic scholars, were concerned both with means to achieve economic development and the sustainability of that development once achieved. This is for example obvious in the works of Ricardo, Marx and John Stuart Mill. Most economists, with the exception of the Marxists, assumed that the system of private property rights would prevail and did not specifically explore the influence of property rights on economic activity. In fact, major interest in this issue amongst economists did not emerge until the second half of the 20th century (for example, Gordon 1954; Ciriacy-Wantrup 1968; see Tisdell and Roy 1997 for further details).

Property rights and governance are closely intertwined. When individuals or groups have property rights in resources, depending on the nature of these rights, they are able to govern the use and allocation of the resources involved. It therefore becomes important as to who has these rights and how they will be enforced. Ease of enforcement may require state or community support for these rights. Otherwise the cost of retaining or obtaining rights may be excessive and subject to brute force rather than the rule of law. Such an uncivilised state of affairs can only have disastrous economic consequences.

Considerable debate exists in Western societies about the extent to which individuals and communities should be governed by higher authorities, especially by central government. This debate has been sharpened in recent years by argument about whether natural resource use should be controlled by central government and its representatives or by local individuals and communities. This has to do with the extent to which individuals should be governed in their use of natural resources and the extent to which local communities should be controlled by higher authorities (Tisdell and Roy 1997).

In a historical context, following Tisdell and Roy (1997), one can identify three different strands of thought relating to governance which in turn have implications for property rights:

- *Hobbes seemed to favour the ultimate allocation of property rights to the crown or absolute central authority (**state control**),*

- *Rousseau favoured control of property by local communities (**communal control**)*
- *Smith, favouring the market system, supported a system of private property rights (**private control**).*

6.3   PROPERTY RIGHTS: DIFFERENT DIMENSIONS

Property rights have many possible dimensions. The existing literature, however, identifies four broad types of property regimes (Tisdell and Roy 1997):

- *private property: property rights rest with an individual or legal entity;*
- *state property (res publica): property rights rest with the government;*
- *communal property (res communes): resource is controlled by an identifiable community of users; and*
- *open-access property (res nullius): access is free and open to all.*

In reality, there are no watertight divisions between these types of property rights. For example, the state may exercise some rights in relation to private property, that is, it may impose an easement on the property, or there may be rights of trespass by the general public on private or state property. When a resource is private property, the right of exclusion exists, as is also the case for state and communal property, for example, the local community may exclude members of other communities or individuals that do not comply with communal regulations. However, as North (1981) points out, exclusion is not always economic and monitoring entails transaction costs. Consequently, property for which exclusion exists as a legal possibility may become *de facto* open-access property or result in opportunistic use of the property by non-owners leading to partial access. Consequently, the type of market failures that occur for open-access property can arise even in the case of private property. This has happened in some cases where state ownership has replaced communal ownership. This is because the state has been less able to enforce or regulate the use of this property than the local community. An example is the transfer of community forests in Nepal to the State Forestry Department with its headquarters in Kathmandu. Whereas the villagers kept deforestation under control, the Forest Department proved to be unable to do this (Mishra 1982). Similar occurrences can be found in forest areas of Bangladesh. In some cases, even when property is made legally state property, it in fact remains under communal control as occurred in some parts of India, and also in some Polynesian and Melanesian communities in the

Pacific. For example, marine areas adjoining villages remained under the communal control of these villages although legally they became crown or state property after colonisation.

Property rights have a significant bearing on resource use and environmental management. As Perrings (1995, p.106) rightly argues, 'the less complete the property rights, the greater is the propensity for resources to be overutilized. The more environmental services/disservices associated with a given pattern of resource use are not the subject of well-defined rights, the greater is the risk of environmental damage'. This is illustrated in Figure 6.1.

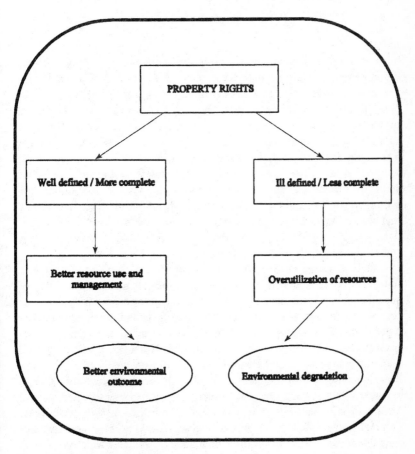

Figure 6.1 Property rights and environmental outcome

6.4   PROPERTY RIGHTS ISSUES: THE WESTERN VIEW

Westerners have largely dismissed communal property as a means of managing resources. In fact, they have tended to treat it synonymously with open-access, arguing that common property results in serious failures in resource allocation and conservation. As is well known, open-access can result in socially damaging abuse of natural resources, lack of investment in protection and husbandry of natural resources and the loss of resources and species which it is socially desirable to retain. This however need not occur if communal governance is the case. Indeed, there will be circumstances in which communal governance offers the best prospect for the optimal conservation and management of a natural resource, such as fish or animals, which migrate in the local community, a forest such as watersource forest which provides positive externalities to the rest of the community, and so on.

British and European practice was in the main to make all property either crown or state property or private property. In Britain itself, the extent of communal rights over property was whittled away with the passing of time, communal land either being enclosed to become private property or being assigned to the crown or the state. This practice was extended to Britain's colonies. Forested land in India, although it actually was communal property and managed by local communities, was widely assigned to the crown and eventually to the Government of India or Indian state governments. Thus, local communities were dispossessed of their traditional resources and their governance of the use thereof. In many cases, this has accelerated environmental deterioration and has been the source of deep social conflict. This is an example of how inappropriate property rights can lead to environmental degradation.

Gadgil and Iyer (1989) argue that prior to British colonial conquest, India had developed systems of communal management which favoured sustainable use of its natural resources. They go on to claim that 'British rule led to disruption of communal organisations and converted communally managed resources into open-access resources. These have subsequently been used in an exhaustive fashion. However, pockets of good resource management under communal control have persisted and are now serving as models for the reassertion of such communal control' (Gadgil and Iyer 1989, p.240). The type of effects described by these authors was not peculiar to the British in India. It was repeated elsewhere by other colonial powers as well as by the British. Furthermore, governments of newly independent countries often continued the policies which reinforced the power of the central government of the nation state. Even in the case of the People's Republic of China, similar issues have arisen, for example, in relation to the governance of the natural resources in Jingpo areas of China (Zhuge and Tisdell 1996).

Although Gadgil and Iyer (1989) suggest that British colonialism in India was a major force in the creation of open-access resources in place of communally managed ones, there is no doubt that the British system, in many cases, dispossessed local communities of their communal property which was then effectively converted into state property, not open-access property, either legally or in practice. Some central governments have continued with this process of dispossession of forest-dwelling communities and tribal groups, for example by attempting to establish areas for nature protection or allowing the forest lands of minorities or tribes to become the private property of dominant groups in the country. The transmigration program in Indonesia is an example of the latter as is the incursion of Bengali farmers onto forested land in the Chittagong Hill Tracts. In Australia, the assignment of aboriginal land to the early white settlers is another example where private property rights were effectively substituted for the communal ones of the indigenous people. Both central and colonial governments were unsympathetic to communal property rights.

6.5 ADMINISTRATION OF RESOURCES BY THE STATE, LOCAL COMMUNITIES AND BY CO-MANAGEMENT

Even though all natural resources exist at a local level, and it is local people who for the main part depend most heavily on these resources for their livelihood and welfare, particularly in developing countries, governments exercise their power to gain control over many natural resources at the local level, and to manage them, as in the case of state forests, or to transfer them to private owners or lease them for economic use. Historically this process has diminished communal control over the management of natural resources. Economists and anthropologists see this process as leading to environmental degradation and undermining the sustainability of natural resource use.

The proponents of communalism claim that it results in practices that 'influence respect, responsibility, and stewardship and are highly participatory. ... They are based on co-operation rather than competition, the collective sharing of a resource rather than the individual attempting to maximise yield without reference to the commodity' (Jacobs 1989, p.vii).

Berkes and Farvar (1989), supporting communalism and traditional communal resource management systems, point out (pp.3–4) that they 'emphasise *responsibility* to the community, rather than unbridled individualism glorified in some Western industrial cultures. Communalism is an important mode of thinking and of managing resources throughout the world from the nomads of the Arabian peninsula to native Amerindian peoples. It is no accident that traditional resource-management systems are often community-based'.

In reality, however, the arguments in favour of communalism are far from watertight. Ideal governance is likely to call for a variety or array of forms of governance:

- *in some cases local community control of resources is ideal,*
- *in others formal state control of resources may be needed,*
- *in many cases co-management by the state and local community may be called for,*
- *in some cases management of natural resources is best left to individuals or households acting on their own free will.*

The important issue is to identify the circumstances in which these different types of governance would be socially ideal.

It is not possible to develop the theory of 'ideal' governance here but factors which should be taken into account in deciding between different forms of governance can be listed. To do so should at least be a start in overcoming preconceptions about ideal forms of governance. Consideration of these factors suggests that co-management or side-by-side management (Tisdell 1995a 1996) of natural resources by the state and local communities is often ideal.

Difference in knowledge can affect the ideal form of management of resources. The set of knowledge of local communities differs as a rule to that available to state authorities particularly those located in central places remote from local communities. In many cases, local knowledge will be more appropriate to the sustainable management of local resources. However, the state *may* have additional valuable knowledge, for example as a result of research work or monitoring. Therefore, it can be important to work out side-by-side procedures to *share* this knowledge effectively.

Local governance, or involvement of local communities in formulation of rules for management of local resources, is likely to result in greater compliance with these rules. This is both because (i) the regulations will have greater acceptance locally (they are more likely to have social legitimacy), the purpose may be more easily comprehended locally as this adds to motivation to comply with the regulations, and

(ii) monitoring may be easier and administration costs lower, when these activities are mainly the responsibility of a local community which supports the regulations.

It needs to be recognised that there are cases in which it is not socially optimal to leave the management of resources to a local community. Consider the following cases:

- *Use of natural resources by a community for its own benefit may damage other communities due to unfavourable external environmental effects. State intervention may be needed to take account of the wider community. However, this needs to be done in an appropriate way and the intervention may fail completely if it is entirely top-down.*
- *The distribution of political power, control over resources and distribution of income in some local communities is far from ideal. Without government intervention, situations of this type can persist. It may be necessary for central government to intervene to change or modify governance structures at the local level, even though this intervention should be sensitively done if required. The actual governance processes that exist at local level are usually the result of a long period of social evolution and may be very sustainable and conducive to resource sustainability. This is why care is needed in trying to impose new social structures. Nevertheless, due to technological changes and exogenous factors, governance and social structures of value at one time in history may be inappropriate at a later time.*

Tisdell and Roy (1997) consider the following factors to be important in cases of resource management:

- *Differences in knowledge about possible management practices and their impacts on productivity, environment and so on.*
- *Differences in knowledge about the social acceptability of various management procedures.*
- *Compliance with regulations – knowledge, monitoring, motivation.*
- *Transaction costs involved in the implementation of management procedures and economics of administration.*
- *Distribution of income and power in community and state governance structure.*
- *The existence of environmental externalities or spillovers extending beyond local communities.*

6.6   SOUTH ASIAN PERSPECTIVE

Despite the negative comment by Gadgil and Iyer (1989) about the role of the British in alienating communal property in India, significant amounts of communal resources remained. In Tamil Nadu, for example, remaining communal lands include *poromboke* or lands incapable of cultivation and set aside for public or communal purposes, and assessed and unassessed wasteland. Blaikie *et al.* (1992) estimated that such land covered almost 20 per cent of the geographical area of Tamil Nadu in 1981–82. Most was forested but smaller portions were used for cultivation and permanent pasture. They find that problems arise from the bureaucratic control of common property resources (CPRs). 'The bureaucratic regulation of CPRs is of particular concern in CPR-dependent villages, for this regulation is often subject to manipulation by local power to the disadvantage of poorer people' (Blaikie *et al.* 1992, pp.262–63).

There is little doubt that 'modern' schemes for community based resource management (CBRM) can become hijacked by politicians, local or central ones. This has led to some despair. Sandalo (1994, p.180) drawing on experience in Palawan in the Philippines observes that, 'Community organising has become almost like a fad, similar to the planned sprouting of NGOs. Every project proponent in an area is organising activities'. He finds that much time is spent in unproductive meetings and that CBRM has become subject to political patronage and interventions. Finally, he finds that government intervention to protect the environment is inconsistent. While in one place CBRM is being fostered to rehabilitate degraded environments, in other places, the natural environment is being destroyed with state permission. He says, 'in Honda Bay [Palawan], for example, mangroves are being rehabilitated simultaneously with the conversion of other existing areas into fishponds, in addition to the indiscriminate and unchecked cutting of trees for housing materials and charcoal making' (Sandalo 1994, p.181).

Communities can vary in many different ways that depend upon variations in social customs and codes. To some extent, castes in Indian society (and tribal groups) form sub-communities, interconnected with a wider community. Gadgil and Iyer (1989) argue that this stratification of Indian society has promoted sustainable use of resources. It divides society into economically complementary groups so overall mutualism exists. They claim the caste system 'promoted sustainable resource use in two ways: by restricting access to many specialised resources of any given locality to just one endogamous group, and by linking together members of different endogamous groups in a network of reciprocal exchanges and mutual obligations' (Gadgil and Iyer 1989, p.242). Berkes (1989, p.237–38) summarises the view of these authors in the following terms: 'Before colonisation, the ecological niche diversification (by varied caste access to different natural resources) ensured monopoly for a local group in the use of specific common-property resources, and was instrumental in the long-term sustainable use of these resources. The historical trend of a deteriorating resource base throughout India is traceable to the forced conversion of communal property into state and private property, increased commercialisation, and the generally increased demand for resources'. While Gandhi had desired to reverse this trend, Nehru reinforced it by increasing the power of the state with the backing of urban middle and trading classes (Gadgil and Iyer 1989, p.251). He favoured top-down policies and industrialisation and paid scant attention to the environment (Roy and Tisdell 1995).

Nevertheless, the caste system still manages to function to some extent and there are at least remote areas of India where different groups still occupy different ecological niches and are involved in the type of exchanges indicated by Gadgil and Iyer. For example, this is so in part of Northeast India (Ramakrishnan 1992; Tisdell 1995b). However, these systems are under stress as a result of increasing population, demands for cash for industrial goods and growing commercialism. It is doubtful if they can be sustained. New institutional arrangements can be expected to emerge, but not necessarily in harmonious fashion.

In a world of change we also have to consider the dynamics of alterations in governance. As technology and other factors alter, the most desirable form of governance is liable to change, irrespective of whether governance is considered at the communal or state level. Major changes occur in property rights and governance over time. Thomson *et al.* (1992) have outlined such changes in relation to land rights in Thailand. From the early 1800s onwards, there was a constant tendency in Thailand to increase the privatisation of land and the security of private tenure of land, particularly in relation to arable land. Much land was also put under state ownership. Consequently, the amount of land used as common property in Thailand has been greatly reduced since the beginning of the last century, a pattern similar to the European one.

In their concluding comments based on the Thai case, Thomson *et al.* (1992, pp.154–55) seem to support the evolution of private property rights by stating that, 'The costs of organising collective management are extremely high and its effectiveness is problematic. Privatization does, however, risk inequality at the subdivision stage when control over the resource itself is allotted to particular individuals. If this is a one-time allocation, with no easy mechanisms to rectify maldistribution, inequities can pose a serious problem. It should be noted that maintaining common-property institutions in no way avoids equity problems; they are simply pushed back a step. They reappear when annual or other increments of reduction from the resource are harvested and distributed to users. Distribution rules specify who gets what, when, and how. The potential for inequity inherent in such regulations and practices is substantial'. They also indicate that community management of common-property resources is only likely to work if the political and economic costs of such management are low.

6.7 ENVIRONMENTAL GOVERNANCE IN BANGLADESH

6.7.1 An overview

Environmental administration in Bangladesh is characterised by a very high degree of centralisation. A large number of ministries, departments and directorates, statutory bodies (Hasan 1996, pp.234–39) are engaged in policies, programmes and actions that directly or indirectly affect the environment. For instance:

- *Policies and programmes pertaining to land and water resources are run by ten ministries, seven directorates/departments and nineteen statutory bodies. Agricultural extension programmes are handled by five ministries, eight directorates/departments and four autonomous bodies.*
- *Environmental management programmes are run directly and indirectly by sixteen ministries, thirteen departments/directorates and thirteen other parastatal organisations.*

The Department of Environment and Forest was created in 1989 to enhance the capability of the government to effectively deal with environmental issues. The Department of Environment was formed by renaming the Department of Environment Pollution Control (DEPC, formed in 1977) and was placed under the Ministry of Environment and Forestry.

The environmental protection programme of the Department of Environment (DOE) has *inter alia* the following objectives (Hasan 1996, p.236):

- *long term sustainable development of the country*
- *conservation of natural heritage in terms of natural resources*
- *a healthy and meaningful living environment for all citizens including the poor.*

The above objectives notwithstanding, environmental management in Bangladesh still revolves around pollution control. The activities that the DOE performs do not reflect this change in aims and broadening of scope. As Hasan (1996, p.237) points out, the formation of the DOE represented a facade and its transformation from the DEPC was structural and did not represent any substantive improvement in environmental governance and management.

Hasan (1996, pp.237–38) provides an illustration of ineffectiveness of environmental administration in Bangladesh. Table 6.1 (Hasan 1996, p.238) shows that the administration of forests rests with two ministries having overlapping jurisdiction and conflicts in management. With too many ministries and departments running the environmental programmes the environmental administration in Bangladesh is not effective and resulted in expanding the bureaucratic machinery. The Department of Environment is supposed to coordinate all the activities relating environmental management. But it does not have the authority over other ministries or departments dealing with environmental regulations and legislations. With different agencies and bodies having their respective chains of command, the coordination aspect of the Department of Environment or even the Ministry of Environment and Forestry becomes

Table 6.1   Pattern of ownership and management of forest in Bangladesh

Category of forest	Area in hectares	Type of forest	Owning and managing agencies
State forest (reserved/ protected/ acquired)	1.3 million	Tropical evergreen Moist or Sal Mangroves	Department of Forest
Unclassed state forest	0.96 million	Tropical evergreen Moist or Sal	District administration of Bandarban, Cox's Bazaar, Khagrachari and Rangamati
Unclassed state forest	32 000	Moist or Sal	District administration of other districts not mentioned above
Unclassed state forest	A few thousand	Tropical evergreen	Ministry of Land
Mini forests, wood lots	0.56 million	Varied	Privately owned and managed

Source: Adapted from Hasan (1996, p.238).

less effective. This state of play of environmental governance and management is reminiscent of the overall effectiveness and priorities of the Bangladesh agricultural research system (Alauddin and Tisdell 1986).

The poor state of environmental administration in Bangladesh is symptomatic of the overall state of administration and governance in Bangladesh. As Hamid (1996, p.13) put it '.. the regulatory regime in Bangladesh entangles in a number of governance issues ... The rules as followed by the bureaucrats are, in most cases, outdated, complicated, ineffective and provides no scope for monitoring, transparency and above all accountability'. (see also Zafarullah 1996; Sobhan 1993). A similar view is echoed by Hasan (1996, p.239). Corruption is endemic in Bangladesh, reminiscent of what Myrdal (1971) calls the 'soft state'. Corruption is ubiquitous. There is a widespread view that '.. if everybody is corrupt why shouldn't I be so?'. In Bangladesh as indeed elsewhere in the developing world 'a common method of exploiting a position of public responsibility for private gain is the threat of obstruction and delay; hence, *corruption impedes the processes of decision-making and execution on all levels. Corruption introduces an element of irrationality in all planning and plan fulfilment* by influencing the actual course of development in a way that deviates from the Plan.' (Myrdal 1971, p.237).

6.7.2   Shrimp culture in Bangladesh: Property rights and resource use

As discussed in Chapter 3 and Chapter 9, shrimp culture in Bangladesh is a very important economic activity and property rights issues have significant bearing on the sustainable use of land and other natural resources in the coastal areas of Bangladesh. Figure 6.2 provides a comprehensive picture of the different forms of property rights that are prevalent in shrimp farming. As can be seen from Figure 6.2, property rights are apparently well defined: The reality however is different. There is a significant divergence between the *de facto* and the *de jure* positions. The divergence seems to vary directly with the divergence between the relative positions of the parties concerned. For instance, the *gher* owners, especially the large ones, are always at an advantageous position *vis-à-vis* the small land owners regardless of the respective *de jure* positions. Thus the property rights are not well defined. Furthermore, they cannot always be enforced given the weaker socio-economic position of the small land owners. This, combined with poor environmental governance and corruption, militates against efficient and sustainable resource use. The process therefore seems to have led to environmental degradation and undermined sustainability of rural communities in the coastal belt of Bangladesh

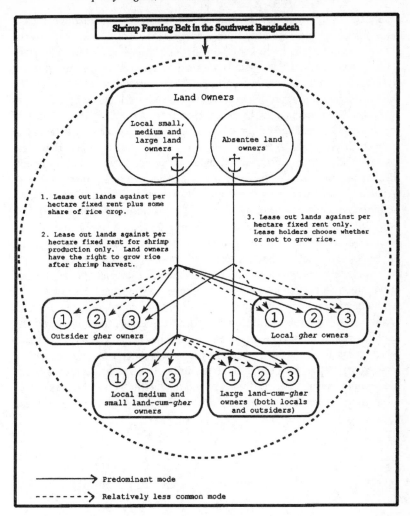

Figure 6.2   Property rights issues in shrimp farming in Bangladesh

6.8   CONCLUDING OBSERVATIONS

Most economists have been slower than other social scientists to come to grips with the complexities of governance, different forms of private property rights and their relationship to sustainable resource use and development. Discussion of examples from various countries including India and

Bangladesh highlights the importance of considering the dynamics of variations in property rights and governance (see also Ostrom 1990). The Indian situation has undergone considerable change. North and Thomas (1973) have argued that socially optimal patterns of property rights are likely to evolve in society and that social evolution is towards the increased creation of private property rights (Axelrod 1984). The latter has certainly been the case in Thailand. However, it is not entirely clear that evolutionary social and political processes result in an ideal distribution of property rights. North (1981; 1990, pp.7, 51–52) modifies his earlier view and recognises that political mechanisms may thwart this process of evolution of ideal patterns of resource ownership. In addition private gain may result in land becoming private property which socially would be better retained as common–property. It is not that evolutionary social processes involving property rights and governance lead invariably to perverse social consequences, but they do not necessarily result in the best of all possible worlds either. Further research is warranted in this regard.

Bangladesh's environmental governance is in poor shape. Numerous government departments are directly or indirectly engaged in environmental management and protection. However, lack of coordination and understanding of the complexities surrounding the issues have rendered the environmental management system largely ineffective. Widespread corruption has further exacerbated the problem. Inadequate, ill-defined and inappropriate property rights have led to environmental degradation and undermined sustainable resource use and the livelihoods of the poorer sections of the community in many parts of rural Bangladesh. Some of these issues are followed up in Chapters 7, 8 and 9.

7 Impact on the Rural Poor of Changing Rural Environments and Technologies: Evidence from India and Bangladesh

7.1 INTRODUCTION: SOME TRENDS

A number of studies have been done on rural poverty in developing Asia and that edited by Quibria (1994) is a major recent contribution. It finds that rural poverty has declined in all developing Asian countries, except Sri Lanka where it showed no change in the 1980s compared to the 1970s. Using poverty lines and a head count basis, rural poverty in Bangladesh was reported to be 41 per cent in 1985–86 compared to 71 per cent in 1973–74. In India, it was found to be 45 per cent in the early 1960s but to have fallen to 25 per cent in 1986–87 (Quibria and Srinivasan 1994, p.6). While such poverty rates are still substantial, their downward trend is encouraging.

Although Quibria and Srinivasan (1994) identify a number of correlates of such poverty (and are careful to stress that they are just that rather than causes) they give virtually no attention to the consequences of environmental change for such poverty nor to variations in the extent of exchange and non-exchange income and their relationship to poverty. In Quibria (1994) the only exception is in relation to the contribution by Gunatilleke *et al.* (1994) on Sri Lanka which states (p.530): 'Policies for environmental protection often fail to take heed of the resulting deprivation of females who depend on forests for firewood, water resources, herb and food gathering (Perera 1990). Environmental degradation, of course, has long-term effects which lead to poverty.' Furthermore, while the contribution dealing with Sri Lanka (Gunatilleke *et al.* 1994) considers gender related aspects of poverty, those covering rural poverty in Bangladesh (Hossain *et al.* 1994) and in India (Dev *et al.* 1994) neglect this aspect even though it is an important dimension of the rural poverty problem (cf. Roy *et al.* 1996).

Taking into account technological and associated environmental changes, this chapter concentrates on possible variations in the relative economic position of the rural poor compared to those who are better off. It summarises some of our earlier findings and draws on the results of village surveys in West Bengal and Bangladesh.

Major environmental changes have occurred in rural India and Bangladesh in recent decades mainly due (but not exclusively) to the introduction of Green Revolution technologies in agriculture and associated population increases which this Revolution has helped to make possible. 'Green Revolution' technologies involve:

- *the introduction of high yielding but environmentally sensitive crop varieties,*
- *greater irrigation and water control for crops,*
- *increased use of artificial fertiliser,*
- *greater mechanisation of agriculture,*
- *increased use of pesticides, and*
- *a rise in the incidence of multiple cropping and in general, greater intensification of agriculture.*

Each one of the above factors has been associated with significant environmental change. Traditional crop varieties have been lost because of their displacement by high yielding varieties (HYVs), thereby reducing biological diversity. The need for water supplies, especially in the dry season, has led to the construction of dams and barrages with adverse consequences for fishing and navigation. Underground water supplies have also been affected, for example, 'excessive' pumping of water from underground sources has had undesirable effects on available supplies. In some areas, salinisation of soil or water has become a problem. The use of artificial fertiliser has resulted in acidification of some soils and loss of organic matter, especially when combined with multiple cropping and use of mechanical equipment (Mahtab and Karim 1992). The use of pesticides has caused the loss of useful insects as well as pests. In some areas, such as Chittagong Hill Tracts, forest loss has increased, so adding to soil erosion. One could easily add to this catalogue of adverse environmental changes in rural areas (Tisdell *et al.* 1992).

These changes have all to some degree involved a loss of natural resources or similar resources. To a large extent, man-made resources and environments have been substituted for natural ones in an effort to increase economic productivity.

At the same time as the above developments have occurred, the market system has become more pervasive in rural areas. Private property rights have been extended and/or are being more rigorously enforced and common or community access to natural resources such as fish has decreased and/or the natural supply of such resources, has declined. As some members of the Chicago School point out (Demsetz 1968), it becomes more economic to enforce private property rights to a resource or set of resources when profit or returns from using this resource or set of resources rises. As a result, there may be less opportunities for the landless or near landless to use natural resources, for example, to collect fodder for their animals from communal land or to obtain free water supplies. A vicious environmental cycle seems to have emerged in parts of India and in Bangladesh, especially the west of Bangladesh where natural gas supplies are not available. Demand for bricks has increased for housing and road building, placing increased strain on natural fuel supplies used in the baking of bricks. At the same time, heightened demands on remaining natural areas of, for example, woodland, have made it more difficult to maintain supplies of for example, fuel from such areas. Furthermore, inland fisheries have not only suffered from over-harvesting but also from unfavourable external effects from the development of agriculture and capital works needed for such development.

New agricultural technologies and the concomitant growth of the market system have encouraged greater specialisation in production, a reduction in the degree of subsistence farming and an increase in road-building to enable marketing to take place at reduced cost. Consequently, social relationships have come to be guided increasingly by market-oriented self-interest rather than by custom or social exchange. Thus erosion of 'community' or traditional communal structures of social support has occurred. At the same time, there has been a reduction in social security provided by access to natural resources (the importance of which has for example been emphasised by Chambers 1987) and local social support may have diminished.

7.2   SOCIO-ECONOMIC ASSESSMENT OF 'GREEN REVOLUTION' TECHNOLOGICAL CHANGE

Socio-economic assessment of Green Revolution technological change is not easy because the impact of such change is multi-dimensional, not single dimensional. The past practice of economists, for example in cost-benefit analysis, has been to try to reduce evaluation to a single dimension specified in monetary units. This is not always possible, but even when it is possible, it is not always satisfactory because knowledge of the way in which attributes behave may be as important as the net result for evaluation.

Alauddin and Tisdell in *The Green Revolution and Economic Development* (1991c), adopt a multi-attribute approach, principally based upon Gordon Conway's (1985a, 1987) suggestion that changes in agricultural technology might be best assessed by taking account of its effect on four characteristics, namely:

- *the level of yields or net returns from agricultural activity,*
- *the variability of the above,*
- *the sustainability of the above, and*
- *the consequences of the technology for income distribution.*

The social desirability of a technique is positively related to the level of yields or net returns which it generates, the stability (lack of fluctuation) of these returns, their sustainability and the degree of reduction in income inequality which it brings about.

Examining these attributes in relation to the adoption of Green Revolution technologies in Bangladesh, Alauddin and Tisdell (1991c) found the following:

- *Crop yields (rice and wheat) were substantially increased by the adoption of these technologies. In addition, the cash income of food grain producers was estimated to have risen by 5–6 per cent in the period 1967–9 and 1980–2 using the model of Hayami and Herdt (Alauddin and Tisdell 1991c, p.107).*
- *The relative variability of annual food grain yields declined substantially. This was partly due to the increase in the incidence of multiple cropping and partly due to a larger proportion of the crop being grown under controlled environmental conditions, for example, with irrigation in the dry season. Multiple cropping increased the number of independent or at least semi-independent events in a year, thereby leading to reduced relative variability of the combined annual results. Furthermore, greater environmental control as a result of man-made investment (e.g. in irrigation), and greater human effort meant that the sensitivity of the yield of HYV crops to variations in environmental conditions was not able to assert itself fully.*
- *On the matter of sustainability of yields, Alauddin and Tisdell (1991c) expressed concern on several grounds. These included deterioration in soil quality as a result of the use of new agricultural technologies:*

*farm soil structure, loss of organic matter, acidification and so on.
Greater use of fertiliser and energy might be necessary in the future to
try to compensate for soil changes. Loss of genetic diversity could also
have long term adverse consequences such as loss of backstop local
varieties of rice. Problems of controlling pests could increase because
of increasing resistance of pests to pesticides and the loss of natural
enemies of pests as a result of the use of modern pesticides. Adverse
externalities may also become more apparent: waterlogging of land or
salinity as a result of irrigation, or unsustainable use of water supplies, especially underground supplies.*

- *The consequences of the Green Revolution for rural income distribution and wealth distribution are complicated because changes in these
variables have a number of different dimensions. Alauddin and Tisdell
(1991c, p.160) found evidence of 'increasing concentration of use and
control of agricultural land in Bangladesh, and of increasing inequality in the ownership of ancillary resources such as irrigation water,
essential for the success of the bulk of Green Revolution technologies.
Increasing landlessness and near landlessness is making the
Bangladeshi rural poor more dependent on wage employment for their
subsistence'. On the whole, wage employment provides less security
than employment based on land ownership and/or access to communal
resources.*

In relation to wage employment in Bangladesh, there appears to have been
very little increase in the number of man-days of casual agricultural
employment and little or no increase in rural real wages (Tisdell and
Alauddin 1992). However, since the advent of the Green Revolution, agricultural employment has become more evenly distributed throughout the
year. Agricultural employment possibilities have not fallen but they have
not increased significantly. Real wages have hardly increased, if at all, but
steadier employment throughout the year is available. While the Green
Revolution has helped to increase non-agricultural employment in
Bangladesh, it has not been harnessed to industrialise Bangladesh on a
major scale.

On the whole, the economic situation of the rural landless and near-
landless may have deteriorated since the Green Revolution. The landless
and the near-landless numbers of the rural community, who tend to be its
poorer members, depend upon two main sources of income: (1) exchange
income, mostly from wage-employment and (2) non-exchange income
such as that obtained from the gathering of fuel, fodder for animals, edible
plants, fish, collection of water from generally accessible 'communal'

places or from larger properties where in the past these commodities might have been provided as a free service or for a low payment. Opportunities to obtain non-exchange income are rapidly disappearing because private property rights are being more rigorously enforced and are being extended as a result of the Green Revolution and population pressure. In addition, unfavourable externalities from this Revolution are reducing the natural productivity of communal property such as the fisheries, and reducing supplies of natural resources due to overuse of shared resources: for example, waterholes pumped dry during the dry season for irrigation. It appears that some impoverishment of the rural landless and near landless has occurred as a result of reduced natural resource availability and reduced opportunities for the poor to gain access to remaining natural resources. This has, for example, happened in the Barind Tract, Rajshahi Division (see also Chapter 8). Communal tanks and water bodies have become silted due to changed land-use and large farmers are now using the silted beds of these for crop growing or are excluding community members from these tanks.

It might be noted that Conway's concept of sustainability (Conway 1985,1987) is based upon the degree of resilience of an agricultural system. Other concepts exist, for example sustainability as intergenerational equity in income distribution (ecological sustainability that is), the maintenance of biodiversity, and the sustainability of community (Tisdell 1993a, 1991b). Achieving sustainability in one of these dimensions may promote its achievement in other dimensions but not always.

7.3   VILLAGE SURVEYS IN WEST BENGAL

In order to gain a better insight into the economic effects of environmental and technological change in rural areas of the type mentioned above, surveys of selected villages in Bangladesh and West Bengal were undertaken in 1992. One of the main purposes of these surveys was to get an indication of the extent of natural resource loss and its consequences for income loss as a function of the economic position (situation) of households. In addition, the questionnaires were designed to elicit information about changes in social obligation, charity and social cohesiveness and the intrusion of the market system into social relationships, migration, environmental change, technological change, the economic position of income and children and the prospects for survival of the village.

In September 1992, three villages (Barakuli, Kamla and Maharajpur) near Mindapur, West Bengal were surveyed. (For further details see Tisdell *et al.* 1996). Direct interviews were undertaken of household heads, using a questionnaire designed by Dr. K.C. Roy and Clem Tisdell. Interviews were supervised by Dr. Roy. Most of the villagers were tribals, in fact Santals. All told, 86 households were surveyed and 98 per cent of their household heads claimed that their income was insufficient to meet their basic needs. Very little charity was given or received. Only one rich family gave charity which took the form of an invitation to a feast. All village members believed that they were more commercial in their dealings with one another than in the past and most (over 80 per cent) believed that there is less community spirit and sharing in their village than in the past. Apart from the 7 per cent who did not respond to this question, the remainder said that their village is more market-oriented than in the past. Furthermore, 70 per cent said that the giving of commodities to satisfy social obligations or needs in their village is less important than in the past.

Apart from the 7 per cent, who did not respond to this question, all of the household heads said that the state of their local environment and the availability of natural resources had deteriorated. Ninety percent said that this had had an unfavourable effect on their economic welfare, 8 per cent said that the changed effect was favourable, and 2 per cent did not respond to this question. Only a few of the very poor or the poor said that environmental change had been favourable for them economically. Seventy-two percent of the households said that if the availability of natural resources and the natural environment was the same as 5–10 years ago, the economic position of their household would be better, whereas 27 per cent said it would be worse and 1 per cent did not respond. Most households claimed to be worse off as a result of environmental change and most households (87 per cent) said that this change had made it more difficult for some members of their households to contribute to the livelihood of their family. On average, the lower the income of the family the more frequently was increased difficulty said to be experienced on the employment side because of environmental change.

In these villages, forest cover has declined and considerable replacement of indigenous forest by introduced eucalyptus has occurred. This has several unfavourable environmental consequences. It now takes householders a longer time to collect a smaller amount of forest product and less opportunities are available to graze animals and collect fodder. More time is spent on water gathering, leaves from eucalyptus trees do not provide income and are unsuitable for fodder.

Several modern technologies have been introduced into the villages in the last 10 years. Seventy-one percent of householders thought that these had a bad impact, 25 per cent considered their impact to be good,

1 per cent said the impact was neutral and 3 per cent did not respond. Ninety-four percent of households said their employment was affected. Eighty-one percent considered the employment effect to be favourable, 17 per cent believed this effect to be unfavourable and 2 per cent gave no response. Those who classified themselves as being in an average economic situation in the village less frequently said that the employment effect had been positive. Eighty-nine percent of respondents considered that it was now easier to obtain paid work as a result of technological change. In most cases it was easier for women to obtain work if allowed by their caste. However, 80 per cent of respondents indicated that it was not easier for children to obtain work.

So we have mixed results: natural resource loss has led to a reduction in real income (or welfare) but technological change has increased the availability of paid work opportunities, according to the villagers surveyed. As mentioned above, more than 90 per cent of respondents believed that their economic welfare had been adversely affected by environmental change in their village.

In order to specify and quantify the significance of environmental and natural resource changes at village level on the economic situation of households, household heads were asked the following:

> Suppose that the availability of natural resources and the natural environment was as it was 5–10 years ago. Would the economic situation of your household be better, worse or the same? If better or worse, 'percentagewise' by how much would it be better or worse?

Nearly all household heads responded that they would be in a better economic position and indicated the extent to which their economic situation would be improved 'percentagewise'. Answers ranged from a 2.5 per cent improvement to a 97.5 per cent improvement, except for respondents indicating no change. On average, respondents in the three Bengali villages believed that their economic situation would be improved by almost 50 per cent (48.9 per cent) by restoration of their pre-existing stock of natural resources and their previous environmental state. Thus clearly householders at the village level consider that the loss of natural and environmental resources is leading to a substantial loss in their opportunities for enhancing their economic welfare. It is uncertain whether the benefits from agricultural development are sufficient to compensate for these lost opportunities.

In addition, it is revealing to consider how the responses to the above query varied with the current economic status of householders within their village. In order to determine the relative economic status of each household in its village, each household head was asked to indicate the percentage of households in their village in a better economic situation and the percentage of those in a worse economic position. The mid-point in the range between these two figures was used as a percentile economic ranking of the household. It is a proxy for the relative economic status or income level of the household. It makes use of the self-ranking method (Sathiendrakumar and Tisdell 1986; Firdausy and Tisdell 1992) which appears in practice to be surprisingly accurate. Similarly, household heads were asked whether they considered their household to be very poor, poor, average, rich or very rich.

Considerable variation exists among households for the percentage improvement in their economic situation to be expected from restoration of their natural environment. The scatter of these percentages are plotted on Figure 7.1 in relation to the percentile ranking of households of their economic position in the village.

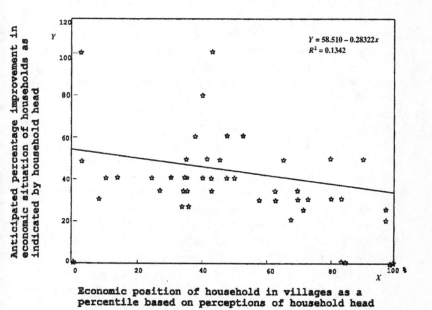

Economic position of household in villages as a
percentile based on perceptions of household head

Figure 7.1   Anticipated improvement in the economic position of households for restoration of natural environment/resources of 5–10 years ago as a function of their relative economic position in the villages of Barakuli, Kamla and Maharajpur, India, September, 1992

A regression line can be fitted to this set of data. The line estimated by least squares is:

$$y = 56.51 - 0.288x \qquad (7.1)$$

where y is the percentage improvement in the economic situation of the household expected by the household head and x is the percentile ranking of the economic position of the household. This line indicates that the poor can be expected to benefit proportionately most by restoration of the natural environment. However, the coefficient of determination for this relationship is low because $R^2 = 0.13$.

Despite the low R^2 value, the general relationship is clear. On average, it seems that relative to their economic situation, the economic cost (or opportunities forgone) by the poorer members of society are greater than for those forgone by the richer ones. Loss of the natural environment seems to have an income regressive effect.

A further observation should be made in relation to Figure 7.1. The scatter of observations for y (the variance of y) is much greater for households in lower income groups than for those in their income groups. This means that *some* poor households do not believe restoration of the previous natural environment of the village would do much for their economic situation but other poor villagers believe that the effect would be substantial for them. The latter is not the case for the richer village members. The poor stand to benefit most it seems in relative terms by environmental or natural resource restoration.

It might be noted that economic development tends to lead to the increased privatisation of natural resources. There is evidence of scheduled classes and tribes being dispossessed of their customary access to land resources by enclosures or variations in property rights, a process which began with British occupation but which has continued in recent times. Because of their relative lack of education and positions of social influence, tribal people have been unable to defend their customary or *de facto* rights to the use of forests and other natural resources. Such a process of systematic dispossession by legal means has not, however, been confined to India. It is a sad indictment of human behaviour that dispossession of tribal people has occurred in many countries both capitalist and non-capitalist in the last few centuries and is still continuing. Nath (1992) has observed, in relation to Orissa:

The landless peasants and agricultural labourers should have been the principal beneficiaries from the land reform measures, but paradoxically it rendered them landless.. Changes in the legal structure in respect of common property resources like land, forest, water, mineral, rivers, stream introduced during the British period and which are continuing today in amended form further alienated them from their traditional source of employment and living. These changes further led to privatisation of common property in favour of some by excluding the vast majority. This is the basic factor in peasant differentiation. (Nath 1993, pp.284–85)

7.4   RESULTS FROM A VILLAGE SURVEY IN BANGLADESH

Data from the village of Durgapur in western Bangladesh collected in 1992 is consistent with the results obtained from India. A similar questionnaire was used and Dr. M. Alauddin arranged for the interviews. Observations were obtained from 127 household heads and on average they indicated that they would expect a 32.36 percent improvement in their economic situation with a return to the natural resource base/natural environment of five to ten years ago. While considerable variation exists in improvement expected, the coefficient of variation of 42.5 per cent was somewhat lower than for the Indian villages for which it was just under 50 per cent. The range of anticipated percentage improvement in economic situation (its variance) of households in Durgapur tended to vary inversely with the economic position of the household, as in the Indian case.

Respondent household heads in Durgapur were asked to locate the economic position of their household in the categories (1) very poor, (2) poor, (3) average (4) rich, and (5) very rich. Table 7.1 shows the average

Table 7.1   Percentage improvement in economic situation expected by household heads in Durgapur, Bangladesh, 1992 from restoration of natural resources to their levels of 5–10 years prior to 1992

Economic group*	No. of households	Income compensation % needed on average
Very poor	18	34.7
Poor	71	32.8
Average	33	30.7
Rich	5	28.0

* No household considered itself to be very rich.

expected improvement in the economic situation of each of these groups for restoration of natural resource loss in the last five to ten years. While the proportionate amount of expected improvement falls with rises in the economic position of families, it does not do so as quickly as in the case of the Indian villages surveyed.

Percentile rankings of the economic position of households were also considered. As in the Indian case the variance of observations tended to be higher for those on lower incomes than for higher incomes. The line of best fit to the data using least squares is

$$y = 33.35 - 0.025x \qquad (7.2)$$

A very weak negative correlation, $R = -0.39$, exists between y and x and only a slight fall occurs in percentage expected improvement with increases in the economic position of the household. However, we can conclude that on average the relative benefit expected by the poor from natural resource restoration is at least as great as for the rich. Hence, given the diminishing marginal utility hypothesis, the relative gain in utility by the poor as a result of natural resource restoration would on average, be greater than for the rich.

7.5   CONCLUDING COMMENTS

From the results above of surveys of rural villages in West Bengal and Bangladesh, the opportunity cost to villagers of natural resource loss and environmental deterioration in the last decade has been substantial. Such costs are often ignored, as is mainly so in Quibria (1994). Both in the Mindapur District and in Durgapur, nearly all villagers indicated that their economic position would be much improved by natural resource restoration. The average percentage improvement for Durgapur was lower than for the three villages in the Mindapur District. The lower figure for Durgapur might be explained by the smaller initial stock of natural resources in Durgapur and the greater dependence of the Santals in the Mindapur District (and elsewhere) on the utilisation of natural resources, compared to Bengalis in Durgapur. However, all the income groups in all the villages claimed on average to have suffered a substantial loss in income opportunity due to natural resource loss and environmental deterioration. Of course, it might be argued that the restoration of the previous environmental situation for the villages is a pipe-dream. This, however, is not the point. The point is to bring out the fact that environmental loss involves economic cost. The percentage loss in income opportunities on average suffered by the poorer members of the villages was greater on average than the claimed loss by the richer members. Thus on average, losses in income opportunities resulting from natural resource/environmental deterioration have been regressive in rural areas judging from the results of the surveys reported here. While it is too early to generalise these results, they should not be ignored. Note that these results do not indicate that the incomes of villagers have been reduced on average as a result of environmental change, but rather that villagers perceive considerable lost economic opportunities as a result of environmental changes. They are very aware of the opportunity cost of 'development' which depletes natural resources and degrades the environment. In their own informal way, they are sensitive to the need for natural resource accounting (cf. Adger and Whitby 1992; Bartelemus 1991; Pearce *et al.* 1990).

8 Agricultural Sustainability in Marginal Areas: Principles, Policies and Examples

8.1 INTRODUCTION

Because of rising populations and advances in agricultural techniques, agriculture on marginal lands in South Asia has intensified and the margin of cultivation has been extended mostly at the expense of natural environments. While doubts have been raised about the sustainability of many modern agricultural practices, such as those associated with the green revolution, on the fertile plains of the Indian subcontinent (Alauddin and Tisdell 1991), it is the upland areas, covering a major portion of the subcontinent, that are especially at risk due to agricultural developments. These areas also contain a high proportion of South Asia's tribal people or its minorities and much of its remaining wildlife.

The purpose of this chapter is to discuss generally the principles of sustainable agriculture and consider case material from two upland areas in South Asia, namely agriculture in the Barind Tract in the Rajshahi Division, Bangladesh and agriculture in the Northeastern hills of India. Unlike the Northeastern hills, the Barind Tract is a relatively low undulating area but nearly all of it is above flood level. In comparison, the hills of Northeastern India rise to considerable elevations (especially in the Himalayan portion bordering China) and are often steep and heavily dissected. In the Chittagong Hill Tracts, the hilly areas of north-east India extend into Bangladesh.

Let us consider the principles of sustainable agriculture in the context of South Asia, followed by case material for the Barind Tract and observations on agriculture in the Northeastern hills of India.

8.2 AGRICULTURAL SUSTAINABILITY: SOME PRINCIPLES

Economic sustainability requires care to be taken of the natural environment, as does agricultural sustainability if agriculture is to remain economically viable in the long-term. If attention is not paid to the sustainability

126

of economic production, future generations may be impoverished and even present generations may experience a decline in their incomes. For example, this result follows when land management results in a rapid rate of soil erosion and loss of valuable topsoil. As explained in Chapter 2, the productivity of economic systems and the state of the natural environment are interconnected. Economic systems (including the agricultural economic sector) may fail to sustain their productivity because they:

- *produces wastes and pollutants which cannot be readily absorbed by the natural environment so reducing the quality or availability of natural resources, or*
- *irreversibly deplete or degrade natural resources.*

In general, increased economic activity, including intensification and extension of agriculture, involves depletion or degeneration of natural resources. Extension of agriculture for example often leads to the loss of natural forests and the use of so called 'wastelands' or *khas* lands in India. These wastelands include wetlands. In the past, it was common to regard 'wastelands' as unproductive but from an environmental and biological point of view they can be extremely productive in their natural state, and often unsuitable for cultivation for very long. Furthermore, intensification of agriculture can easily result in declining long-term productivity. For example, artificial fertilizers may cause the soil to become acidic, soil structure may deteriorate due to excessive cultivation, valuable topsoil may be eroded away and soil nutrients may be mined quickly on light or poor soils such as those of the Barind Tract discussed below.

The main factor able to offset declining economic productivity due to environmental deterioration is technological progress. It usually enables greater economic production to be achieved using fewer inputs. It has enabled economic production to increase despite natural resource depletion and deterioration. While optimists take continuing technological progress for granted, in reality the likely extent of such future progress remains uncertain.

An additional factor that may offset the impacts on economic production of resource depletion is investment in man-made capital. But production of man-made capital involves the conversion of some natural resource stocks into such capital and so these stocks are further depleted. Furthermore, all man-made capital has a limited life. Consequently, unrestrained accumulation of man-made capital may not be a suitable long-term offset to or substitute for natural resource depletion (Pearce 1993). In the early stages of depletion of natural resources such substitution is likely to be beneficial from an economic point of view, but as substitution proceeds and natural resource stocks are reduced, substitution becomes more problematic from an economic standpoint. Because many Asian countries have already depleted their natural resource stocks considerably, they might enter the problematic trade-off zone much earlier than anticipated by their political leaders.

Environmental economists differ about how much caution is needed in promoting economic changes affecting the natural environment. Nevertheless a group favouring sustainable development stress the importance of applying the precautionary principle, that is of planning which anticipates future possible environmental consequences. This is because many environmental changes which can be brought about by economic activity are irreversible (for example, extinction of species) or can only be reversed at great cost. Furthermore, many of these changes are uncertain and some may not provide signs of adverse environmental consequences until it is too late to adopt preventative or countervailing measures.

In relation to agricultural development, adverse environmental consequences can be very costly or uneconomic to reverse e.g. desertification, salinisation of soils, or soil erosion.

8.3   SUSTAINABLE AGRICULTURAL TECHNIQUES AND SYSTEMS OF LAND MANAGEMENT

The sustainable use of an agricultural technique of production depends not only on its biophysical sustainability in use but also on its economic viability and social acceptability. Whether or not a technique is likely to be sustainably used appears to depend on three factors:

- *the biophysical sustainability of its use,*
- *its economic viability, and*
- *its social acceptability.*

Thus a sustainable agricultural technique would be one that is economically viable, socially acceptable and biophysically sustainable. In Figure 8.1, if A represents the set of available economically viable techniques, B is the set of socially acceptable techniques and C is the set of biophysically sustainable techniques, only those techniques in the overlapping set (dotted) would be fully sustainable. In practice, we cannot be sure that such sets will overlap. However, it is possible that they *may be made to do* so as a result of extra research and development effort. Many agricultural research bodies

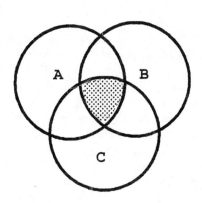

Figure 8.1 Basic requirements for the sustainability of agricultural techniques. Only techniques or projects in the overlapping sections (dotted) satisfy all the requirements for sustainability

(including international research bodies such as those belonging to CAGIAR group) have now included sustainability of agricultural techniques as an objective in their research agenda.

This discussion can be extended by considering what would be required for economic viability, social acceptability and for biophysical sustainability. Different authors appear to have somewhat different suggestions about these requirements.

Gordon Conway (1985b, 1987), for example, in considering the evaluation of agricultural systems, measures:

- *their economic viability by their level of returns or yields also taking account of the degree of instability of these,*
- *their social acceptability by the impact of these techniques on the distribution of income, and*
- *their biophysical sustainability by the ability of yields to recover to former levels after being subjected to an environmental shock.*

Conway considers that traditional agricultural techniques are generally more sustainable and have a better impact on income distribution than modern agricultural techniques. On the other hand, they give lower levels of returns than modern techniques but their returns may be more stable.

Nevertheless, basically Conway defines sustainability in biophysical terms, that is the ability of yields to return to former levels after experiencing an ecological shock. For the cases illustrated in Figure 8.2, (A) indicates a sustainable case and (B) illustrates an unsustainable case.

Somewhat different and more complex views have also been expressed about what may be required for social sustainability and for economic sustainability (Tisdell 1993, Ch.9). Some writers, Douglass (1984) for

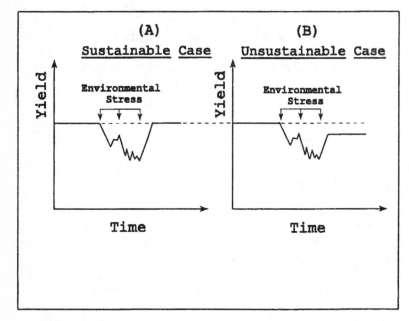

Figure 8.2 Illustrations of sustainable and unsustainable agricultural systems according to Conway (1985, 1987)

example, have suggested that 'community' or communal cohesion must be retained for social sustainability to be achieved.

8.3.1   Normative and positive attitudes to agricultural sustainability – what is versus what ought to be

It is possible to consider whether something *is* sustainable such as income or yields from cultivating a crop using a particular technique. This is a *positive* approach to analysing sustainability. Another approach is to consider whether it is *desirable* for some particular thing to be sustained. This is a normative approach.

Very often a clear distinction is not made between what it is *desirable* to sustain and what *can be* sustained, that is between normative and positive statements. One needs to look critically at discussions from this point of view. For example, those recommending strong conditions for sustainability (*emphasizing the importance of conserving natural resources*) may do so because they:

- *have ecocentric values or*
- *they believe that given current conditions, any further reduction of natural environmental stocks will threaten the economic well-being of future generations or*
- *they hold both viewpoints.*

It cannot be overstressed that the goal of sustainability is of little value in itself and rather meaningless unless we specify sustainability of what. Indeed, there are some situations which it is undesirable to sustain, for example, poverty.

8.3.2   Economics and sustainability of agricultural production

According to neoclassical economic theory, economic activity will only be sustained by the private sector as long as it is profitable. Unfortunately, private economic decisions do not always ensure long-term sustainability of environmental resources or production.

Private economic greed can threaten sustainability

Desire to make large short-term profits may motivate individuals to destroy natural resources such as forests, drive species to extinction and mine the land. This could also occur because people are desperately poor but in this case their power to transform the natural environment is rather limited because they lack capital. These changes may even happen when private rights to property are fully secured in land and natural resources. This is not to say that market economic systems do not support conservation of natural resources in some cases. They do but only if this is privately profitable.

Inappropriate property rights threaten sustainability

In some cases, *lack of property rights* is a disaster from a conservation or sustainability point of view. This is so for *open-access* resources, that is a resource which all are free to exploit, if they are in strong demand. In the past, fishing stocks were brought to extinction or close to extinction by open-access (consider, for example, the stock of whales). In Asia, access to many water resources, especially underground water has been open, and this is resulting in their excessive and inappropriate use from an economic point of view.

Private economic viability versus social economic benefit

Private economic profitability of the use of a technique or agricultural system is necessary in most economies if the use of the technique is to be sustained. However, this does not mean that the technique is socially desirable or that its social economic return is positive. The private costs of using a technique may be less than its social cost because some of the costs are passed onto others without compensation and consequently economic externalities or spillovers occur. For example, the clearing of land for agriculture may increase water run off and increase flooding and erosion downstream imposing costs on other farmers. The flow of streams may also become more erratic and so impose additional costs on others. This is a problem arising from increased cultivation of hilly areas of much of South Asia.

Similar problems may occur in shared water bodies. Wastes may be disposed of into such bodies by economic agents and impose costs on others. The uncontrolled withdrawal of water from such bodies for irrigation can result in water shortages and a decline in agricultural production dependent on such irrigation. Examples are available from many areas in South Asia and some are given later.

Private and social returns from projects or economic activity need not coincide. This will be the case when significant environmental spillovers or externalities arise from private economic activity. Thus three possibilities exist:

- *Projects that are economically viable privately but give a negative social economic return.*
- *Projects that are privately economically viable and also give a positive social economic return.*
- *Projects that are not privately economically viable but which give a positive social return. These three possibilities are represented by the Venn diagram shown in Figure 8.3.*

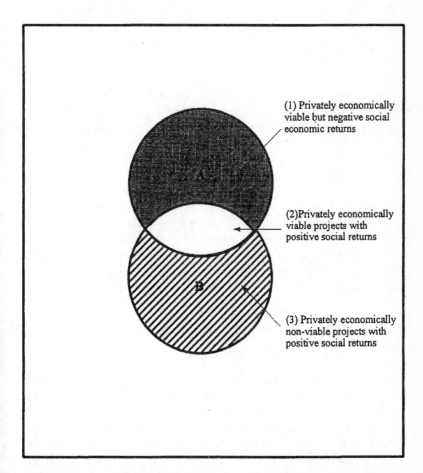

Figure 8.3 Due to environmental spillovers or externalities, private and social benefits from economic projects may differ. This diagram indicates three alternative possibilities

Projects in Group 1 are unsatisfactory from a social point of view and are likely to threaten the sustainability of production. The government should consider measures to prevent economic entities, such as farmers, from engaging in these activities. Projects in group (2) are socially desirable and are likely to be adopted by farmers if known to them. Projects in group (3) are socially beneficial but will not be undertaken by private business. It may be desirable for the government to adopt policies to make these projects privately economically viable (for example, they might be subsidised by the government) or in some cases, these projects might be undertaken by the government.

Sustainability of use of agricultural techniques in a dynamic context

The world is subject to continual change. Consequently agricultural techniques of production which seem to be sustainable in a stationary setting or one of little change may not be viable in a changing world. For example, shifting or swidden agriculture may be very sustainable at low levels of population density (Ramakrishan 1992), but becomes unsustainable as population densities increase and the length of the cultivation cycle becomes shorter. This has happened in a number of parts of the world where shifting agriculture is practised, for instance in Northeast India. In such circumstances, it is important to search for alternative agricultural techniques which may prove to be more sustainable in the changing circumstances. This illustrates the importance from a policy point of view, of making the best adjustment to attain sustainability of production when particular trends are apparent and cannot be counteracted. This will for instance be apparent for the study below of Northeast India.

8.4   AGRICULTURAL SUSTAINABILITY IN THE BARIND TRACT, NORTHWEST BANGLADESH

The Barind Tract covers much of the Northwestern region (Rajshahi Division) of Bangladesh (Figure 8.4) and extends into West Bengal, India. In Bangladesh, the total area of the Tract is 7296 sq km. While most of Bangladesh consists of flood-prone riverine plains and some is hilly (for example, the Chittagong Hill Tracts, and parts of Sylhet), the Barind Tract is an elevated, undulating terraced area and is flood free. Its physical features have been described in detail by Rashid (1991, pp.13–15) and by Brammer (1996).

Compared to the rest of Bangladesh, its Northwest has relatively unfavourable climatic conditions for agriculture. Ninety per cent of its

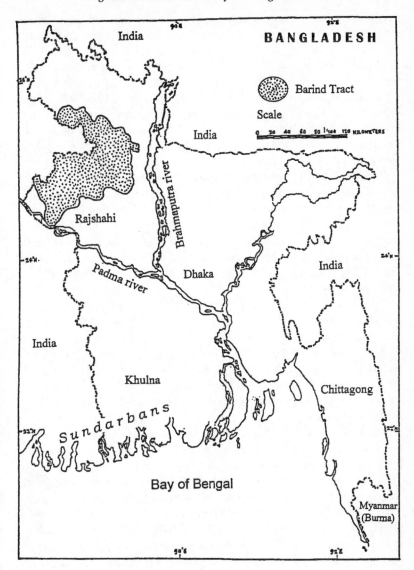

Figure 8.4 Map of Bangladesh showing the general location of the Barind Tract

rainfall of 1200 to 1400 mm occurs within the three month period, June to August. Because of the nature of the soils (discussed below) and the monsoonal downpour, much of this rainfall is lost as surface runoff and causes considerable soil erosion. During the dry period of seven to eight months, evapotranspiration exceeds precipitation. In addition, the length of the monsoon varies considerably and extremes of temperature are experienced with many summer days above 40°C and several winter days below 5°C.

Zuberi (1992) reports the topsoil is very thin (often sandy) and beneath there is a hard clay pan. The clay pan impedes the penetration of water to underground areas and the water holding capacity of the soil is low. Furthermore Zuberi (1992) points out that the organic content of the soil is low (organic matter accounts for only 0.5 to 0.7 per cent of the soil content) and that the soil is deficient in plant nutrients such as nitrogen, in zinc and sulphur and trace elements.

Considering all these aspects, Northwest Bangladesh is a marginal area for agriculture, particularly crop growing. Nevertheless, cultivation in this area has expanded and more than three-quarters of the land in Northwest Bangladesh is under cultivation, a higher percentage of land than in the more fertile Northeast (Dhaka Division) which has about 71 per cent of its area under cultivation. In the Southwest area (Chittagong Division) 43 per cent of land is under cultivation and in the Southwest area (Khulna Division) 63 per cent.

Table 8.1 specifies land use patterns in the four divisions of Bangladesh. It highlights the high degree of cultivation in the Rajshahi Division and indicates little scope for extension of cultivation in this region. The extent of the forested area in this division is the lowest in Bangladesh at approximately 0.4 per cent of its land area. The Chittagong Division shows greatest forestation (Chittagong Hill Tracts and mangrove forests) and Khulna, the second highest degree of forestation mainly because of the presence of the Sunderbarns.

About 100 years ago, less than 50 per cent of the land in the Barind Tract was under cultivation. Zuberi (1992, p.6) states that 'in the past, there was a long sustained, stable land use system as indicated from the historical accounts; the comparatively flat areas were cultivated with Aman (rainfed) rice while the elevated high lands and slopes were grass lands and low jungles covered with fuel and fruit frees.' Elsewhere Zuberi (1993, p.5) maintains that 'North Western Bangladesh practically has no forest cover at all. But recent historical accounts show that more than 50 percent of the area was covered with natural vegetation.' Hunter (1877) reported that this area was fairly well wooded. But with the expansion of agriculture and increased population, most of these natural areas have been destroyed, along with the rich biodiversity associated with these.

Loss of natural vegetation cover has reduced additions to soil organic matter, disrupted natural nutrient cycles and has exposed the soil to the elements resulting in rapid erosion of topsoil. In addition, rapid heating of the topsoil occurs thereby quickly oxidising organic matter remaining in

Table 8.1   Land utilisation in Bangladesh (1989–90): Area in 1000s of hectares

Item	North West		North East		South East		South West		Bangladesh	
	area	%	area	%	area	%	area	%	area	%
Total land area	3457	–	3643	–	3172	–	4026	–	14289	–
Not available for cultivation	731	21.0	718	21.0	402	12.7	868	21.6	2782	19.5
Forest	14	0.4	176	4.8	1350	42.6	603	15.0	2134	15.0
Cultivable waste	77	2.3	83	2.3	54	1.7	21	.05	235	1.6
Current fallow	110	3.0	182	5.0	135	4.3	90	2.2	517	3.6
Net cropped area	2525		2412	66.2	1231	38.8	2444	60.7	8612	60.3
Net cultivable area[a]	2635	76.0	2594	71.2	1366	43.1	2534	62.9	9124	63.9
Net cultivable area[b]	2773	80.0	2778	76.2	1261	39.8	2744	68.2	9562	66.9

[a] Net cropped area + current fallow (5 + 6).
[b] Upzilla maximum area of crop.

Source: Based on data from Bangaladesh Statistical Service.

the soil. Water retention and penetration of the soil has also been reduced by loss of natural vegetation cover, especially reduced tree cover.

Since the early 1940s cultivation of the Barind Tract has expanded at the expense of forested land, 'wasteland', grazing land, by the increased use of areas formerly used as ponds but either deliberately filled with soil or filled by silt from increased soil erosion.

The major portion of the cropland of the Barind Tract is used for rice production and most of this rice land is now sown with High Yielding Varieties (HYV) of rice. But paddy is a high user of water and encouragement of its production in a water-scarce region is risky, especially since it may quickly degrade the poor soil of this region.

Government policy has been to encourage intensification of cropping in this region, including the increased cultivation of HYV rice. To this end, it established the Barind Integrated Area Development Project (BIADP) within the Ministry of Agriculture. Against advice from foreign experts, deep tube wells are being installed in this region under this project (*The Daily Star*, July 13 1996). One problem is that the use of water from underground sources is liable to exceed the rate of recharge of the aquifers. The actual and planned water supplies from these sources are in all probability unsustainable in the long-term. Already watertables have fallen in some areas. For example, mango trees are reported to have died in some areas around Rajshahi due to falling watertables.

Irrigation from underground sources has enabled the area double cropped and triple cropped to be substantially increased. This raises the rate of depletion of soil nutrients and accelerates soil erosion. Hence 'reports of HYV (rice) yields of 2.6 t/ha decreasing to around 2.0 t/ha or lower (even only 1.2 t/ha) in many areas, are common in recent years' (Zuberi 1993, p.6). Consequently several reports and papers highlight the lack of sustainability of current agricultural practices in this region and there is significant land degradation with evidence of desertification in some areas (Ministry of Environment and Forestry and IUCN 1991). In addition, it seems probable that current and planned use of underground water for irrigation are unsustainable. Thus the longer term prognosis for agricultural production in this region are bleak and the possibility of future environmental refugees from this region cannot be dismissed. This raises several questions in political economy. In particular why should the government support agricultural developments which, on the face of it, result in unsustainable increases in income?

There are several possible explanations. First, governments tend to be myopic in their decision-making. Existing government is able to claim credit for increases in income in the short to medium term. In the long term, if incomes have fallen, the government has usually changed and the issue of responsibility for projects which prove to be environmentally unsustainable becomes confused, particularly if there is initial uncertainty about whether the projects involved are sustainable. Furthermore, policies to restrict use of resources such as use of underground irrigation water are liable to be politically unpopular e.g. to introduce pricing which reflects user-costs. Consequently, political mechanisms are unlikely to favour conservation and sustainability. This appears to have been the case in the Barind Tract.

It may also be that low incomes in this region result in a strong time preference for present consumption and a belief that the long-term will somehow take care of itself. Whether it does or not will depend on whether increases in man-made capital (combined with technological progress) compensate for the decline in natural resources in the Barind Tract. There is no indication that this is going to happen. This would not, however, be a problem if adequate capital accumulation were to occur in Bangladesh as a whole since there could be outward migration from the Barind Tract should its capital stock (natural resource stock plus man-made capital) and incomes decline. However, these possibilities do not seem to have been considered by those determining land use in the Barind Tract. There is no guarantee that the rest of Bangladesh will be able to provide adequate income for environmental refugees from the Barind Tract.

8.5 THE SUSTAINABILITY OF AGRICULTURE AND RELATED LAND-USES ON THE NORTH EASTERN HILLS OF THE INDIAN SUBCONTINENT

Much of the Northeast of India is hilly and in parts these hills extend into Bangladesh, for example, the Chittagong Hills. The majority of the population of these hills consists of tribal people, and shifting agriculture and forest resources play a major role in their life. The incidence of poverty is high. The situation is not unlike that in the hilly areas of Yunnan (Zhuge and Tisdell 1996) and in Myanmar.

Most of Northeast India consists of hills or mountains deeply dissected by rivers and streams due to the uplifting of the land. This makes travel in this region slow and difficult. Of the seven hill states of Northeast India (Arunachal Pradesh, Assam, Manipur, Meghalaya, Mizoram, Nagaland and Tripura, shown in Figure 8.5), Assam is the least hilly because much

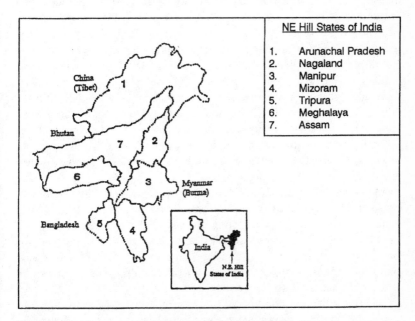

Figure 8.5 The seven North-East Hill States of India. They are Arunachal Pradesh (1), Nagaland (2), Manipur (3), Mizoram (4), Tripura (5), Meghalaya (6) and Assam (7)

of it lies in the plains of the Brahmaputra and there are fewer tribal people in this state than in the others. In the hilly areas of Northeast India, traditional shifting agriculture is becoming unsustainable.

In general, the levels of per capita income in the Northeast Indian states are lower than elsewhere in India but compare favourably with that of some other Indian states (e.g. Bihar). For example, it is estimated (Ministry of Finance 1994, Table 1.8, p.S–12) that for 1990–91 the per capita net state domestic product for Bihar was 2650 rupees, whereas for Manipur it was 3893, for Mizoram (in 1989–90) 4135, for Meghalaya 4190, for Assam 3932, for Arunachal Pradesh 5046 and for Tripura 3328. rupees. However, by contrast Delhi recorded a figure of 10 638 Rupees. Per capita incomes in the Northeast are still considered to be low but are not dramatically below the overall level of incomes in India.

The rate of population growth in the Northeast is rapid and overall is above the Indian average. It ranged in 1981–91 from an average exponential growth rate of 2.17 per cent for Assam to 4.45 per cent for Nagaland. Mizoram recorded a 3.34 per cent growth rate (Ministry of Finance 1994, Table 9, p.S–115). Population densities in the Northeast are low by Indian standards and range from 10 people per square km in Arunachal Pradesh to 286 in Assam. Mizoram had a low density in 1991 of 33 people per square km (Ministry of Finance 1994, Table 9. p.S–115). Nevertheless, with such rapid rates of population increase, population density is clearly rising rapidly and continuing to affect the region's natural environment. In addition, income aspirations are rising. Furthermore, densities are not low in relation to the quality of agricultural land available.

Agriculture and forests are important for economic welfare in Northeast India where the vast majority of the people are engaged in rural pursuits. However, a number of the agricultural practices used in the Northeast are becoming increasingly unsustainable and will continue to do so as population densities rise there and demands for higher incomes result in activities intensifying economic production.

As pointed out by Ramakrishnan (1992) and others, shifting agriculture (slash-and-burn agriculture, or *jhum* agriculture) which is practised by a number of tribal groups is becoming less sustainable as cultivation cycles are shortened due to population pressures. Once this cycle goes below 10–12 years it seems that it is no longer an economic form of agriculture compared to possible types of settled agriculture. In some cases the length of the cycle has fallen to 3–5 years.

This raises the question then of just how sustainable is settled agriculture in the Northeast taking into account the monsoonal nature of the area, the prevalence of sloping lands and the nature of soils. Certainly *modified* forms of settled agriculture are likely to be called for in this region to improve agricultural sustainability: mixed systems of cultivation as in permacultures, use of hedgerows for soil erosion control and so on. These are all matters worthy of investigation.

The above underlines the point that strategies for sustainable development must be based upon anticipation and that flexibility is needed. Given that population levels are going to increase in the Northeast of India, then policies for sustainable development, including sustainable agricultural development, need to be designed *taking this into account*. A *dynamic* approach to planning for sustainability is required.

A reduction in the length of *jhum* cycles has a number of adverse environmental consequences. It reduces biodiversity and it increases the rate of soil erosion, apart from its unfavourable economic consequences for the cultivator. While the slash-and-burn technique appears to be relatively sustainable and not a major environmental danger when population densities are low, this is not the case for higher population densities.

Inroads continue to be made into forested and woody areas in Northeast India as population pressures and desires for economic development increase.

Ramakrishnan (1992, p.386) reports:

In Northeastern India, large-scale disturbance of the rain forest ecosystem has resulted in varied levels of degraded arrested bamboo forests, with weed take-over or a totally bald landscape. During the last few decades, large-scale timber extraction for industrial purposes has cleared vast areas of land for invasion by exotic weeds... Thus exotic weeds such as *Eupatorium* spp., and *Mikania micrantha* have taken over vast tracts of cleared land along with native weeds such as *Imperata cylindrica* and *Thysanolaena maxima*. Once this large-scale invasion has occurred, the jhum farmer is even more limited by the land area available for his jhum system of agriculture, as he prefers to avoid sites of high weed density. Because of this and increased population pressure, jhum cycle has dropped drastically in length from a more favourable 20 years or more, to an extremely short 5 years or even less. Having no other option, in the absence of an alternate agricultural technology that is viable from an ecological and social angle, the jhum farmer perforce had to resort to very short jhum cycles although the system operates below subsistence level and has caused further environmental degradation. Large-scale timber extraction and very short jhum cycles of 4–5 years have resulted in an arrested succession of weeds in Northeastern India.

In some cases, deforestation has led to desertification in Northeast India. Ramakrishnan (1992, pp.386–87) suggests that desertification in Cherrapunji in Meghalaya has been rapid and sudden mainly due to past deforestation. Reforestation has been arrested. Furthermore, in other areas, reforestation has been attenuated, for example by the growth of bamboo. Forested areas are trapped in a bamboo successional stage with 'obvious adverse consequences for biological diversity in the region'. Ramakrishnan, (1992, p.387) suggests that mixed plantation forests may be needed to re-establish forest succession and help in increasing biological diversity. There are clearly many other issues that need to be investigated as far as the sustainability of forests in Northeast India is concerned. Forests are especially important in Northeast India because they play a substantial role in providing economic support for many tribal groups and are an important source of fuel. They also play a major role in maintaining biodiversity and in providing environmental services such as improving waterflows and reducing soil erosion.

It is often argued that sustainable development is not just a matter of achieving economic sustainability and that sustainability must be considered in relation to at least three dimensions. These dimensions are:

- *the biophysical,*
- *the economic, and*
- *the social.*

For this reason, it is usually recommended that strategies for sustainable development be studied on a holistic basis employing an interdisciplinary approach. Sustainable development strategies should ideally satisfy sustainability conditions for all of the above *three* dimensions.

Views differ about what constitutes social sustainability but it involves the maintenance of a sense of community and of cohesion in society. It also requires the continuing ability of the society to avoid disintegration and to respond effectively to changes which call for a communal response. Irrespective of the exact definition adopted, it is clear that the social dimension cannot be ignored in planning and implementing development strategies.

Ramakrishnan (1992, Ch.3) has described social patterns in Northeast India as being ones involving economic mutualism between different tribal and ethnic groups, using somewhat different techniques of obtaining a livelihood and utilising different sets of resources so that competition between them is reduced and they are able to more easily retain their separate identities and communities. While some exchange occurs between groups, subsistence activities play a dominant role in the Northeast. Ramakrishnan (1992, p.88) points out that although it is difficult to generalise about village organisation and formation in this region, 'diverse communities often coexisting in the same area have evolved ways in which they are able to do so, sharing resources in a highly complementary manner'.

However, the equilibrium of communities can easily be shattered by resource-depletion and increasing resource scarcity which can render some ways of life and some communities unsustainable. For example, with diminishing forest resources in the Northeast, those communities heavily specialised in using these resources could find their communities endangered. Gathering from forests still plays a significant role in the subsistence of some tribal groups. One group, the *Sulungs* of Arunachal Pradesh, obtains almost half of its food requirements from hunting and gathering (Ramakrishnan 1992, p.117). Hill tribes such as the *Garos* and the *Khasis* in Meghalaya and the *Nithis*, the *Karbis*, the *Kacharis* and the *Chakmas* all show significant dependence on forest resources for food and fuel, a dependence that rises during poor seasons. These societies are liable to be disrupted by loss of forest resources.

It was suggested above that in hilly areas where shifting agriculture is becoming economically and ecologically unsustainable, there may be a case for promoting relatively sustainable forms of settled agriculture. Some such relatively sustainable forms include alley cropping with hedgerows (Jha 1995), agroforestry, and perennial crops, such as fruit trees. Research to develop sustainable agriculture systems appropriate to this region is required.

However, it is one thing to develop ecologically sustainable agricultural techniques. It is another to have them adopted. They may fail to be adopted for economic reasons or because of social constraints.

A number of forms of conservation agriculture, such as alley cropping with hedgerows, require an investment. Many poor farmers are not in a position to undertake such investment (Tisdell 1996) because of their lack of capital or of access to credit, or because at the time the conservation measures can be implemented, their labour is required for cropping activities and the opportunity cost of withdrawing it for implementation of conservation measures is too high.

The main constraint to the introduction of settled conservation-type agriculture in the region is a social one. Tribal social systems have evolved around shifting agriculture and in many cases, tenure of individuals or households in land does not exist. The Mizos of Mizoram for example allocate land to households as the village shifts its cultivation from one area to another in its territory by ballot. Consequently, a family may be allocated a different portion of land when the village returns to the same area after cultivation completes one cycle. This discourages a household from undertaking any long term investment in the land which it temporarily occupies. In these circumstances, there is no incentive to plant perennials such as trees and there is no scope to introduce hedgerows and alley cropping. Furthermore, possibilities for credit are limited because of lack of collateral. Note, however, that forms of shifting agriculture differ in Northeast India and property rights also show some variation. In Arunachal Pradesh, for example, amongst some tribes individual households are assigned fixed or definite parcels of land throughout the territory of their villages for use for shifting agriculture. This provides greater scope for development of settled agriculture since it increases private property rights.

Changing property rights in this region is not easy because of vested interests in the existing systems. Furthermore, social systems and economic systems are interrelated. Changing to settled agriculture involves substantial alterations in the social system, and if serious social disruption is to be avoided, new systems need to evolve.

Nevertheless, in several areas near sizeable urban populations, for instance, near Aizawl in Mizoram, *de facto* private property rights and relatively settled forms of agriculture are emerging because of the availability of nearby urban markets for production. Commercialisation and market-related agriculture are evolving and are encouraging the establishment of private property.

The Government of Mizoram under its New Land Use Plan (Leanzela 1995, Ch.9) has assigned a limited number of small parcels of land to some individuals (as private property) and has provided them with an initial subsidy to engage in settled forms of agriculture, like the growing of fruit trees such as bananas and mangoes. This is a transitional type of policy and because it is on a small scale unlikely to be socially disruptive.

Shifting agriculture as now practiced in Northeast India appears to be unsustainable and results in a magnification of adverse environmental externalities. Apart from increasing biodiversity loss, it reduce natural vegetation cover because of shorter cultivation cycles (that is reduced fallow periods). Therefore, it results in increased soil erosion and greater fluctuations in streamflows so that both flooding in wet seasons and lack of availability of water in streams in dry seasons become more pronounced.

Note, however, that this situation would not necessarily be rectified merely by the provision of private property rights in land and the adoption of methods of settled agriculture. The latter methods need to be economic and environmentally appropriate. For example, a number of Bengalis have migrated to the foothills of the Chittagong Hill Tracts and are employing the same agricultural techniques as they used on the plains. These techniques are resulting in severe soil erosion (Alauddin *et al.* 1995).

8.6 CONCLUDING COMMENTS

Issues involved in agricultural sustainability are very wide ones, and they have been placed in a general context in this chapter and related to case studies for two marginal agricultural regions, mainly the Barind Tract situated mainly in Northwest Bangladesh and the Northeast hills of India. The case study for the Barind Tract illustrates how modern agricultural technologies promoted by government can threaten agricultural sustainability. By contrast, the case material for Northeast India illustrates a traditional agricultural system that is becoming unsustainable with population growth and rising income aspirations. It highlights the point also that changing agricultural techniques in this situation is not easy because of existing social systems and the inertia of current institutional and cultural arrangements. In each of these cases, socio-economic challenges as well as scientific and technological ones are involved in devising strategies for sustainable development.

9 Sustainability of Rice–shrimp Farming Systems: Environmental and Distributional Conflicts

9.1 INTRODUCTION AND OVERVIEW

The case studies of agricultural and environmental changes reported in Chapters 7 and 8 are for inland areas of Bangladesh and India. By contrast the case material presented here is for land use in the deltaic areas of Khulna in southwest Bangladesh where rice production and shrimp aquaculture often alternate on the same piece of land. Although the government of Bangladesh has encouraged the aquaculture of shrimp, it is doubtful whether this aquaculture is sustainable using current production methods. Furthermore, shrimp culture in the Khulna region is reducing rice yields and having adverse environmental spillovers on agricultural production and other rural pursuits. In the Chittagong region, shrimp culture has reduced salt production, decreased tree cover, and production of goods dependent on forests e.g. mangrove forests and removal of trees, has exposed coastal communities to the risk of greater damage from cyclones. Mangroves and similar coastal forests act as protective buffers against tidal surges and the force of the sea. The main areas of Bangladesh where shrimp culture occurs are shown in Figure 9.1.

Rice–shrimp farming in the Khulna region is basically along the following lines:

- *In the wet season, the fields grow paddy.*
- *In the dry season, once the rice is harvested and stubble removed, they are flooded with brackish water containing shrimp post-larvae from nearby rivers and streams. Shrimp fields are then stocked, in most cases, with shrimp fry caught from the wild and occasionally with the hatchery-bred ones. These are raised extensively until they are ready for the market.*

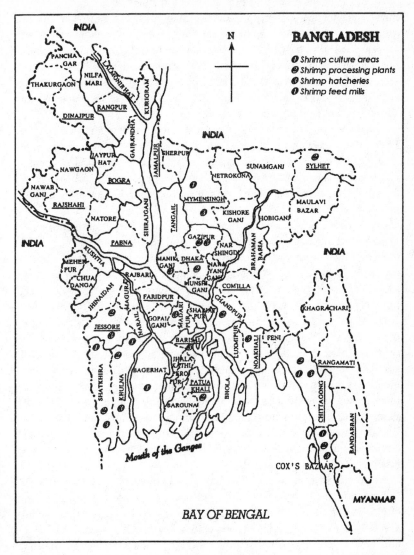

Figure 9.1 Shrimp farming areas and locations of other sub-sectors of the shrimp industry in Bangladesh

- *The mature shrimp are harvested and the ponds are drained before the end of the dry season. The land is then able to be prepared for the rice crop grown in the wet season. The cycle then repeats itself.*

Similar production systems are used in other parts of Asia, for instance in parts of India and Sri Lanka (see for example Alagarswami 1995; Jayasinghe 1995). Not only does rice–shrimp farming have adverse consequences for the sustainability of economic production, it also may result in serious deterioration in the distribution of income. Before considering such matters, utilising survey data from the Khulna region, let us review shrimp culture in Bangladesh generally.

The fisheries sub-sector is of critical importance to the economy of Bangladesh. Fish is a staple food which ranks next to rice and constitutes about 80 per cent of the animal protein intake. It accounts for 4 per cent of GDP and 12 per cent of export earnings and employs 1.2 million people on a full-time basis. An additional ten million people are employed on a part-time basis (DOF 1995).

Shrimp culture is central to the fisheries sub-sector. Shrimp cultivation experienced a spectacular boost from a negligible base in the early 1970s to become a major export industry in recent years. This represents a significant change in the structure and composition of Bangladesh's export trade. This is largely due to the effects of various government policies and high export demand. The shrimp industry is influenced by a range of government policies and institutional arrangements that have been designed over time to achieve various individual socio-economic objectives. The measures used in the industry include subsidised credit to promote diffusion of intensive and semi-intensive technologies and leasing of government land for shrimp farming. These and other arrangements are in place to achieve a range of objectives including raising production/productivity in shrimp farms, generating employment and earning foreign exchange. Expanding shrimp cultivation consistent with ecologically sustainable development is a priority area identified by the government (MOF and FAO 1992; Rahman *et al.* 1995).

Although shrimp cultivation has great potential in some areas of Bangladesh, the current level of yield is very low. According to Mazid (1995) shrimp aquaculture is practised mostly by extensive (traditional) and only occasionally by improved extensive (improved traditional) technology and semi-intensive technologies. Under the extensive method the annual yield ranges between 60–200 kilogrammes per hectare. The yields per hectare for the improved extensive and the semi-intensive techniques are respectively 0.60–1.00 and 2.00–6.00 metric tonnes. On very rare occasions intensive cultivation is practised. Under this technology yields can go as high as 5 to 10 metric tonnes per hectare (Mazid 1995). All shrimp areas in Bangladesh, however, are not suitable for intensive shrimp aquaculture (Rahman *et al.* 1995). Table 9.1 sets out characteristic

Table 9.1 Shrimp farming methods in Bangladesh

Farming methods	% of total area (138 000 ha)	Farm size (ha)	Liming fertilisation	Water management	Screening	Type of feed	Stocking density* (pl/m^2)	Annual yield (kg/ha)
Extensive	75	2–100	No	Tide fed	Nil – imperfectly	Natural	1–1.5	150–200
Improved Extensive	24	1–10	Yes	Tide+pump	Moderately	Supplemental	1.5–8	250–750
Semi-intensive/ Intensive	1	0.5–2	Yes	Tide+pump+ aeration	Perfectly – very perfectly	Formulated feeds	20–50	3000–6000

* Karim and Aftabuzzaman (1995) suggested a stocking density for improved extensive and semi-intensive/ intensive methods as 1.5–3 pl/m^2 and 20–40 pl/m^2 respectively.

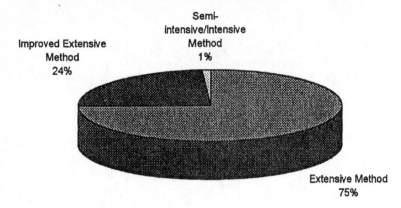

Figure 9.2   Relative shares of different shrimp farming methods in Bangladesh

features of different shrimp farming methods while Figure 9.2 graphically illustrates the spread of these technologies. According to a Master Plan Organisation (MPO 1986) estimate, total area under shrimp culture is expected to increase from 96 048 hectares in 1990 to 135 000 hectares in the year 2005.

What seems unclear, however, is whether or not the government has taken explicit account of the medium and longer term costs of expanding shrimp cultivation. It is entirely possible that the likely environmental degradation and natural resource depletion following shrimp cultivation could outweigh the short and medium term gains of export-led growth. As seen in Chapter 2, the current national income is perhaps overestimated given that it does not account for the depletion and degradation of the stock of natural resources (Repetto *et al.* 1989).

Against this background and the empirical evidence presented in preceding chapters this chapter provides a special case study of environmental impacts of shrimp (prawn) cultivation in Bangladesh since it has significant environmental consequences. The existing literature pays scant attention to its possible adverse impact on the ecology, environment and agriculture. This study is an attempt to counterbalance this. It proceeds first of all with a broad overview of the shrimp sector. This is followed by a brief review of the existing literature. Farm-level evidence is then presented employing primary data from three areas in the greater Khulna region. The objective is to identify gainers and losers from shrimp aquaculture. It investigates: employment gain/loss due to shrimp cultivation, effect on the environment, income distribution, and possible conflicts between agriculture and aquaculture, conflicts of interests between landowners and shrimp farm owners.

9.2   A BRIEF REVIEW OF LITERATURE

The rice–shrimp integrated farming system on a large scale in Bangladesh is a relatively new phenomenon. To date there has not been any comprehensive study incorporating environmental costs and benefits, social cost–benefit analysis, allocative and technical efficiencies and an analytically rigorous analysis of the short-term and medium-term implications of government policies. Nor has there been any study on the sustainability of the process of *rice–shrimp* integrated farming systems.

Some earlier studies on the resource availability and production potentialities of brackish water aquaculture operation were conducted by Cook and Schmidt (1979). They gave only the description of the production process, the size and ownership of shrimp ponds in the coastal areas of Bangladesh. The study conducted by Islam (1983) indicated the growing conflicts between rice farming and shrimp culture in the Khulna region. These conflicts relate to those in resource use as well as the interests of various groups engaged in the process. Some later studies (Chowdhury 1988, Das 1992) identified similar problems. The findings indicated that due to the effect of shrimp cultivation, the yield of both paddy and salt decreased in Khulna and Cox's Bazaar respectively as well as uneven distribution of gains from shrimp culture.

Analytic literature on shrimp culture in Bangladesh to date seems to concentrate primarily on the socio-economic aspects in that it emphasises the social and economic backgrounds of the different groups affected by the process of shrimp farming: *gher* owners, land owners and landless labourers. These studies provide useful insights into the sociology of the relevant rural society and could provide useful pointers to the resulting income distribution pattern.

However, there is little detailed discussion of the effects of environmental changes using rigorous analytical techniques [see, for example, Ali (1991), Chowdhury (1988), Rahman (1989, 1990, 1992), Rahman *et al.* 1992]. Rahman *et al.* (1995) correctly identified important environmental problems associated with shrimp cultivation but like many preceding studies do not provide a detailed analysis of their effects on the sustainability of shrimp farming. The literature on policy discussion (Chong *et al.* 1991, World Bank 1991) also seems to be based on scant empirical evidence and only provides a general overview of shrimp farming: microlevel analysis does not feature very prominently. The available literature also do not pay adequate attention to the effects of economic and institutional variables, such as input and output prices, competitiveness of Bangladesh's shrimps, property rights issues on sustainability of shrimp farming.

Many of the above studies may be substantial in respect of providing basic information on some aspects, like socio-economic changes and description of environmental changes. On closer analysis, however, one can find that they lack comprehensiveness and therefore provide only a partial picture instead of an integrated view encompassing technology, institutions, policy and the environment which are critical to the broader issue of sustainability of the existing rice–shrimp farming systems/practices and their implications for policy measures (for further details see Alauddin and Hamid 1996).

To sum up, the existing literature suffers from limitations in that it does not :

- *quantify environmental benefits and costs;*
- *establish a proper linkage between the effects of environmental degradation and resource depletion on sustainability of the process and sustainability of rural communities;*
- *assess policy implications with sufficient analytical rigour.*

In the light of the preceding discussion and government policy priority (MOF and FAO 1992), one can clearly identify the need for an integrated study encompassing socio-economic, environmental and institutional aspects to provide a sound basis for policy formation.

The present study does not claim to fill all the gaps in the existing literature, but goes some way towards this. Based on primary data and techniques such as discriminant analysis and statistical techniques, it identifies some of the implications of shrimp cultivation for income distribution and sustainable development.

9.3   THE SHRIMP SECTOR: A BROAD PICTURE

This section records the changing structure and composition of Bangladesh's exports during the last two decades. Table 9.2 sets out the broad composition of Bangladesh's total exports (**EXPORT**) in terms of primary (**PRIMARY**) versus manufacturing goods (**MANUFAC**). The relative shares of shrimp, raw jute and readymade garments are also presented. **PCSHRIMP** and **PCRJUTE** respectively represent relative shares of shrimp and raw jute in the primary goods category while **SHRMPCEX** and **PCGARMENT** refer to relative shares of shrimp and readymade garments in total exports (**EXPORT**). Trends in relative shares of different categories of exports are also presented in Figure 9.3.

A careful inspection of the information contained in Table 9.2 and illustrated in Figure 9.3 reveals that there is a progressive decline in the share

Table 9.2 Shrimp in Bangladesh's export trade: 1972–73 to 1993–94

YEAR	EXPORT	PRIMARY	MANUFAC	SHRMPCEX	PCGARMENT	PCSHRIMP	PCRJUTE
1972	2711	1165	1546	0.85	0.00	1.97	89.36
1973	2974	1226	1749	1.11	0.00	2.69	83.47
1974	3061	977	2084	0.78	0.00	2.46	75.33
1975	5517	2323	3194	2.63	0.00	6.24	79.14
1976	6255	2679	3576	3.93	0.00	9.18	65.89
1977	7406	2551	4855	3.42	0.01	9.92	57.00
1978	9283	3534	5749	4.80	0.02	12.62	61.65
1979	11242	3457	7784	4.71	0.09	15.30	64.24
1980	11599	3419	8180	4.74	0.46	16.09	56.84
1981	13209	4882	8327	6.84	1.06	18.52	41.74
1982	16162	5724	10438	9.27	1.58	26.19	45.16
1983	19902	6909	12993	7.81	3.89	22.51	41.63
1984	24155	8185	15970	8.26	12.44	24.38	47.63
1985	24314	8884	15430	11.08	16.05	30.31	41.39
1986	32632	9044	23588	10.47	27.82	37.79	34.95
1987	38081	8867	29214	9.49	35.24	40.73	28.09
1988	40968	9539	31430	9.32	36.47	40.05	32.35
1989	49764	10548	39216	8.33	39.99	39.28	38.59
1990	60561	10794	49767	7.45	42.83	41.80	34.04
1991	75908	10175	65733	6.00	53.36	44.79	31.99
1992	92575	12195	80380	6.52	52.06	49.53	23.68
1993	100975	13820	87156	7.80	50.97	57.00	16.44

Notes: 1972 means financial year beginning July 1972 etc. **EXPORT** is total export. **PRIMARY** is
export of primary goods while **MANUFAC** is manufacturing export. **EXPORT, PRIMARY** and
MANUFAC are expressed in millions of takas in current prices. **PCSHRIMP** and **PCRJUTE**
respectively refer to relative shares (percentages) of shrimp and raw jute in primary exports.
SHRMPCEX and **PCGARMENT** refer to relative shares of shrimps and readymade garments
in total export respectively.

Sources: EPBB (1991, 1995); BBS (1979, 1990a, 1993).

of **PRIMARY** (raw jute, shrimp and other agro-based exports). This is
despite a significant increase in shrimp exports which now contributes
nearly half of the primary exports items suggesting considerable decline in
raw-jute exports from over 80 per cent in the early 1970s to only a third of
the total primary exports in recent years. By implication manufacturing
exports have shown considerable growth (from about 60 per cent to more
than 80 per cent of the total) over the same period. As for shrimp, its share
in total exports (**SHRMPCEX**) grew from next to nothing in the early
1970s to contribute about 8 per cent in the early 1990s. Its share rose to as
high as 11 per cent in the mid-1980s.

Thus Bangladesh appears to have moved away from its traditional
dependence on the export of jute-based items. From a closer examination
of the movements in the relative shares of the various broad components
of the primary goods category, it is clear that while the share of raw jute

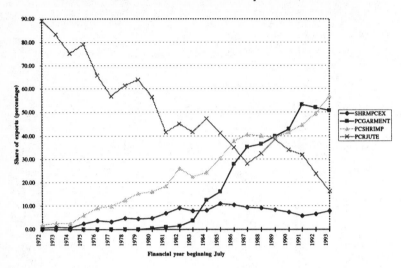

Figure 9.3   Shrimp in export trade: 1972–73 to 1993–94

export has continuously declined, that of shrimp has increased quite considerably. By the second half of the 1980s shrimp exports surpassed raw jute in relative importance. On the other hand the relative shares of the remaining items of this category after considerable fluctuations and a somewhat increasing tendency up until the early 1980s have declined and seem to have stabilised to about a quarter of the total exports in the last few years. Thus in the primary goods category shrimp has replaced jute as the dominant item of exports.

Shrimps are grown primarily for international market. Prior to Bangladesh's entry into the international shrimp market, shrimp was much cheaper than fish in Bangladesh (Karim and Aftabuzzaman 1995). Now it is quite expensive and beyond the buying capacity of average people. However, local demands are now met mostly from open water shrimp catches, that are not exclusively destined for overseas market. Bangladesh's shrimps are well recognised for their flavour, taste and texture since they are grown in a 100 per cent natural environment (BFFEA 1995). Since the bulk of the production comes from extensive culture methods that involve none to very little of the modern technologies, it is logical to say that harvested crops are devoid of chemicals, particularly artificial growth hormones. Even though Bangladesh is a small player in terms of its share in international markets, providing 4.2 per cent of the world production of farmed shrimp, it is the seventh largest cultured shrimp producer in the world. Figure 9.4 captures this phenomenon.

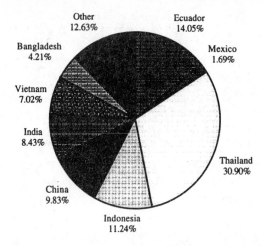

Figure 9.4 Major shrimp farming countries with their relative contribution to world production (per cent)

Table 9.3 sets out information on the land under shrimp culture along with its regional distribution, total area and production as well as productivity per hectare. Figure 9.5 brings into sharper focus regional distribution of area and production. Shrimp cultivation is almost exclusively concentrated in the four districts of Satkhira, Khulna, Bagerhat and Cox's Bazaar. Over 70 per cent of the total number of farms (**PCFARM**) is located in the greater Khulna district (Satkhira, Khulna and Bagerhat) accounting for 74 per cent of land area under shrimp cultivation and 77 per cent of its total output. The remainder of the farms, area under cultivation and output are almost entirely accounted for by Cox's Bazaar.

Two types of farming systems normally dominate shrimp culture in the costal belt in Bangladesh: (i) in the Khulna region paddy cultivation alternates with shrimp culture; (ii) in the Cox's Bazaar region salt production alternates with shrimp cultivation.

9.4   FARM-LEVEL EVIDENCE

Rahman *et al.* (1995) argue that despite the destruction of mangroves in Chokoria the issue of environmental degradation is less pronounced in the Cox's Bazaar region than in the Khulna region. Partly because of this and partly because of the longer history and greater relative importance of shrimp culture, the present study relies on primary data from the Khulna region. Employing a direct questionnaire method, we collected farm-level data. The field work was conducted from December 1992 to March 1993

Table 9.3   Structure, regional distribution of area and output and yield of shrimp in Bangladesh

REGION	NFARM	AREA	FARMSIZE	OUTPUT	YIELD	PCAREA	PCPROD	PCFARM
KHULNA	813	23759	29.22	3801.88	160	21.94	20.73	12.43
SATKHIRA	1123	21207	18.88	4368.64	206	19.58	23.82	17.17
BAGERHAT	2648	35483	13.40	6032.11	170	32.76	32.89	40.49
COX'S BAZAAR	1879	27069	14.49	4060.35	150	24.99	22.14	28.73
CHITTAGONG	44	383	8.70	50.56	132	0.35	0.28	0.67
NOAKHALI	14	61	4.36	3.78	62	0.06	0.02	0.21
BHOLA	1	12	12.00	0.86	72	0.01	0.00	0.02
PATUAKHALI	18	326	18.11	1.19	65	0.30	0.12	0.28
TOTAL	6540	108300	16.56	18339.37	169	100.00	100.00	100.00

Notes: **NFARM** is number of shrimp farms (*ghers*); **AREA** is land area under shrimp farming (hectares); **FARMSIZE** is average size of *gher* (hectares); **OUTPUT** is shrimp output (tonnes); **YIELD** is shrimp yield per hectare (kilogrammes); **PCAREA** is percentage of total shrimp area; **PCPROD** is percentage of total output; **PCFARM** is percentage of total number of *ghers*.

Source: Adapted from Rahman *et al.* (1995).

Shrimp area

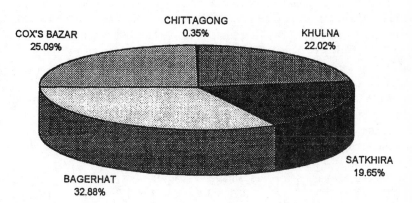

Shrimp output

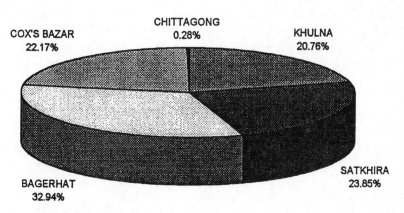

Figure 9.5   Regional distribution of shrimp area and output, 1992

in the coastal region of greater Khulna district (Satkhira, Khulna and Bagerhat). Primary data were collected on more than five hundred households in three different categories: shrimp farm owners, known as *gher* owners (107); landowners (262) and landless labourers (216).

9.4.1   Data analysis for the *gher* owners

More often than not the *gher* owners are not the owners of the land under shrimp culture. In general, the *gher* owners practise shrimp cultivation under leasing arrangements (Alauddin and Hamid 1996) with the landowners for a specified period of time on payment of an annual rent that varies across regions. The duration of agreement between land owners and *gher* owners ranged from 1 year to 7 years with an average of 4.35 years and a modal value of 5 years. Depending on the contractual arrangements as to whether the landowners had the right to only an annual lease fee, or to a combination of an annual lease fee and a share of the rice crop, or to the rice crop only, the fee varied from 0 taka to 15 000 taka per hectare, the average being 6300 taka per hectare. In our sample it was found that many of the *gher* owners practised shrimp cultivation on their own land.

Let us consider the percentage distribution of own land in *gher* (**PCOWNLND**). Table 9.4 sets out the relevant information. It can be seen that about 30 per cent of the *gher* owners were engaged in shrimp farming on land leased in from landowners. As the **PCOWNLND** tends to increase the percentage of *gher* owners tends to decrease. Only 2.8 per cent of *gher* owners cultivated shrimp on **PCOWNLND** in the 75 to < 100 per cent category while only 1.9 per cent of the *gher* owners did not lease in any land from others. There was wide variation of **PCOWNLND** with the average being 27 per cent and a standard deviation of 28 per cent. Table 9.5 provides information on the size distribution of *ghers*. Nearly a quarter of the *ghers* in the sample were below 10 hectares in size while 32.7 per cent of the *ghers* ranged between 10 and 20 hectares. Toward the

Table 9.4   Distribution of percentage of own land in *gher*

PCOWNLND	PCGHEROWN	CUMPERCENT
nil	29.9	29.9
up to 25%	27.1	57.0
25.01 to 50%	22.4	79.4
50.01 to 75%	15.9	95.3
75.01 to < 100%	2.8	98.1
100 per cent	1.9	100.0

Notes: **PCGHEROWN** is percentage of *gher* owners and **CUMPERCENT** is cumulative percentage.

Table 9.5   Distribution of percentage of size of *ghers*

GHERSIZE	PCOWNERS	CUMPERCENT
Up to 10 hectares	23.4	23.4
10.01 to 20 hectares	32.7	56.1
20.01 to 40 hectares	14.0	70.1
40.01 to 80 hectares	15.9	86.9
80.01 to 160 hectares	9.4	96.3
Above 160 hectares	3.7	100.0

Notes: **GHERSIZE** is size of *gher* in hectares, **PCOWNERS** is percentage of
gher owners and **CUMPERCENT** is cumulative percentage.

upper end of the scale, 13 per cent of the *ghers* were above 80 hectares in size. This represents unevenness in the size distribution of *ghers* with a mean of 36 hectares and a standard deviation of 43 hectares. The size of *ghers* ranged between as small as 0.28 hectare to as large as 182 hectares. From the sample, size of *ghers* (**GHERSIZE**) seems to vary somewhat inversely with the percentage of own land in the *gher* (**PCOWNLND**) as indicated by the negative correlation between the two variables of the order of -0.2743 (significant at 0.2 per cent level). This seems to support the hypothesis that larger *gher* owners tend to lease in a greater percentage of the land under their *ghers*.

Many of the *gher* owners are based in the main in the urban centres and for many of them shrimp culture represent no more than a side business. They represent a class of people with resources at their disposal wielding considerable socio-political power in the local community. A majority of the *gher* owners in our sample did not reveal their political identity and those that did had affiliations with the major political parties, especially the party in power at the national level. However, most of the *gher* owners in the sample were revealed to have readier access to and influence over the higher echelons of the local (regional) administration and the law enforcing agencies.

In terms of the impact of shrimp farms the *gher* owners were asked questions on various aspects of the process. These includes *inter alia* whether the local community has had improved economic conditions after *gher*, and whether there had been any adverse effect on the environment, for example on green vegetation and species of indigenous fish.

Almost all of the *gher* owners suggested that shrimp farming has had a favourable impact on the economic condition of the community in general.

Table 9.6   Discriminant analysis for *gher* owners on groups defined by
ECONOMY

Discriminating variable	Standardised canonical discriminant function coefficients	Value at group means	
		Group 1	Group 2
EMPLOY	1.000 (0.7327)	–0.1046	3.4174

Notes: The figure in parenthesis is Wilks' lambda value. The coefficent is highly significant at 0.001 per cent level.

This was further analysed using discriminant analysis for *gher* owners on groups defined by a dichotomous variable **ECONOMY** (1 for improvement and 2 for deterioration in economic condition following shrimp cultivation). The results are set out in Table 9.6. The discriminant function was estimated to identify the variables that differentiate the groups of respondents. We started with several variables such as **EMPLOY** (employment opportunities), **PCOWNLND** (percentage of own land in the *gher*), **PART** (percentage of ownership in the *gher*), **PCHIND** (percentage of Hindu owners of land in the *gher*) and **PCMUSLIM** (percentage of Muslim owners of land in the *gher*). A stepwise run of discriminant analysis identified **EMPLOY** as the only discriminating variable. In other words, improved economic conditions resulted from increased employment opportunities. This contrasted with the *gher* owners' opinion on the environmental impact of the process of shrimp culture. It was gathered that while these recorded employment and export gains seem highly impressive, they have been achieved at considerable costs. These relate to environmental and ecological problems in the form of loss of green vegetation, loss of genetic diversity (loss or extinction of indigenous species of fishes) and declining rice yields in shrimp farms.

At this stage it would be useful to ask: how significant was the difference between average rice yields (1) in pre and post *gher* phases; and (2) on and off shrimp farms? Employing *t*-tests for paired sample it was confirmed that there was a significant decline in rice yields in the post *gher* phase compared to the period preceding the process of shrimp cultivation. Also rice yields off the shrimp farms were significantly higher than those on the farms. The results of the exercise are presented in Table 9.7.

Table 9.7   Rice yields on and off shrimp farms and pre and post *gher* phases: *t*-tests of paired samples for *gher* owners

Paired variable	*t*-value		
	1990	1991	1992
Rice yield on and off *gher*	13.42	10.59	15.26
Rice yield in pre and post *gher* periods	5.67	5.63	5.55

Notes: All the *t*-values are highly significant at 0.001 per cent level.

9.4.2   Data analysis for the land owners

In contrast to the distribution of ownership of the *ghers*, land distribution is dominated by a very large number of small owners. This can be clearly seen from the information contained in Table 9.8. Nearly 60 per cent of the farms are below 2 hectares in size. Tables 9.9 and 9.10 set out information on the percentage of landowners having land area inside as well as outside the *ghers*. Many of these landowners (about 47 per cent) have their entire land resource within the *ghers*. About 34 per cent of the landowners have up to 50 per cent of their land within the *ghers* while the remaining

Table 9.8   Distribution of land ownership pattern

HECOWNL	PCLANDOWN	CUMPERCENT
0.01–0.25	11.8	11.8
0.26–0.50	8.0	19.8
0.51–0.75	13.4	33.2
0.76–1.00	9.2	42.4
1.01–2.00	15.5	59.9
2.01–4.00	17.2	77.1
4.01–10.00	11.8	88.9
Above 10.00 hectares	11.1	100.0

Notes: **HECOWNL** is hectare of land owned, **PCLANDOWN** is percentage of land owners and **CUMPERCENT** is cumulative percentage.

Table 9.9   Distribution of land area in the *gher*

HECINL	PCLANDOWN	CUMPERCENT
0.01–0.25	13.0	13.0
0.26–0.50	17.5	30.5
0.51–0.75	14.9	45.4
0.76–1.00	9.9	55.3
1.01–2.00	23.7	79.0
2.01–4.00	11.8	90.8
4.01–10.00	6.5	97.3
Above 10.00 hectares	2.7	100.0

Notes: **HECINL** is hectare of land in *gher*, **PCLANDOWN** is percentage of land owners and **CUMPERCENT** is cumulative percentage.

Table 9.10   Distribution of land area outside of the *gher*

HECOUTL	PCLANDOWN	CUMPERCENT
NIL	46.7	46.7
0.01–0.25	6.6	53.3
0.26–0.50	6.5	59.8
0.51–0.75	4.6	64.4
0.76–1.00	5.7	70.1
1.01–2.00	8.4	78.5
2.01–4.00	8.1	86.6
4.01–10.00	8.0	94.6
Above 10.00 hectares	5.4	100.0

Notes: **HECOUTL** is hectare of land in *gher*, **PCLANDOWN** is percentage of land owners and **CUMPERCENT** is cumulative percentage.

19 per cent of the landowners have 50–99 per cent of their entire land leased out for shrimp cultivation.

In conformity with the discriminant analysis for *gher* owners in the preceding section, we conducted discriminant analyses for landowners on groups defined by **ECONOMY** (1 for improvement and 2 for deterioration in economic condition) as well as **FAVOUR** (1 for those who favour the continuation of *ghers* and 2 for discontinuation). The results are set out in Tables 9.11and 9.12. In deriving these results a stepwise method

Table 9.11 Discriminant analysis for land owners on groups defined by ECONOMY

Discriminating variable	Standardised canonical discriminant function coefficients	Value at group means	
		Group 1	Group 2
EMPLOY	0.5353 (0.7519)	–0.2955	1.0932
PORTION	–0.8371 (0.8093)		
RENT	1.0558 (0.9088)		

Notes: The figures in parentheses are Wilks' lambda values. The coefficents are highly significant at 0.001 per cent level. **EMPLOY, RENT** and **PORTION** respectively refer to employment impact (1 for more opportunities, 2 for fewer opportunities), lease fee paid per hectare to the landowner by the *gher* owner and percentage share in the ownership of the *gher*.

Table 9.12 Discriminant analysis for land owners on groups defined by FAVOUR

Discriminating variable	Standardised canonical discriminant function coefficients	Value at group means	
		Group 1	Group 2
RENT	0.6727 (0.7364)	2.3763	–0.1912
PORTION	0.5207 (0.6830)		

Notes: The figures in parentheses are Wilks' lambda values. The coefficents are highly significant at 0.001 per cent level. **RENT** and **PORTION** respectively refer to lease fee paid per hectare to the landowner by the *gher* owner and percentage share in the ownership of the *gher*.

embodied in the SPSS package was employed. It involved an iterative procedure which ultimately settled for **EMPLOY, PORTION** (percentage of ownership in the *gher*) and **RENT** (amount per hectare per year payable to the landowners by the *gher* owners) as the discriminating variables for the grouping variable **ECONOMY**. The same procedure identified **PORTION** and **RENT** as the two most discriminating variables for the other grouping variable **FAVOUR**.

It could be inferred from the above that employment is a key factor separating the two groups categorised by **ECONOMY**. **RENT** and **PORTION** are the other two discriminating variables that differentiate between the groups classified by **ECONOMY** as well as favour. Thus share in the *gher*, amount of rent received and employment generation seem to be critical determinants of landowners' perception of the impact of their economic condition as well as their attitude towards the continuation or otherwise of use of land for the purpose of shrimp cultivation.

Table 9.13 presents results of t-tests for paired samples for landowners on the differences in paddy yields on and off shrimp farms as well as pre and post *gher* phases. The statistical qualities of the estimates clearly support the view that paddy yields on shrimp farms are significantly lower than those off the shrimp farms. The same conclusion applies to the paddy yields in the pre and post *gher* periods. This is consistent with the results discussed earlier on the samples from *gher* owners. Landowners expressed the opinion that shrimp cultivation had unfavourable impact on the environment. This is consistent with the view expressed by the *gher* owners.

9.4.3   Data analysis for the landless

Let us now consider the information on the landless. For the purpose of this study landless is defined as owning 0.25 hectares or less of cultivable land, with or without homestead land. About 60 per cent of the landless in

Table 9.13   Rice yields on and off shrimp farms and pre and post *gher* phases: *t*-tests of paired samples for land owners

Paired variable	*t*-value		
	1990	1991	1992
Rice yield on and off *gher*	11.05	9.18	11.16
Rice yield in pre and post *gher* periods	−23.05	−23.28	−23.75

Notes: All the *t*-values are highly significant at 0.001 per cent level.

the sample seemed to have experienced improvement in their economic condition since the introduction of shrimp farming in their area, while the remaining 40 per cent had an experience to the contrary. A discriminant analysis for the landless on the grouping variable defined by **ECONOMY** identified **YEARGHER** (year in which *gher* started in the area), **PERCENT** (percentage increase in income), CAUSINCR (cause of increase in income, *Gher* = 1, Others = 2, NA = 0) and **CAUSDECR** (cause of decrease in income, *Gher* = 1, Others ≥ 2, NA = 0) are set out in Table 9.14 Thus the process of shrimp cultivation has had a significant influence on the well being of the landless in the survey area.

9.5 SOME FURTHER OBSERVATIONS

Shrimp cultivation, through a network of backward and forward linkages, has created substantial volume of employment in shrimp farms as well as ancillary activities like trade/commerce, processing and marketing.

Table 9.14 Discriminant analysis for landless on groups defined by ECONOMY

Discriminating variable	Standardised canonical discriminant function coefficients	Value at group means	
		Group 1	Group 2
CAUSDEC	−0.5425 (0.0331)	3.7114	−8.6820
CAUSINCR	0.8236 (0.0464)		
PERCENT	0.2388 (0.0309)		
YEARGHER	−0.1911 (0.0298)		

Notes: The figures in parentheses are Wilks' lambda values. The coefficents are highly significant at 0.001 per cent level. **YERGHER** and **PERCENT** respectively refer to year in which *gher* started in the area and percentage increase in income. **CAUSINCR** and **CAUSDECR** respectivley refer to cause of increase in income (*Gher* = 1, others = 2, NA = 0) and cause of decrease in income (*Gher* = 1, Others ≥ 2, NA = 0).

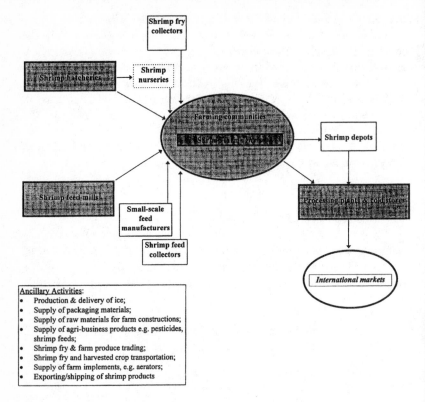

Figure 9.6   Schematic diagram of Bangladesh's shrimp industry showing sectoral linkages

Sectoral linkages of Bangladesh's shrimp industry are portrayed in Figure 9.6. It was estimated that in 1983, 4.1 million person days of employment were created on-farm for 51 000 hectares of shrimp farms in the coastal areas of Bangladesh. Off-farm employment was 5.1 million person days. As of 1990, shrimp farming was extended to 108 000 hectares with total employment implication (on and off shrimp farms) of about 22.2 million person days (MPO 1986; DOF 1994). While these recorded employment and export gains seem highly impressive, they have been achieved at considerable costs. Our findings and field observations indicate: (i) uneven gains between *gher owners* and land owners especially the small land owning households, (ii) adverse environmental spillovers in the form of loss of green vegetation (vegetables, coconut trees, bamboo plantation), loss of genetic diversity (loss or extinction of indigenous species of fishes), declining rice yields, (iii) increased employment opportunities off the shrimp farms – overall increased employment. These findings are supported by Mazid (1995) and Rahman *et al.* (1995).

In case of any ecological or environmental disasters resulting from shrimp farming those who have the least to lose are the shrimp farm owners who often are not the owners of the land under shrimp culture. In sum, shrimp farm owners represent a very powerful class of people who can easily accumulate funds in other occupations in urban locations in the event of their being forced to quit shrimp farming, leaving a legacy of environmental crisis.

In contrast, those with the most to lose from any possible irreversible damages to the environment are *primarily the small and marginal landowning and the landless households*. For these two classes of people the land and water-based activity, that is, agriculture and related activity, and subsistence fishing represent major occupations.

World Bank estimates (World Bank 1989) indicate that there are over 10 million additional people carry out subsistence fishing. To quote one important study 'A vital aspect of the subsistence fishing is its role in cushioning poverty. The significance of the small miscellaneous fish species as distinct from the principal commercial species – is that the "miscellaneous species" constitute the main part of the catch in the subsistence fishery and as such are a key resource for the rural poor. They can be seen as poor people's fish and their economic and nutritional value for rural poor people must not be underrated, though they are of less commercial significance' (ODA 1990, quoted in Ali 1991, p.17).

Even though shrimp cultivation and ancillary activities have provided employment and income gains for these groups of households, they may have been achieved at the cost of the future. Thus it is at odds with the concept of sustainable development as defined in WCED (1987, p.43).

The process of shrimp cultivation therefore epitomises conflicting resource-use patterns. Under extensive farming systems, which is the most common practice, more land is required. Given the extreme scarcity of arable land in Bangladesh, this threatens the potential to expand and sustain rice supply (or salt production). Increased salinity and soil acidification are believed to have led to decreased rice yields in addition to having adverse implications for other forms of vegetation or biodiversity. Furthermore, the decline in shrimp yields due to continuous use of the same land and use of chemicals are impediments to sustainable land use in the shrimp belt with potentially serious implications for sustainability of rural livelihoods and of rural communities.

9.6   CONCLUDING OBSERVATIONS

Both rice and shrimp farming are of enormous significance to the economy of Bangladesh. Rice is the staple food, while shrimp is an important export item and has created a significant volume of employment including employment for women (Hamid and Alauddin 1996). This notwithstanding, there are costs that need to be taken into consideration in any assessment of the sustainability of the rice–shrimp farming systems. The costs include (1) environmental degradation resulting from: conversion of mangroves into shrimp farms; increased salinity; dumping of pond effluent and use of chemicals affecting neighbouring ecosystems; loss of biodiversity, (2) declining production/yield of rice and other crops, and (3) greater income polarisation. All of these impact on the sustainability of livelihoods and on the sustainability of rural communities.

10 Energy Resources in Bangladesh: Issues and Options

10.1 INTRODUCTION

The importance of energy in economic development can hardly be overstated. Energy is often considered to be a key factor in industrialisation and modernisation, which is a *sine qua non* for overall socio-economic development. Bangladesh, or for that matter South Asia, is no exception in this regard. This chapter examines energy issues in Bangladesh particularly, and in South Asia generally. By way of background we proceed first of all with a broad overview of the South Asian energy situation. This is followed by a discussion of the sources and pattern of energy use in Bangladesh. Commercial and non-commercial energy resources are identified. Institutional factors, such as pricing and distribution policies, affecting exploitation of energy resources are critically discussed. Implications of any energy crisis are also examined.

10.2 ENERGY USE IN SOUTH ASIA: A BROAD OVERVIEW

Based on UNDP (1996) and World Bank (1996a), Table 10.1 sets out information on energy use, energy consumption and industrial pollution in the four major South Asian economies. Several observations can be made:

- *In per capita terms Bangladesh is the lowest energy-using country among her south Asian neighbours. Her per capita energy use is about a fourth of both India and Pakistan, marginally above half of Sri Lanka in 1994. Bangladesh has experienced highest growth rate in per capita energy use during the 1980–90 period. All countries experienced higher rates of energy use in the 1980–90 period compared to the 1990–94 period.*
- *Bangladesh's net energy imports, as a percentage of energy consumption, were the second highest in 1980 (60 per cent compared to 91 per cent for Sri Lanka). This declined quite considerably in 1994*

while for other countries in the sample it has remained much the same. As of 1994 Bangladesh had the second lowest import intensity in South Asia.

- Production of commercial energy has experienced high growth rates during the 1971–80 and 1980–93 periods. It is the highest for Bangladesh, compared to her other South Asian neighbours. For all the countries except Sri Lanka the growth rate is higher in the latter period than in the former.

- Bangladesh's commercial energy consumption on a per capita basis is much lower in Bangladesh compared to her subcontinental neighbours. As of 1993 Bangladesh's per capita commercial energy consumption is about a fourth of both India and Pakistan while the corresponding figure for Sri Lanka is about twice that of Bangladesh. It is worth noting however that Bangladesh's per capita commercial energy consumption has grown at a much faster rate than that of any of the other countries under consideration.

- Commercial energy imports as a percentage of merchandise exports is the second highest among the South Asian countries. As of 1993 more than a quarter of its merchandise exports were used for import of commercial energy. For India the corresponding figure was 36 per cent. It might be noted that Bangladesh's commercial energy imports though quite high in 1993 were considerably lower than in 1985 when energy imports accounted for nearly 60 per cent of exports earnings (BPC 1991, p.xii–6).

- Closely related to energy use is the extent of pollution as indicated by carbon dioxide (CO_2) emissions. For all the major South Asian countries (Sri Lanka excepted) CO_2 emission has more than doubled between 1980 and 1992. In per capita terms Bangladesh's CO_2 is about a sixth of India's and a fourth of Pakistan's and nearly half of Sri Lanka's. India has the highest per capita CO_2 emission, followed by Pakistan.

10.3   SOURCES AND PATTERN OF ENERGY USE IN BANGLADESH

10.3.1   Biomass

According to BPC (1991, p.xii–1) Bangladesh is a low energy-using subsistence economy, with energy use dominated by non-commercial biomass fuels, accounting for 65.4 per cent of the total, while commercial

Energy use

Table 10.1 Commercial energy use, consumption and industrial pollution in major South Asian countries

| | Energy use (oil equivalent) | | | | | | GDP per kg. ($) | | Net energy imports as % of energy consumption | | CO$_2$ emissions* | | | |
| | Total (thousand metric tonnes) | | Per capita (kg) | | Average annual growth rate (%) | | | | | | Total (mill. metric tons) | | Per capita (metric tons) | |
	1980	1994	1980	1994	1980–90	1990–94	1980	1994	1980	1994	1980	1992	1980	1992
Bangladesh	2,809	7,700	32	65	9.0	5.8	4.6	3.4	60	31	7.6	17.2	0.09	0.15
India	93,907	222,262	137	243	6.9	4.8	1.8	1.3	21	20	350.1	769.4	0.51	0.87
Pakistan	11,698	32,247	142	255	8.0	6.4	2.0	1.6	38	38	31.7	71.9	0.38	0.60
Sri Lanka	1,411	1,979	96	111	0.5	7.5	2.9	5.9	91	83	3.4	5.0	0.23	0.29

Energy consumption

Table 10.1 (*Continued*)

	Production as % of national energy reserves			Commercial energy production average annual growth rate (%)		Commercial energy consumption average annual growth rate (%)		Commercial energy use (oil equivalent)				Commercial energy imports (as % of merchandise exports)	
								Kilograms per capita		GDP output per kg (US$)			
	Coal 1991	Natural gas 1991	Crude oil 1991	1971–80	1980–93	1971–80	1980–93	1971	1993	1971	1993	1971	1993
Bangladesh	(.)	1.4	(.)	11	12	9	8	18	59	5.2	3.5	..	26
India	0.4	1.5	3.9	5	7	5	7	111	242	1.0	1.2	8	36
Pakistan	0.6	1.7	11	7	7	6	7	103	209	1.5	1.9	11	24
Sri Lanka	..	..	..	8	7	2	2	80	110	2.3	5.3	..	13

* Less than half the unit shown.

.. Data not available.

Source: World Bank (1996a, pp.202); UNDP (1996, pp.182–83).

fuels account for 34.6 per cent. Agricultural waste is central to the non-commercial biomass fuel, accounting for a relative share of 73.4 per cent in its type while fuelwood and cow dung account for the remaining 26.6 per cent. In the commercial fuel category (primary energy), about 62 per cent of the total supply is accounted for by natural gas. Petroleum products account for 32 per cent while only 6 per cent of commercial energy originate from coal and hydroelectricity.

It is widely acknowledged that traditional fuel supply in Bangladesh is in crisis. According to the Bangladesh Planning Commission (BPC 1991, pp.xii:1–2) 'increased flooding, erosion and siltation are the most dramatic symptoms of widespread deforestation and its consequences.' The important consequences associated with the above are (BPC 1991, pp.xii:1–2):

- *removal of tree cover within agricultural areas;*
- *gradual shift to more ecologically damaging fuel collection practices that divert essential nutrients and organic matters away from the soil.*

Bangladesh's biomass originates from three sources (as identified in Table 10.2):

Table 10.2   Biomass fuels in Bangladesh, 1981

Type of fuel	Gross weight (million tonnes)	Energy content (peta joules)	Relative share (per cent of gross weight)	Relative share (per cent of energy content)
Forest	0.68	10.30	1.79	2.15
Not available for cultivation	0.08	1.20	0.21	0.25
Village forests	4.66	65.60	12.27	13.69
Culturable wastes	0.15	2.00	0.39	0.42
Current fallow	0.33	4.70	0.87	0.98
Net crop	23.08	288.48	60.77	60.19
Subtotal	**28.98**	**372.28**	**76.30**	**77.67**
Livestock	6.70	77.72	17.64	16.22
Recycle biomass	2.30	29.30	6.06	6.11
Total	**37.98**	**479.30**	**100.00**	**100.00**

Source: Adapted from Task Force Report (1991, p.92).

- *forests (village and reserve),*
- *landmass, including culturable waste, current fallow and area not available for cultivation,*
- *agricultural crop residues and livestock.*

Agricultural crop residues provide the most important source of Bangladesh's biomass, followed by forests and livestock. The information set out in Table 10.2 relates to 1981. However, there has been very little change in the overall supply of biomass in recent years, even though there has been some change in composition with the relative share of agricultural crop residues increasing at the expense of contribution of forests in 1990 (BPC 1991, p.xii–2; see also BBS 1994a). Thus even in the absence of the latest figures it can be surmised that the overall supply position of biomass or its composition have not experienced any significant change.

10.3.2   Electricity

Table 10.3 sets out information on electricity generation, energy sold and systems loss over a period of two decades encompassing 1972–73 to 1993–94. Significant increase in gross generation of electricity can be observed. During the period under consideration Bangladesh has experienced a nine-fold increase in electricity generation. Overall systems loss is very high, even though in the last few years it has shown a declining tendency. Figure 10.1 illustrates trends in systems loss and overall power generation. According to ADB (1987) Bangladesh experienced a system loss of nearly 38 per cent in the financial year ending June 1987 compared to nearly 25 per cent for India, 31 per cent by Nepal and 23 per cent by Pakistan, 8 per cent by Thailand. In general the East Asian countries experience lower rates of system loss compared to those reported for South Asian countries. The high system loss suffered by Bangladesh is due to a host of factors ranging from technical to non-technical reasons (Task Force Report 1991, pp.37–38). Loss due to technical factors may be inherent in the technologies which may not be used efficiently. The loss is multiplied because of non-technical factors which include absence of proper metering devices, use of faulty metering devices, inefficient system management, and massive corruption at both the suppliers' and users' ends. *Thus the high incidence of system loss is the result of relatively less efficient technologies, the inefficient use of these technologies and poor governance symptomatic of poor governance elsewhere in Bangladesh* (see also Chapter 6).

   Bangladesh is a power-deficit country. As a result, in Bangladesh load-shedding and power failure are ubiquitous phenomena. It is claimed by

Table 10.3 Power generation and consumption in Bangladesh, 1972–73
to 1993–94

Year	Gross generation (GWH) (1)	Station use (GWH) (2)	Net sent out (GWH) (3)	Energy sold (GWH) (4)	Energy losses (GWH) (5)	T and D loss (%) (6)	Gross loss (%) (7)
1972–73	1086	43	1043	623	420	40.27	42.63
1973–74	1265	66	1199	828	371	30.94	34.55
1974–75	1322	71	1251	835	416	33.25	36.84
1975–76	1460	89	1371	932	439	32.02	36.16
1976–77	1619	93	1526	1013	513	33.62	37.43
1977–78	1913	94	1819	1205	614	33.75	37.01
1978–79	2122	105	2017	1381	636	31.53	34.92
1979–80	2353	116	2237	1405	832	37.19	40.29
1980–81	2662	122	2540	1740	800	31.50	34.64
1981–82	3035	141	2894	2028	866	29.92	33.18
1982–83	3422	184	3238	2374	864	26.68	30.63
1983–84	3966	210	3756	2705	1051	27.98	31.80
1984–85	4528	202	4326	2841	1485	34.33	37.26
1985–86	4800	227	4573	3307	1266	27.68	31.10
1986–87	5587	285	5302	3485	1817	34.27	37.62
1987–88	6541	400	6141	3773	2368	38.56	42.32
1988–89	7115	398	6717	4695	2022	30.10	34.01
1989–90	7732	430	7302	4705	2597	35.57	39.15
1990–91	8270	447	7823	4871	2952	37.73	41.10
1991–92	8890	511	8379	6021	2358	28.14	32.27
1992–93	9206	506	8700	6906	1794	20.62	24.98
1993–94	9785	566	9219	7458	1761	19.10	23.78

Note: GWH is gega watt hours. T and D loss is transmission and distribution
loss. Col. (6)=Col. (5)/Col. (3)X100. Col (7)=[Col. (2)+Col.
(5)]/Col. (1).

Source: Adapted from Task Force Report (1991, p.110) and World Bank
(1995b, p.110).

the government (AMITECH) that the current load shedding is partly due
to the government's decision to provide uninterrupted power supply at
night-time between 11 pm and 6 am for irrigation during the current crop
season which is expected to continue until mid-April (of 1997).

According to EIU (1996, p.22) 'The average daily shortfall has been
150 MW at peak times when demand for electricity rises to around
2100 MW. The country's theoretical power capacity is around 2900 MW
but only around 1950 MW is ever produced at one time, about half of

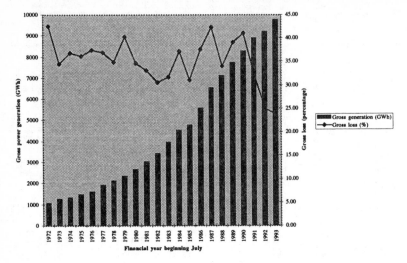

Figure 10.1   Power generation and gross power loss: Bangladesh, 1972–73 to 1993–94

what the country needs'. With the rehabilitation of some power plants and likely commissioning of new power plants power supply should improve. According to the latest available information (AMITECH), the Bangladesh government is moving ahead on a faster track to alleviate existing power shortage and meeting growing demand. The government has decided to put in place several new power plants to raise Bangladesh's power generation capacity to 3530 MW by the year 2000 and 4659 mw by the year 2005. It might be noted that given the projected pace of urbanisation, industrialisation and growth in other sectors of the economy, Bangladesh needs to raise its power generation capacity to at least 3150 MW by 2000 and to 4600 MW by 2005. The AMITECH news report also suggests that some of the plants will be operational by early 1998.

Table 10.4 sets out electricity consumption by sectors as well as total consumption since the mid-1980s. Electricity consumption has more than doubled over the period. The time series set out in Table 10.4 has two parts. Since October 1991 the Dhaka Electric Supply Authority (DESA) is separated from Bangladesh Power Development Board (BPDB). The domestic commercial and industrial consumption figures since 1991–92 exclude those for Dhaka and hence the sudden changes.

There is widespread dissatisfaction with electricity supply in Bangladesh. A recent survey by the World Bank (World Bank 1996b, p.5) of electricity consumers in Bangladesh reports low mean consumer satisfaction rate, even though satisfaction rates are higher in rural areas (60 per

Table 10.4   Total and sectoral consumption of electricity in Bangladesh, 1985–86 to 1993–94

Year	Consumption by sector					
	Domestic	Commercial	Industrial	Agriculture	Others[*]	Total
1985–86	716	278	1563	51	699	3307
1986–87	826	309	1728	56	566	3485
1987–88	885	391	1843	63	590	3772
1988–89	1044	531	2331	95	694	4695
1989–90	1165	380	2504	74	582	4705
1990–91	1384	425	2256	91	714	4870
1991–92	1070	421	1471	85	2974	6021
1992–93	1089	362	1256	101	4098	6906
1993–94	1206	357	1197	139	4559	7458

[*] Includes bulk sale to DESA (Dhaka Electric Supply Authority separated from the Bangladesh Power Development Board and functioning since October 1991); and REB (Rural Electrification Board).

Source: Adapted from Task Force Report (1991, p.110) and World Bank (1995b, p.110).

cent) than in the urban areas (40 per cent). This phenomenon is the result of 'intermittent and frequent power cuts, voltage fluctuations (urban areas) and excessive billing' (World Bank 1996b, p.5). One might also note that 97 per cent of the urban respondents and 9 per cent of the rural respondents had access to electricity. The rural electrification programme is much more successful than the electric supply in urban areas. In the financial year 1994–95, whereas the Dhaka electric supply registered a system loss of 31 per cent the *Palli Biddut Samity* (PBS, rural electric cooperative) registered a system loss of only 15 per cent. World Bank (1996b, p.36) uses some other indicators which suggests striking contrasts between the performances of DESA and PBS. Based on information relating to 1994–95, these can be summed up as follows:

- *Collection as a percentage of billing was 78 per cent for DESA and 98 per cent for PBS.*
- *Collection-purchase ratio was 54 per cent for DESA compared to 83 per cent for PBS.*
- *Each DESA employee served 92 customers compared to 188 by each employee of PBS.*

- *Due to poor collection effort, DESA's accounts receivable was equivalent to 7.6 months of average billing while for PBS it was a mere 2.2 months.*

Institutional factors such as reward and punishment, and greater accountability for PBS employees, compared to DESA employees, characterised by strong unionism, provide scope for greater efficiency in PBS in comparison to DESA.

10.3.3   Natural gas

Natural gas is Bangladesh's most abundant energy resource but it is also a non-renewable resource. As of October 1990 the total gas reserve is estimated to be about 37 trillion cubic feet. This includes about 26 trillion cubic feet of proven and probable reserves and 11 trillion cubic feet of possible reserves (Task Force Report 1991, p.131). However actual gas reserve at the beginning of 1990–91 was estimated to be 16 trillion cubic feet (Task Force Report 1991, p.132). Since then there has been some further discovery of gas fields (AMITECH). The Task Force Report (1991, p.132) forecasts demand for a fifty-year period encompassing 1990–91 to 2040–41. Given the demand forecast the cumulative gas consumption in year 2041 is estimated to be 18.883 trillion cubic feet which will go close to exhausting Bangladesh's actual gas reserve unless the probable and possible reserves translate into reality.

Table 10.5A presents natural gas production and consumption in Bangladesh for the 1983–84 to 1992–93 period. Information on gas

Table 10.5A   Trend in natural gas production and consumption in Bangladesh, 1983–84 to 1992–93

Year	Index of total production	Indices of consumption for					Total consumption
		Power	Fertilisers	Industrial	Commercial	Households	
1983	100	100	100	100	100	100	100
1984	113	127	97	128	108	109	113
1985	127	132	111	159	119	117	126
1986	150	172	119	186	133	118	148
1987	177	206	160	166	142	131	176
1988	187	216	168	147	152	160	182
1989	201	247	176	147	151	176	198
1990	207	270	170	143	143	182	204
1991	226	305	182	139	141	198	223
1992	253	309	216	145	145	228	241

Table 10.5B   Changing pattern of natural gas usage in Bangladesh,
1983–84 to 1992–93

Year	Power	Fertilisers	Industrial	Commercial	Households
1983	37.57	39.65	13.01	2.56	7.21
1984	42.03	33.91	14.67	2.45	6.94
1985	39.36	35.03	16.45	2.43	6.73
1986	43.66	31.93	16.34	2.30	5.76
1987	44.05	36.18	12.31	2.08	5.39
1988	44.53	36.51	10.50	2.14	6.33
1989	46.85	35.16	9.64	1.95	6.40
1990	49.69	33.01	9.09	1.79	6.41
1991	51.42	32.39	8.15	1.63	6.41
1992	48.22	35.61	7.82	1.54	6.80

Note: 1983 means financial year beginning July 1983 etc. The indices are
constructed with 1983–84 as the base year.

Source: Based on data from World Bank (1995a, p.228).

consumption in different sectors is also presented. Table 10.5B sets out the
changing pattern of natural gas usage in different sectors. Figures 10.2
and 10.3 illustrate these trends and patterns. From a careful inspection of
the information contained in Tables 10.5A and 10.5B and Figures 10.2
and 10.3 the following observations could be made:

- *Both production and consumption of natural gas in Bangladesh have
more than doubled over the decade beginning 1983–84.*
- *Natural gas consumption for sectoral utilisation has recorded varying
trends. While gas consumption for power generation has more than
trebled, those for fertiliser production and household usage have more
than doubled.*
- *Industrial and commercial use of natural gas has grown much more
slowly. Furthermore industrial usage has fluctuated somewhat.
Compared to 1983–84 it nearly doubled in 1986–87. However, in the
light of the trend in subsequent years, the figure for 1986–87 could be
considered as an aberration with relatively minor fluctuations.*
- *The use of natural gas is dominated by its usage in power generation
and fertiliser production. In the early 1990s these two sectors consumed
more than 80 per cent of the gas used. This shows an increase in the
relative share of compared to that in the early 1980s. The combined relative share industrial, commercial and household use has declined from
over 22 per cent in 1983–84 to around 16 per cent in 1992–93.*

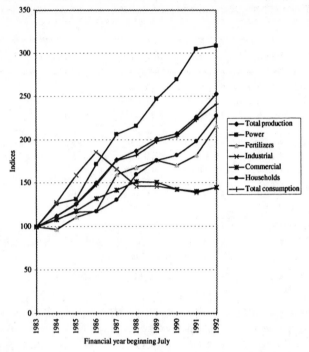

Figure 10.2   Trend in production and consumption of natural gas in Bangladesh, 1983–84 to 1992–93

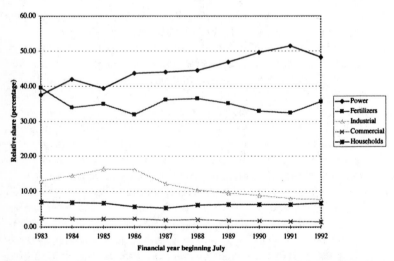

Figure 10.3   Changing pattern of use of natural gas in Bangladesh: 1983–84 to 1992–9

*Commercial and industrial usages have registered the sharpest declines
in their relative shares. One might also note that 'the consumption of
gas per unit of product (whether it is fertiliser or electricity) is much
higher than in the developed world, (BPC 1991, p.xii–6).*

10.4 ENERGY PRICING

The international market has recorded sharp rises in energy prices in the
1970s and in the first half of the 1980s. This notwithstanding, prices of
energy commodities in Bangladesh have been pegged at a level below that
of world economic prices even though some periodic upward revisions
have been made. However since the fall of crude oil prices in the international market in FY1985–86, the domestic market did not see a significant
lowering of prices, only minor adjustments were made on some occasions
although gas and electricity prices rose on average by 15 and 10 per cent
respectively.

Scant regard for economic principles epitomises Bangladesh' energy
pricing policies. Pricing of energy commodities, especially natural gas and
electricity, do not conform to established economic norms. Apparently
economic rationale becomes the casuality to the so-called community
service obligations which are often loosely termed as social welfare considerations. Task Force Report (1991, pp.50–53) provides an excellent critique of energy pricing in Bangladesh. Based on this report let us
summarise the salient features of energy pricing in Bangladesh.

- *In theory agencies dealing with different forms of energy can set their
  own prices. In practice, however, it is fully regulated by the government. The energy-supplying agencies such as Power Development
  Board, Petrobangla, Rural Electrification Board and Bangladesh
  Petroleum Corporationare government entities. The major objective
  of these agencies seems to be based on the premise that 'the energy
  industry must under no circumstances be allowed to be an exploitative
  monopoly' (p.50).*

The guiding principles of energy pricing include *inter alia* the following
(p.51):

- *to operate as financially viable organisations but not to earn above
  normal profits;*
- *to keep prices as low as possible – equity rather than profit
  maximisation;*

- *to provide adequate service to the entire public even if it requires cross-subsidisation of different consumer groups.*

The above seem to suggest a pricing strategy that is based more on equity than on economic logic. This is similar to energy pricing strategies in some other LDCs (see for example Kumar 1987). However the energy pricing policy embodied in the above principles has entailed a process of distortions, even though some may be unavoidable due to socio-economic considerations.

As the Task Force report (1991) correctly points out, the most important source of distortion lies in heavy underpricing of natural gas. Whereas the economic price of 1000 cubic feet of natural gas should be at least 132 taka, it sells at 80 taka to the domestic sector and at 37 taka to the power sector implying subsidies per 1000 cubic feet of 52 taka and 95 taka respectively (pp.52–53).

The above seems to have resulted from:

- *a rather mistaken view that Bangladesh has a relatively unlimited supply of gas; and*
- *the view that gas is Bangladesh's own resource and therefore can be supplied at cost price. However, the cost price calculations employed by the agency concerned imply that price is set far below the 'economic price', with the further implication that it entails sacrificing the 'economic value' of this non-renewable resource.*

Thus the energy pricing policy itself has led to significant inefficient use of energy resources. Energy prices do not reflect their social marginal costs. The system of 'user pays' does not seem to have adhered to pricing of energy resources in Bangladesh.

10.5   ENERGY, THE ENVIRONMENT AND RELATED ISSUES

As emphasised in Chapter 1 and Chapter 2, environmental considerations have assumed renewed significance in any economic development strategy since the publication of the Brundtland Report (WCED 1987). Energy and the environment are inextricably linked. Environmental considerations are of critical importance in each and every step of the fuel cycle: exploration, extraction, transportation, conversion and consumption. This applies to all types of fuel and energy conversion systems (Task Force Report 1991, p.44).

Bangladesh's energy planners and policy makers seem to have been concerned with environmental and conservation issues since the mid-1980s. According to BPC (1991, p.xii–6) the Third Five Year Plan (1985–90) sought to evolve a regime of energy prices that were likely to reflect economic values, reduce inefficiency in the form of excessive energy use and foster conservation of scarce fuels. The Fourth Five Year Plan (1990–95) set objectives along much the same line keeping in view better inter-fuel substitution. However, while efforts have been made to promote use of equipment and process which are energy efficient these have been piecemeal and ineffective due to the virtual absence of an inter-grated policy (BPC 1991, p.xii–6). The Task Force Report (1991) echoed a similar view.

The Task Force Report (1991, pp.116–24) projected energy demand at five yearly intervals up to the year 2010. It envisages two scenarios: *with* and *without* conservation. These are set out in summary form in Table 10.6. Three main categories of energy sources are presented. An examination of Table 10.6 suggests greater reliance on saving biomass energy sources as the key element in the energy demand projection model. Given Bangladesh's limited landmass and growing population the pressure on biomass supply will increase (Parikh 1988). As discussed in

Table 10.6 Total projected energy demand for selected energy sources with and without conservation: Bangladesh 1995 to 2010

Year	Conservation strategy	Gas (MMCF)	Electricity (GWh)	Agricultural residues (000 tons)	Woodfuel (000 tons)	Animal dung (000 tons)
1995	without	139000	10044	27694	9836	6339
	with	133490	9764	25269	9124	5831
	savings (%)	*3.96*	*2.79*	*8.76*	*7.24*	*8.01*
2000	without	198000	19106	30775	10733	6662
	with	188100	18164	26780	9329	5248
	savings (%)	*5.00*	*4.93*	*12.98*	*13.08*	*21.22*
2005	without	233000	28382	32931	11447	7000
	with	221330	27236	27296	9496	5600
	savings (%)	*5.01*	*4.04*	*17.11*	*17.04*	*20.00*
2010	without	265000	40400	35756	12326	7200
	with	252150	38868	28130	9611	5400
	savings (%)	*4.85*	*3.79*	*21.33*	*22.03*	*25.00*

Source: Adapted from Task Force Report (1991, pp.116–124).

Chapter 3 and Chapter 9, loss of tree cover due to large scale deforestation and loss of green vegetation and mangroves due to shrimp farming in the coastal areas of Bangladesh are likely to compound the problem. In several parts of Bangladesh, for example, the northern and southwestern districts, there is a fuel wood crisis (UNDP-World Bank 1982). Uneven regional distribution of energy resources in Bangladesh also aggravates the situation. For instance, all the gas fields are located in the eastern zone and more than 80 per cent of the existing power generation capacity is located in the eastern zone (Task Force Report 1991, p.33).

Although government regulations forbid the burning of timber in brick-kilns the people of these areas have no alternative and this adds to the increasing loss of the few remaining trees. The situation may improve somewhat with the operation of the Jamuna Multipurpose Bridge, which will also have gas pipelines for the northern and western regions of Bangladesh (Task Force Report 1991, pp.334–35).

Bangladesh Planning Commission (BPC 1991, p.xii–6) cites a report of the Bangladesh Energy Planning Project regarding utilisation and conser-vation of energy. According to the findings of the report that there is a con-servation potential of 15–20 per cent in the industrial sector and 25 per cent in the transport sector. In the domestic sector, consumption of natural gas could be reduced by 25 per cent and fuelwood and kerosene by 40 and 30 per cent respectively with the use of more energy efficient cooking stoves.

Let us consider the conservation of natural gas once again. Because, as can be seen in Table 10.5B, the domestic and industrial sectors use only a small fraction of natural gas consumption, prospects for gas conservation is unlikely to be bright if one were to concentrate primarily on these sectors. The bulk of gas consumption is accounted for by fertiliser produc-tion and electricity generation. Unless production efficiency can be enhanced in these sectors gas conservation on a significant scale is unlikely. It is interesting to note from Table 10.6 that the Task Force Report (1991) did not seem to envisage any significant savings of gas in its energy demand forecast.

10.6   CONCLUDING OBSERVATIONS

Bangladesh is a low energy-using country. At the same time Bangladesh is an inefficient user of energy resources. Bangladesh's system loss in power generation is one of the highest in the developing world.

Bangladesh's energy conservation strategy to date seems to lack comprehensiveness and success seems to have been limited due to the piecemeal nature of energy planning, bordering on short-term considerations resulting from lack of clear understanding of the intricate issues surrounding the balance between use of energy resources and sustainable development. To date, energy planning efforts have been directed primarily to augmenting supply to meet increased demand. Inadequate attention has been paid to formulating a comprehensive energy conservation strategy incorporating efficient energy use and overall environmental management. While Bangladesh's recent efforts to augment power supply to meet growing need is long overdue, it is unclear whether environmental considerations have been adequately factored in.

Bangladesh is an energy-deficient country and energy is a scarce resource yet it is underpriced. Energy pricing in Bangladesh defies economic logic and norm. Institutional arrangements involving energy pricing are not conducive to rational economic pricing.

Carbon dioxide emission is on the increase even though well below some of Bangladesh's neighbours. Projected energy demand will stretch the environment to the limit. A rural energy crisis is foreshadowed by Parikh (1988) and UNDP-World Bank (1982). Energy crisis is likely to affect the rural and urban poor more adversely compared to their relatively richer counterparts. Those at the lower end of the income group spend a significant percentage of their monthly expenditure on fuel and lighting. According to the 1989–90 household expenditure survey reported in BBS (1994, p.664), the lowest per capita monthly income group for Bangladesh as a whole spent nearly 11 per cent of their income on energy. The corresponding figures for the rural poorest and the urban poorest were respectively nearly 11 per cent and more than 15 per cent. These were more than twice the overall Bangladesh average and the rural average but the urban poorest spent more than three times the overall urban percentage spend on energy.

Thus energy and the environment, and by implication the livelihoods of many communities, are inextricably interlinked. In the light of the preceding discussion Bangladesh's energy crisis, especially in rural areas, may not be a long way off. This could seriously undermine the delicate balance between the use of energy resources and the environment. Thus while one should not be unduly pessimistic there is cause for concern.

11 Sectoral Change, Urbanisation and South Asia's Environment in a Global Context

11.1 INTRODUCTION

As indicated in the previous chapter, energy production and consumption in South Asia have expanded substantially. This is partly a consequence of expanding populations, rising incomes, and increased industrialisation and urbanisation. The purpose of this chapter is to consider the nature of sectoral change and urbanisation on the Indian subcontinent and the implications of these for sustainable development and the state of the environment. Consideration of these matters is followed by a discussion of the global environmental impacts of economic change in South Asia and conversely possible consequences of global environmental change on South Asia.

As countries develop economically, the relative size of their agricultural sector declines and their manufacturing (industrial) and service sectors grow (Clark 1940). Before economic development begins, the agricultural sector is the dominant sector, but once high incomes are obtained, it becomes a relatively minor sector in terms of its contribution to GDP and aggregate employment. After economic development, both the manufacturing and service sectors are much greater in size and eventually the service sector becomes dominant.

This structural change stimulates urbanisation because manufacturing and service industries tend to be *urban-centric*. They usually prosper where there are concentrations of people and an agglomeration of industries and services. They may gravitate towards existing urban centres, but new growth centres may also arise which become nuclei for urbanisation. While there may be strong attractions of industry and migrants to existing urban centres (Tisdell 1975), new urban growth centres do rise and in due course often become substantial in size. Examples in Asia in the last 200 years or so include Calcutta, Shanghai and Singapore.

The urban centricity of the economic sectors which grow most with economic development has several environmental and sustainability implications. Wastes associated with human populations and economic activity become geographically concentrated and often exceed the capacity of natural environments to assimilate them and concentrations of pollutants can reach levels that are injurious to human health. Public action is required to dispose of, or manage, such wastes. Pollution becomes a serious issue. In addition, public action is required to deal with traffic congestion. Traffic congestion has become a major problem in many Asian cities, most of which lack adequate means of mass transit.

It is possible for growing pollution problems in metropolitan areas to threaten sustainable economic development. However, a more important consideration for the sustainable development of urban areas is the state of the infrastructure for their economic interdependence with surrounding areas and more distant communities. No large urban community is able to be self-sufficient. The wealth and survival of urban communities is very dependent on exchanges with other communities, urban and non-urban. These are facilitated by appropriate infrastructures for communication and by freedom of trade.

As a rule, urban communities depend upon their peripheries for water, waste disposal and supplies of food and raw materials, and for markets for part of their production. However, they can also depend on more distant markets. In a few cases, links with their hinterland can be small and their major links may be through foreign trade, as in the case of Singapore, for example.

Given the nature of urban areas, their growth is likely to favour the expansion of market systems and greater division of labour and specialisation in production. Market-making is favoured as are changes which reduce market transaction costs, such as infrastructures which reduce transport costs and/or improve the reliability of transport. All these changes bring with them environmental change. Rural areas become more closely connected to urban areas for their economic well being and both urban and rural communities see mutual advantages in the improvement of transport and communication systems.

With the growth of cities, supplies of public utilities, such as water, electricity and sewage disposal works, assume increasing importance. The large investment in infrastructure occurring in Asia, especially East Asia, partly reflects growing demand for public utilities. The supply of such infrastructure has substantial environmental impact.

Urbanisation brings with it new health problems and hazards. However, incomes in urban areas, although unequally distributed, tend to be higher than in rural areas. Furthermore, length of life is often higher in urban areas and morbidity lower than in rural areas (cf. WRI 1996). Nevertheless, environmental health problems occur in urban areas which are absent in the countryside.

Rates of population growth are normally lower in urban areas than in rural ones. This is partly due to changed lifestyles and greater individual freedom in cities. A contributing factor is the fact that the economic costs of raising children in urban areas is higher and the economic benefits of having them are lower than in rural areas. Therefore, on the basis of Becker's theory (Becker 1960) one would expect family sizes to be smaller in cities than in rural areas. Thus, urbanisation reduces the rate of population growth in a country and lowers this potential demand on its natural resources and the environment. It can, therefore, favour sustainable development.

11.2　THE RELATIVE DECLINE OF AGRICULTURE AND THE EXPANSION OF MANUFACTURING AND SERVICE SECTORS IN SOUTH ASIA

From Table 11.1, a substantial decline in the proportion of the labour force employed in agriculture in South Asia is evident in recent decades. Employment in industry has risen in relative terms with the increases being greatest for Bangladesh, India and Sri Lanka. The service sector has also grown substantially in relative importance.

Similar trends are apparent in the distribution of GDP by sectors. However, on this measure of sectoral size, agriculture's relative contribution to GDP is much lower than its proportionate employment of the

Table 11.1　Labour force distribution in selected South Asian economies

	Percentage of labour force in								
	Agriculture			Industry			Services		
Countries	1960	1985–88	1990	1960	1985–88	1990	1960	1985–88	1990
Bangladesh	86	56.5	65	5	9.8	16	9	33.7	18
India	74	62.6	64	11	10.8	16	15	26.6	20
Pakistan	61	41.3	52	18	10.2	19	21	48.5	30
Sri Lanka	57	42.6	48	13	11.7	21	30	45.7	31

Source: Based on UNDP (1991, 1996).

Table 11.2   Structure of production in selected South Asian countries

	Distribution of GDP(%)											
	Agriculture			Industry			Manufacturing			Services		
Countries	1970	1980	1994	1970	1980	1994	1970	1980	1994	1970	1980	1994
Bangladesh	55	50	30	9	16	18	6	11	10	37	34	52
India	45	38	30	22	26	28	15	18	18	33	36	42
Pakistan	37	30	25	22	25	25	16	16	18	41	46	50
Sri Lanka	28	28	24	24	30	25	17	18	16	48	43	51

Source: Based on World Bank (1995a, 1996a).

labour force and the opposite is the case for the other sectors. Note the relatively large size of the service sector in these low income countries.

If the structure of industry, say by the distribution of labour force, happened to be the sole determinant of urbanisation, we would expect about one-third to a half of the population in South Asia to live in urban areas. In fact, the proportion of urban population is considerably lower. Nevertheless, there appears to be a positive, but not perfect, correlation between the relative size of the non-agricultural sector of economies and the degree of their urbanisation.

11.3   URBANISATION IN SOUTH ASIA

Table 11.3 provides information on urbanisation for selected South Asian countries and comparisons with low-income countries as a whole. It can be seen that, except for Pakistan, the percentage of the urban population to total population is lower for South Asian countries than for low-income countries as a whole, but in the case of India the difference is small. Compared to low-income countries as a group, the rate of urbanisation in India and Sri Lanka is slower, but it is faster in Bangladesh, Pakistan and Nepal. A faster rate of urbanisation usually results in an increase in the seriousness of urban environmental problems because it is difficult to expand the urban infrastructure at a rate matching the urban influx of population.

In addition, it is not only the broad rate of growth of urban populations that is likely to be significant from an environmental point of view, but also the concentration of that urbanisation. Even if the overall rate of urbanisation is low, the growth may, for example, be concentrated in a

Table 11.3   Urbanisation statistics for selected South Asian countries

Country	Urban population		% of total population in cities of 1 million or more
	As % of total 1994	By rate of growth 1990–94	
Bangladesh	18	4.9	8
India	27	2.9	9
Pakistan	34	4.7	18
Nepal	13	7.4	0
Sri Lanka	22	2.2	0
Low income countries	28	3.8	10

Source: Based on World Bank (1996a, Table 9, p.204).

few very large cities and these may experience very high rates of population growth and an inability to expand infrastructure fast enough to avoid serious environmental problems. This appears to be the case in a number of South Asia's larger cities, for example, Calcutta.

The extent of urban agglomeration can also have environmental consequences. In 1994, 8 per cent of the population of Bangladesh was located in cities of 1 million or more. The comparable figures are 9 per cent in India and 18 per cent in Pakistan. However, South Asia is home to five of the world's twenty-five largest cities. Bombay, Calcutta, Delhi, Karachi and Dhaka are all megacities. Their comparative size is indicated in Table 11.4. Many of these cities, for example Dhaka, continue to grow at a rapid rate.

Views differ about the economic advantages and disadvantages of very large urban agglomerations. Nevertheless, the following observation by Jones (1991, pp.24–25) is pertinent:

> Even if it is true that national economic growth would be maximized by allowing the larger metropolises to grow to vast size, planners might nevertheless opt for slower national growth if faster metropolitan growth meant seriously widened regional income disparities, or that the quality of life would be lowered in ways not captured by income measures, or that clear problems of governance and political instability might result, or that the environmental sustainability of megacities is suspect in the longer run.

Table 11.4   The world's twenty-five largest cities, 1995

City	Population (millions)
Tokyo, Japan	26.8
Sao Paulo, Brazil	16.4
New York, United States of America	16.3
Mexico City, Mexico	15.6
* Bombay, India	15.1
Shanghai, China	15.1
Los Angeles, United States of America	12.4
Beijing, China	12.4
* Calcutta, India	11.7
Seoul, Republic of Korea	11.6
Jakarta, Indonesia	11.5
Buenos Aires, Argentina	11.0
Tianjin, China	10.7
Osaka, Japan	10.6
Lagos, Nigeria	10.3
Rio de Janeiro, Brazil	9.9
* Delhi, India	9.9
* Karachi, Pakistan	9.9
Cairo, Egypt	9.7
Paris, France	9.5
Metro Manila, Philippines	9.3
Moscow, Russian Federation	7.5
* Dhaka, Bangladesh	7.8
Istanbul, Turkey	7.8
Lima, Peru	7.5

* South Asian city.

Source: Based on UN Population Division, *World Urbanisation Prospects 1994 Revision*, United Nations, New York.

According to *World Resources 1996–97* (WRI 1996), cities account for a disproportionate share of national income. Furthermore 'urbanization is associated with higher incomes, improved health, higher literacy, and improved quality of life. Other benefits of urban life are less tangible, but no less real: access to information, diversity, creativity and innovation'. The main reason why there is migration from rural to urban areas, including cities, is that overall socio-economic conditions are judged by the migrants to be better in the urban areas.

Nevertheless, most of the cities in low-income countries experience severe environmental problems, particularly in South Asia. The general observation made in *World Resources 1996–97* applies to most South Asian cities. It observes that:

> Especially where population growth is rapid, local governments are unable to provide for even the most basic needs of their citizens. Throughout the developing world, the urban poor live in life-threatening conditions. At least 220 million urban dwellers lack access to clean drinking water; more than 420 million do not have access to the simplest latrines. Between one and two-thirds of the solid waste generated is not collected. It piles up on streets and in drains, contributing to flooding and the spread of disease. The problems of urban poverty exact an enormous toll in largely preventable deaths and diseases. *(WRI 1996)*

A feature of South Asian cities is that air pollution is well in excess of health standards and domestic and industrial effluents are released to waterways with little or no treatment. Water quality is therefore very poor and a threat to human health and aquatic life. In most cases there are also vast squatter settlements and these are often located in areas experiencing the most environmental problems. Therefore, the poor in cities not only have very low incomes, but also live in the worst environmental conditions, often on land that no one wants because of the environmental hazards associated with it.

In India, only about a quarter of all wastewater generated in major river basins is collected and even less is given any treatment at all (cf. Bowonder 1995, p.161). In the case of the Ganges Basin, which receives more than half of the waste water generated in India in major basins and contains 80 cities, less than a quarter of the wastewater is collected and treated. While India has extensive pollution control measures, compliance with these measures is poor. Up to a half of industrial firms may fail to comply with environmental standards (Bowonder 1995, p.158).

The Hindu Survey of the Environment reports that:

> The city of Calcutta is suffering from serious environmental disorder. Collapsing sewer lines, stagnant canals, obsolete pumping stations, waterlogging, heaps of garbage, increasing noise, air and water pollution, rise in malaria and gastro-enteric diseases and shrinking wet lands are just a few problems plaguing the city. (Battacharya 1995, p.146)

Cholera has become endemic due to water pollution.

Urban waste management (or lack of it) is a serious problem throughout India. Even hospital waste is not disposed of in a safe manner. *The Hindu*

Survey of the Environment 1995 (Ravi 1995) provides general evidence and case studies for 25 towns and cities throughout India, showing the appalling state of most urban environments.

Not only is the availability of sewerage in Calcutta low and Calcutta's drainage problems severe due to human-induced environmental changes, its air quality is also very poor. On average, the particulate matter in its air exceeds the standards set by the World Health Organization on 268 days of the year. In this respect, its air quality is worse than that of Bangkok, Jakarta, Manila or Shanghai (Stubbs and Clarke 1996, Vol. 1, p.533). Particulate matter is a major contributor to respiratory diseases. The main source of such particulate matter in Calcutta is the burning of coal for industrial and domestic purposes. Furthermore, significant emissions of sulphur dioxide and nitrous oxide occur. Although these emissions are lower than in major Chinese cities or Bangkok, they are a cause for concern.

11.4   URBANISATION IN BANGLADESH AND ASSOCIATED ENVIRONMENTAL PROBLEMS

Although urban environmental problems in South Asia could be illustrated by taking any country in South Asia, or any of its major cities, it is convenient, given the focus of this book, to take Bangladesh as an example. It has a rapid rate of urbanisation and its major city, Dhaka, is already a megacity. With a population of around eight million, Dhaka accounts for almost a quarter of Bangladesh's urban population. Bangladesh's second largest city, Chittagong, has a population of around three million. Its other two large cities are Khulna and Rajshahi.

According to Khan and Hasan (1996), only 16 per cent of houses in urban areas in Bangladesh are durable. Many are built with bamboo posts and use bamboo mats for walls. These mats and walls require repair and renovation after one or two monsoons. They constitute a serious fire hazard, especially in slum areas where extreme crowding may occur. For instance, it is reported that up to 6000 people live on a hectare in the Islambad slum area of Dhaka. Basic sewers and amenities are lacking in many of these areas.

Water and sanitation facilities in Bangladesh's urban areas are poorly developed. Only about 10 per cent of its urban population have access to piped water and sanitation. As poor as the sanitation is in Dhaka, it is even worse in Chittagong and in smaller urban centres, as can be seen from

Table 11.5   Coverage of urban water supply in Bangladesh: Per cent of population

Urban centre	House connection	Public standpost	Hand tube well	Unspecified sources
Dhaka	49	10	–	41
Chittagong	29	8	10	53
District towns	14	9	29	48
Thana centre	4	–	25	71

Source: Based on Khan and Hasan (1996) p.223.

Table 11.6   Coverage of sewerage disposal in Bangladesh: Per cent of population

Urban centre	Sewerage	Septic tank	Bucket latrine	Pit latrine	Others
Dhaka	15	40	–	15	30
Chittagong	–	31	15	5	49
District towns	–	22	26	16	16
Thana Centre	–	6	*n/a	16	78

*n/a = statistic not available.

Source: Based on Khan and Hasan (1996, p.223).

Tables 11.5 and 11.6. Concerning sewerage, it is clear, given the larger 'Other' category, that many people use open spaces to defecate and urinate. Khan and Hasan (1996, p.215) note:

> Due to unplanned growth and illegal settlements, the urban centres in Bangladesh have grown with miserably poor and primitive sanitation systems. The built drainage system is faulty. Further, the natural drainage system and flood retention areas have been choked by water weeds or encroached upon by building construction. The result is excessive flooding even with moderate rainfall.

Given lack of adequate sanitation and safe water in Bangladesh, water borne diseases are common.

Virtually no provision exists for the removal of solid wastes (garbage) in urban Bangladesh. It is therefore commonly dumped on streets where recyclers, scavengers and vermin of various kinds reduce its volume.

In Dhaka, the municipal authority only has the capacity to collect about half of the solid wastes generated every day. In slum areas, little or no municipal collection of garbage occurs. A major part of the garbage left in the streets is not collected by the city and is 'left behind either to rot or to be collected by informal groups (or to be eaten by scavenging animals and vermin). However, scavengers, rag pickers, and *tokais* (young street children who work as collectors of waste and throw away pieces) reduce the quantity of waste for collection and disposal' (Islam 1996, Vol. 2, p.71).

Most of the solid waste is organic material, unlike in high income countries, but the quality of inorganic material is increasing. Polyethylene bags, for instance, are becoming more common and often block drains when disposed of. Hasan and Mulamsottil (1994, p.196) report that 'In some areas, the residents throw their garbage into open drains. The garbage decomposes in these blocked drains and provides breeding grounds for mosquitoes and flies.' In fact, garbage may be thrown into any open space including ponds and watercourses. Hasan and Mulamsottil (1994) also report poor air quality in Dhaka and that Dhaka has a high incidence of bronchitis and other respiratory diseases (United Nations 1987).

While average incomes in cities such as Dhaka are higher than for the remainder of the country, income is very unevenly distributed. A recent study found that around 50 per cent of the population of Dhaka is below the poverty line and that 30 per cent is in extreme poverty (Islam 1996). Most of this latter group live in slum and squatter settlements which house about 3 million people, or approximately one-third of the population of Dhaka. These are also the groups most likely to be without public utilities and municipal services. Apart from inadequate water supplies and facilities for sanitation, they are likely to be without access to electricity. In Dhaka 64 per cent of households are located in areas which do not have electricity supply. Furthermore, traffic congestion and noise are increasing problems in Dhaka and are likely to become worse.

Coordination of the planning and development of Dhaka leaves much to be desired. Different public agencies are overseeing different aspects of Dhaka's development and maintenance of its infrastructure. Their activities are not coordinated and personnel are lacking in required skills. There is considerable inefficiency in the use of funds set aside for the development of Dhaka. Governance problems, including corruption, add to the inefficiency with which public funds are used in developing Dhaka. It may be possible to increase the efficiency of Dhaka's development by privatising the supply of some municipal services, or contracting out their supply. In addition, greater participation by local communities in taking care of their own local environment could help. At least a side-by-side approach would be preferable to a complete top-down system in improving some local environments in Dhaka. Since cities involve a high degree of interdependence in living conditions and a high degree of externalities, the quality of governance of cities is a major influence on the quality of living conditions and the supply of urban services within them. Unfortunately, low levels of economic development and poor governance often go hand in hand.

11.5   TRANSBOUNDARY AND GLOBAL ASPECTS OF ENVIRONMENTAL CHANGE IN SOUTH ASIA

Transboundary and global aspects of environmental change are assuming growing importance in South Asia, but a number of transboundary environmental issues have been of importance in South Asia for several decades. In particular, shared water resources have been a bone of contention.

For instance, a number of rivers are shared between more than one country, for example, the Indus between India and Pakistan, the Ganges/Padma between India and Bangladesh, and the Bhramaputra between China, India and Bangladesh. Agreement was reached between India and Pakistan on sharing the water of the Indus in 1960 (The Indus River Treaty) and after years of acrimony, India and Bangladesh have reached agreement on sharing of the waters of the Ganges. While agreement extends to sharing of the waterflows, there does not appear to be any agreement on the control of pollution emissions to these rivers. Consequently, the waters of the Indus, for example, are becoming increasingly polluted. The Bhramaputra does not appear to have been the source of international agreement, presumably because its waterflows are adequate to meet current needs. Nevertheless, deforestation in its headwaters appears to be increasing its sediment load and this has potential international environmental effects, for example, siltation and deforestation in its headwaters may be increasing the seasonal variability of the Bhramaputra's flow (see also Chapter 3).

The treaty between India and Bangladesh (entered into December 1996) on the sharing of the waters of the Ganges at Farakka, involves sharing on a 50/50 basis if the flow at Farakka of the Ganges is 70 000 cusecs or less in a ten day period, 35 000 cusecs to Bangladesh if the flow is 70 000–75 000 cusecs, with India's maximum off-take being 40 000 cusecs in a ten day period with excess water being available to

Bangladesh. It makes no provision for the quality of the water entering Bangladesh. As pointed out above, the Ganges is seriously polluted. Nevertheless, the Treaty represents progress in the sharing of a trans-boundary natural resource.

As pointed out in Chapter 2, substantial biodiversity loss has occurred in South Asia and is continuing. Nevertheless, India, in relation to other low-income countries, has a relatively high proportion of its land in pro-tected areas, whereas Bangladesh is poorly served in this regard.

To the extent that the international community values biodiversity, loss of biodiversity in South Asia has global consequences. The preservation of biodiversity can, however, impose high costs on low-income countries, although there can be circumstances where they themselves benefit econ-omically from the conservation of natural environments. Each case must be assessed individually. Where a local community would be disadvan-taged economically by engaging in nature conservation, but the interna-tional community's gain from conservation would exceed the loss of the locals, all could gain if the international community were to compensate locals adequately for any loss from engaging in nature conservation. However, it is sometimes difficult to devise suitable income transfer mechanisms. Furthermore, such transfers involve transaction costs which have to be offset against any benefits otherwise obtained.

In relation to air pollution, South Asian countries are rapidly increasing their use of fossil fuels. In particular, India's use of fossil fuels is now substantial by world standards. Consequently, acid rain occurs in parts of India and there is increasing potential for their transport internationally (Foell 1994). Furthermore, India's use of fossil fuels is making a significant global contribution to greenhouse gas emissions and that is expected to grow as its fossil fuel consumption expands.

In the period 1990–96, commercial energy use in Nepal expanded on average at 16.4 per cent per annum, in Bangladesh at 5.8 per cent, in India at 4.8 per cent, in Pakistan at 6.4 per cent and in Sri Lanka at 7.5 per cent (World Bank 1996, p.202). These are rates of increase significantly higher than those for low income countries as a whole.

In 1992, India emitted 769 million tonnes of carbon dioxide from its use of commercial energy. This is about one-third of the level for China, but it exceeded that of many high income countries, for example, the United Kingdom (566.2 million tonnes). However, the emissions of the U.S. at 4625 million tonnes were much higher and the emissions of Japan were somewhat higher (World Bank 1996). Nevertheless, on a per capita basis, the carbon dioxide emissions of India were only a fraction of those of all high income countries.

At the same time as South Asia is becoming an increasingly important source of greenhouse gas emissions, it is likely to be seriously affected by a rise in the sea level. For example, Buchdal (1996) reports that 'a rise in the sea level of 1.5 metres would flood one fifth of all farmland of Bangladesh, equivalent to a 21.3 per cent loss in agricultural production.'

11.6   CONCLUDING COMMENTS

There is widespread support for Kuznets' hypothesis concerning the state of the environment and economic development. This hypothesis is that pollution and environmental degradation intensities at first rise with economic development, but eventually decline as income levels reach higher levels. This, therefore, suggests that, broadly speaking, economic growth is the eventual solution to increased economic welfare and improved environmental conditions. The historical experience of many high income countries today supports this view. It indicates that South Asian countries should try to emulate the growth patterns that were adopted by Western countries. These involve polluting now and cleaning up later and converting the 'maximum' amount of natural resource capital into man-made capital.

However, there are a number of possible difficulties for this approach which involves very weak conditions for sustainable development. These are:

- *The global environmental impact of all countries following this strategy could be disastrous given that it will result in a rapid accumulation of greenhouse gases. With economic growth, South Asia, like China, will become a major contributor to greenhouse gas emissions.*
- *Even if pollution intensities fall, total pollution levels may continue to rise. The flow of total pollution emissions may continue to rise because, even though the level of emission per unit of output falls, the marginal increase remains positive. Furthermore, for those pollutants where levels depend on their stocks rather than their flows, any current emissions will increase their accumulation.*
- *Some environmental impacts can be irreversible and this needs to be taken into account.*
- *Environmental and natural resources provide economic services and an appropriate balance must be struck between these and other resources such as man-made capital. The appropriate composition can vary from country to country. It may be that it would be economically advantageous to South Asia, for example, to retain a higher*

ratio of natural resources and environmental capital in proportion to other resources than in Europe.

- *It cannot be assumed that low-income countries will all be able to sustain sufficient development to achieve high-income status. Premature attempts to do so involving depletion of natural and environmental resources, while initially raising incomes, may prove unsustainable. Economic growth and development can then be attenuated. The country then ends up with a poorer environment and little prospect for achieving high income levels. It is caught in a low-level income equilibrium trap (Leibenstein 1957) and the possibility of ever escaping from the trap is made harder as a result of natural resource depletion. Thus, the strategy of depleting natural resource capital for a great economic leap forward proves to be abortive. While this may not occur in South Asia, it is always a risk. South Asian countries can ill afford to engage in profligate and unsustainable uses of their natural resources.*

The sustainable development of a country does not require sustainable development in every region of it (if migration is possible and economic), but if development is not ecologically sustainable in most regions, the sustainability of national development is likely to be jeopardized. As the case studies in this book indicate, regional development in several parts of India and Bangladesh are unsustainable. There is little doubt that other cases could be added for South Asia.

While urbanisation and the growth of urban-centric industries may seem to be the answer to sustainable development problems in areas such as South Asia, one must be careful not to be too glib about this. Urban areas depend upon rural ones for their economic sustainability. Economic and ecological systems are interdependent and becoming more so as market systems expand and economic globalisation occurs. Thus the economic and ecological problems of South Asian economic development are interdependent and the welfare of this region as a whole depends on the sustainability of its parts and in becoming increasingly linked with that of the whole world. Growing regional and global interdependence is occurring.

Bibliography

ADB (1987) *Electric Utilities Data Book for the Asian and Pacific Region.* Manila: Asian Development Bank.

Adger, N. and Whitby, M. (1991) 'Accounting for the Impact of Agriculture on Environmental Quality', *European Economic Review,* 35, pp.629–47.

Ahmad, Y.J., El Serafy, S. and Lutz, E. (eds. 1989) *Environmental Accounting for Sustainable Development,* A UNEP – World Bank Symposium, Washington, D.C.: World Bank.

Ahmed, A. and Reazuddin, M. (1990) 'Industrial Pollution of Water Systems in Bangladesh', in Rahman *et al.* (eds.), pp.177–80.

Ahmed, A.H.M.M. (1985) *Economics of Coastal Shrimp Culture in a Mixed Farming Systems: A Study of Chittagong–Cox's Bazaar Region in Bangladesh.* M.S. Dissertation. Malaysia: University Pertanian Malaysia.

Ahmed I. (1995) 'Sustainable Livelihoods and Employment: Pragmatic Approaches', in Ahmed and Doeleman (eds. 1995), pp.317–62.

Ahmed, I. and Doeleman, J.A. (eds. 1995) *Beyond Rio: Environmental Crisis and Sustainable Livelihoods in the Third World.* London: Macmillan.

Ahmed, M. (1986) 'The Use and Abuse of Pesticides and the Protection of Environment', in BMOE, pp.89–95.

Ahmed, M.F. (1986) 'Modern Agriculture and Its Impact on Environmental Degradation', in BMOE, pp.42–49.

Ahmed, R. (1981) 'Agricultural Price Policies under Complex Socioeconomic and Natural Constraints: The Case of Bangladesh', Research Report, No. 27. Washington, D.C.: International Food Policy Research Institute.

Ahmed, R. (1992) 'Overview of Environmental Legislation, Their Constraints and Suggested Measures for Effective Implementation', in *Training Manual on Environmental Management in Bangladesh.* Dhaka: Department of Environment.

Alagarswami, K. (1995) 'India' Country Paper, in FAO/NACA, pp.141–86.

Alauddin, M. (1986) 'Identification of Key Sectors in the Bangladesh Economy: A Linkage Analysis Approach', *Applied Economics,* 18, pp.421–42.

Alauddin, M. (1997) 'The Readymade Garment Industry and Changing Structure of Bangladesh's Foreign Trade', in Roy *et al.* (eds. 1997) pp.139–50.

Alauddin, M. and Hamid, M.A. (1996) 'Economic, Social and Environmental Implications of Shrimp Farming in Bangladesh: An Overview of Issues and Agenda for Research', in Alauddin and Hasan (eds.), pp.278–99.

Alauddin, M. and Hasan, S. (eds. 1996), *Bangladesh: Economy, People, and the Environment,* Economics Conference Monograph Series 1. Brisbane, Queensland: Department of Economics, The University of Queensland.

Alauddin, M. and Tisdell, C.A. (1986a) 'Bangladesh and International Agricultural Research: Administrative and Economic Issues', *Agricultural Administration,* pp.1–20.

Alauddin, M. and Tisdell, C.A. (1986b) 'Market Analysis, Technical Change and Income Distribution in a Semi-Subsistence Agriculture: The Case of Bangladesh', *Agricultural Economics,* 1(1), pp.1–18.

200

Alauddin, M. and Tisdell, C.A. (1989) 'Poverty, Resource Distribution and Security: The Impact of New Agricultural Technology in Rural Bangladesh', *Journal of Development Studies*, 25(4), pp.550–70.

Alauddin, M. and Tisdell, C.A. (1991a) 'Welfare Consequences of Green Revolution Technology: Changes in Bangladeshi Food Production and Diet', *Development and Change*, 22(3), pp.497–517.

Alauddin, M. and Tisdell, C.A. (1991b) 'The "Green Revolution" and Labour Absorption in Bangladesh Agriculture: The Relevance of East Asian Experience', *Pakistan Development Review* 30(2), pp.173–88.

Alauddin, M. and Tisdell, C.A. (1991c) *The Green Revolution and Economic Development: The Process and Its Impact in Bangladesh.* London: Macmillan.

Alauddin, M. and Tisdell, C.A. (1995) 'Labour Absorption and Agricultural Development: Bangladesh's Experience and Predicament', *World Development*, 23(2), pp.281–297.

Alauddin, M., Mujeri, M.K. and Tisdell, C.A. (1995) 'Technology–Environment–Employment Linkages and the Rural Poor of Bangladesh: Insights from Farm-Level Data', in Ahmed and Doeleman (eds), pp.221–255.

Alcala, C.A. and Vande Vusse, F.J. (1994) 'The Role of the Government in Coastal Resources and Management', in Pomeroy (ed.), pp.12–19.

Ali, M.Y. (1990) 'Open Water Fisheries and Environmental Changes', in Rahman *et al.* pp.145–165.

Ali, M.Y. (1991) *Towards Sustainable Development: Fisheries Resource of Bangladesh.* Dhaka: Ministry of Environment and Forestry and National Conservation Strategy Secretariat.

AMITECH: Internet News of Bangladesh.

Axelrod, R. (1984) *The Evolution of Cooperation.* New York: Basic Books.

Bangladesh Agriculture Sector Review (1989) *Main Report – Bangladesh Agriculture: Policies and Performance*, United Nations Development Programme, Dhaka.

Barbier, E.B. (1987) 'The Concept of Sustainable Economic Development', *Environmental Conservation*, 14(2), pp.101–10.

Barbier, E.B. (ed. 1993) *Economics and Ecology.* London: Chapman and Hall.

Barbier, E.B. and Markandya, A. (1993) 'Environmentally Sustainable Development: Optimal Economic Conditions' in Barbier (ed.) pp.11–28.

Barker, R. and Cordova, V.G. (1978) 'Labour Utilization in Rice Production', in IRRI *Economic Consequences of the New Rice Technology.* Los Banos, Philippines: International Rice Research Institute.

Bartelemus, P.L. (1992) 'Environmental Accounting and Statistics', *Natural Resources Forum*, February, pp.77–84.

Bayliss-Smith, T.P. and Wanmali, S. (eds. 1984) *Understanding Green Revolutions: Agrarian Change and Development Planning in South Asia.* Cambridge, U.K.: Cambridge University Press.

BBS (1976) *Agricultural Production Levels of Bangladesh 1947–72.* Dhaka: Bangladesh Bureau of Statistics.

BBS (1978) *Statistical Pocket Book of Bangladesh 1978.* Dhaka: Bangladesh Bureau of Statistics.

BBS (1979) *Statistical Year Book of Bangladesh 1979.* Dhaka: Bangladesh Bureau of Statistics.

BBS (1980) *Year Book of Agricultural Statistics of Bangladesh 1979–80*. Dhaka: Bangladesh Bureau of Statistics.

BBS (1984a) *Monthly Statistical Bulletin of Bangladesh, March 1984*. Dhaka: Bangladesh Bureau of Statistics.

BBS (1984b) *Statistical Year Book of Bangladesh 1983–84*. Dhaka: Bangladesh Bureau of Statistics.

BBS (1985a) *1983–84 Year Book of Agricultural Statistics of Bangladesh*. Dhaka: Bangladesh Bureau of Statistics.

BBS (1985b) *1984–85 Statistical Year Book of Bangladesh*. Dhaka: Bangladesh Bureau of Statistics.

BBS (1985c) *1984–85 Year Book of Agricultural Statistics of Bangladesh*. Dhaka: Bangladesh Bureau of Statistics.

BBS (1986a) *Monthly Statistical Bulletin of Bangladesh, May 1986*. Dhaka: Bangladesh Bureau of Statistics.

BBS (1986b) *Monthly Statistical Bulletin of Bangladesh, November 1986*. Dhaka: Bangladesh Bureau of Statistics.

BBS (1990a) *Statistical Yearbook of Bangladesh 1990*. Dhaka: Bangladesh Bureau of Statistics.

BBS (1990b) *Monthly Statistical Bulletin of Bangladesh, December 1990*. Dhaka: Bangladesh Bureau of Statistics.

BBS (1991a) *Report on the Use of Agricultural Inputs for Major Crops in Bangladesh 1989–90: Crop – Aus, June 1991*. Dhaka: Bangladesh Bureau of Statistics.

BBS (1991b) *Report on the Use of Agricultural Inputs for Major Crops in Bangladesh 1989–90: Crop – Aman, June 1991*. Dhaka: Bangladesh Bureau of Statistics.

BBS (1992a) *Report on Labour Force Survey 1989*. Dhaka: Bangladesh Bureau of Statistics.

BBS (1992b) *Report on the Use of Agricultural Inputs for Major Crops in Bangladesh 1989–90: Crop – Boro, July 1992*. Dhaka: Bangladesh Bureau of Statistics.

BBS (1992c) *Monthly Statistical Bulletin of Bangladesh, October 1992*. Dhaka: Bangladesh Bureau of Statistics.

BBS (1993) *Statistical Pocket Book of Bangladesh 92*. Dhaka: Bangladesh Bureau of Statistics.

BBS (1994a) *1993 Statistical Yearbook of Bangladesh*. Dhaka: Bangladesh Bureau of Statistics.

BBS (1994b) *Monthly Statistical Bulletin of Bangladesh, December 1994*. Dhaka: Bangladesh Bureau of Statistics.

Becker, G. (1960) 'An Economic Analysis of Fertility' in National Bureau o Economic Research, *Demographic and Economic Change in Developed Countries*, Princeton: Princeton University Press.

Bell, L.S. (1992) 'Farming, Sericulture and Peasant Rationality in Wuxi County', in Rawski and Li (eds.), pp.207–42.

Bergson, A. (1938) 'A Reformulation of Certain Aspects of Welfare Economics', *Quarterly Journal of Economics*, 52, pp.310–14.

Berkes, F. (1989) 'Multiple-Resource Cases and Integration Development', in Berkes (ed.), pp.237–39.

Berkes, F. (1994) 'Property Rights and Coastal Fisheries' in Pomeroy (ed.), pp.52–62.

Berkes, F. (ed. 1989) *Common Property Resources: Ecology and Community-based Sustainable Development*. London: Belhaven Press.

Berkes, F. and Farvar, M.T., (1989) 'Introduction and Overview', in Berkes (ed.), pp.1–17.

BFFEA (1995) Leaflet. Dhaka: Bangladesh Frozen Foods Exporters Association.

Bhalla, A.S. (ed. 1992) *Employment, Environment and Development*. Geneva: International Labour Office.

Bhattacharya, M. (1995) 'What Ails the City of Joy?', in Ravi (ed.), pp.146–148.

Biggs, S.D. and Clay, E.J. (1981) 'Sources of Innovation in Agricultural Technology', *World Development*, 9(4), pp.321–36.

Binswanger, H.P. and Ruttan, V.W. (eds. 1978) *Induced Innovation: Technology, Institutions and Development*. Baltimore, Md.: John Hopkins University Press.

Blackorby, C. and Donaldson, D. (1992). 'Pigs and Guinea Pigs: A Note on the Ethics of Animal Exploitation', *Economic Journal*, **102**, pp.1345–69.

Blaikie, P., Harris, J. and Pain, A. (1992) 'The Management and Use of Common-Property Resources in Tamil Nadu, India', in Bromley (ed.), pp.247–64.

BMOA (1994) *Handbook of Agricultural Statistics*. Dhaka: Bangladesh Ministry of Agriculture.

BMOA (1995) *Handbook of Agricultural Statistics*. Dhaka: Bangladesh Ministry of Agriculture.

BMOE (1986) *Protection of Environment from Degradation*, Proceedings of South Asian Association for Regional Cooperation (SAARC). Dhaka: Bangladesh Ministry of Education, Science and Technology Division.

Booth, A. (ed. 1992) *The Oil Boom and After: Indonesian Economic Policy and Performance in the Soeharto Era*. Singapore: Oxford University Press.

Bowonder, B. (1995) 'Environmental Management: Redefining Perspectives', in Ravi (ed.), pp.157–61.

BPC (1985) *The Third Five Year Plan 1985–90*. Dhaka: Bangladesh Planning Commission.

BPC (1990) *The Draft Fourth Five Year Plan 1990–95*. Dhaka: Bangladesh Planning Commission.

BPC (Undated) 'A Study on All Agricultural Crops', *Second Plan/Perspective Plan Study Report Series*. Dhaka: Bangladesh Planning Commission.

Brammer, H. (1996) 'The Agroecology of Bangladesh's Terrace Areas Part 1: Physiography and Soils', *Asia Pacific Journal on Environment and Development*, 3(1), pp.1–14.

Brandon, C. and Ramankutty, R. (1993) *Toward an Environmental Strategy for Asia*. World Bank Discussion Paper No. 224. Washington, D.C.: World Bank.

Bromley, D.W. (ed. 1992), *Making the Commons Work*. San Francisco: Institute for Contemporary Studies.

Bromley, D.W. and Cernea, M.M. (1989) 'The Management of Common Property Natural Resources', World Bank Discussion Paper No. 57. Washington, D.C.: World Bank.

Buchdal, J. (1996) 'Global Change and its Impact on World Agriculture', Global Change Information Programme, http://www.doc.mmv.ac.uk/cric/agricul.html.

Cao, Yang and Tisdell, C.A. (1991) *China's Surplus Agricultural Labour Force*, Discussion Paper in Economics No. 50. Brisbane: Department of Economics, University of Queensland.

Chakravaty, S. (1990) 'Development Strategies for Growth with Equity: The South Asian Experience', *Asian Development Review*, 8(1), pp.133–59.

Chambers, R. (1987), *Sustainable Livelihoods, Environment and Development: Putting Poor Rural People First*, IDS Discussion Paper No. 240. Brighton: University of Sussex Institute of Development Studies.

Chambers, R.G. (1988) *Poverty in India: Concepts, Research and Reality*, IDS Discussion Paper No. 241. Brighton: University of Sussex Institute of Development Studies.

Chayanov, A.V. (1966) *The Theory of Peasant Economy*. Homewood, Illinois: Irwin.

Chong, K-C., Islam, N. and Begum, M. (1991) *Analysis of Constraints to and Potentials and Opportunities for Expanded Fish Production in Bangladesh*. Dhaka: Ministry of Fisheries and Livestock, Department of Fisheries, Government of Bangladesh.

Chowdhury, M.A.M. (1988) 'Socio-Economic Consequences of Shrimp Cultivation in Bangladesh: A Case Study of Satkhira, Chakaria and Maheshkhali', *Bangladesh Journal of Public Administration*, 2(2), pp.49–76.

Ciriacy-Wantrup, S.V. (1968) *Resource Conservation: Economics and Policies*, 3rd edn, Division of Agricultural Sciences, University of California, Berkeley, C.A.

Clark, C. (1940) *The Conditions of Economic Progress*, 1st edn, London: Macmillan.

Conway, G.R. (1985a) 'Agroecosystem Analysis', *Agricultural Administration*, 20, pp.31–55.

Conway, G.R. (1985b) 'Agricultural Ecology and Farming Systems Research', in J.V. Remenyi (ed.) *Agricultural Systems Research for Developing Countries*, ACIAR Proceedings No. 11. Canberra: Australian Center for International Agricultural Research.

Conway, G.R. (1986) *Agroecosystem Analysis for Research and Development*. Bangkok: Winrock International.

Conway, G.R. (1987), 'The Properties of Agroecosystem', *Agricultural Systems*, 24, pp.95–118.

Cook, N.L. and Schmidt, V.W. (1979) *Shrimp Culture for Small-Scale Fishermen in Bangladesh*, Report of a Mission to Study the Feasibility of Involving small-scale Fishermen in Shrimp Culture in Bangladesh, Aquaculture Development and Coordination Programme. Dhaka: FAO.

Dalal-Clayton, C. (1990) *Aspects of Bangladesh's Flood Action Plan*, Issue Series No. 1. London: International Institute for Environment and Development.

Daly, H. (1980) *Economics, Ecology and Ethics: Essay towards a Steady-state Economy*. San Francisco: Freeman.

Das, R.K. (1992) *A Study on Social and Economic Aspects of Shrimp Prawn Cultivation in Bangladesh*, Master of Agricultural Science Thesis in Agricultural Economics. Mymensingh: Bangladesh Agricultural University.

Dasgupta, P. (1992) 'Population, Resources and Poverty', *Ambio*, 21(1), pp.95–101.

DCCI (not dated) 'Readymade Garments: Present and Future', Dhaka: Dhaka Chamber of Commerce and Industry.

Denison, E.F. (1962) *Sources of Economic Growth and the Alternatives before Us*. New York: Committee for Economic Development.

Dev, M.S., Parika, K. and Suryanarayana, M.H. (1994) 'India' in Quibria (ed.), pp.190–354.

DOF (1994) 'Districtwise Area and Number of Shrimp Farms', DOF Document. Dhaka: Department of Fisheries.

DOF (1995) *Fish Fortnight '95*: Leaflet. Dhaka: Department of Fisheries.

Douglass, G.K. (1984) 'Introduction', in Douglass (ed), pp.3–29.

Douglass, G.K. (ed. 1984) *Agricultural Sustainability in a Changing World Order.* Boulder, CO. Westview Press.

Ehrlich, P.R. (1970) *The Population Bomb*. New York: Ballantine Books.

EIU (1996) *EIU Country Report*, Bangladesh Third Quarter 1996. London: Economist Intelligence Unit.

EIU (1996) *EIU Country Report, Bangladesh Third Quarter 1996*. London: Economist Intelligence Unit.

El Serafy, S. and Lutz, E. (1989) 'Environmental and Resource Accounting: An Overview', in Ahmad, *et al*. (eds.), pp.1–7.

Engels, F. (1959) 'Outlines of a Critique of Political Economy' in K. Marx, *Economic and Philosophic Manuscripts of 1844*. Moscow: Foreign Languages Publishing House.

EPBB (1991) *Export From Bangladesh 1972–73 to 1991*. Dhaka: Export Promotion Bureau, Bangladesh.

EPBB (1992) *Bangladesh Export Statistics 1991–92*. Dhaka: Export Promotion Bureau, Bangladesh.

EPBB (1995) *Exports From Bangladesh 1972–73 to 1993–94*. Dhaka: Export Promotion Bureau, Bangladesh.

FAO/NACA Regional Study and Workshop on the Environmental Assessment and Management of Aquaculture Development (TCP/RAS/2253), *NACA Environment and Aquaculture Development Series*, No. 1. Bangkok, Thailand: Network of Aquaculture Centres in Asia-Pacific.

Firdausy, C. and Tisdell, C.A. (1992),'Rural Poverty and its Measurement: A Comparative Study of Villages in Nusa Penida, Bali', *Bulletin of Indonesia Studies*, **28**(2), pp.75–93.

Foell, W.K. (1994) 'Acid Rain in Asia: Regional Analysis and Policies' in T. Sterner (ed.), *Economic Policies for Sustainable Development*. Dordrecht: Kluwer The Netherlands, pp.227–39.

Gadgil, M. and Iyer, P. (1989) 'On the Diversification of Common Property Resource Use by Indian Society', in Berkes (ed.), pp.240–55.

Georgescu-Roegen, N. (1971) *The Entropy Law and the Economic Process*. Cambridge, Mass.: Harvard University Press.

Georgescu-Roegen, N. (1976) *Energy and Economic Myths: Institutional and Analytical Economic Essays*. New York: Pergamon Press.

Ghosh, R.N., Melotte, Y.M. and Siddique, M.A.B. (eds. 1996) *Economic Development and Change: South Asia and the Third World*. New Delhi: New Age.

Gibbons, M., Gummett, P. and Udgaonkar, B. (eds. 1984) *Science and Technology Policy in the 1980s and Beyond*. London: Longman.

Gill, G.J. (1991) *Seasonality and Agriculture in the Developing World*. Cambridge, U.K.: Cambridge University Press.

GOB (1995) *Bangladesh: Economic Review June 1995. Dhaka: Finance Division, Ministry of Finance.*

GOB (1996) *Bangladesh Economic Review June 1995*. Dhaka: Finance Division, Ministry of Finance.

Gordon, H.S. (1954) 'The Economic Theory of a Common Property Resource: The Fishery', *Journal of Political Economy*, **62**, pp.124–44.

Gujarati, D. (1988) *Basic Econometrics*. New York: McGraw-Hill.

Gunatilleke, M.G., Perera, M., Wanigaratne, R.A.M.C, Fernando, R.E., Lakhsman, W.D., Chandrasiri, J.K.M.D. and Wanigaratne, R.D. (1994) 'Sri Lanka', in Quibria (ed.), pp.355–543.

Hamid, M.A. (1996) 'Governance Issues and Sustainable Development: The Case of Regulatory Maze in Bangladesh', Paper for the conference on Governance Issues and Sustainable Development in the Indian Ocean Rim Countries. 28–30 October. Perth: University of Western Australia.

Hamid, M.A. and Alauddin, M. (1996) 'The Shrimp Industry and Employment Generation in Bangladesh', in Alauddin and Hasan (eds.), pp.301–321.

Hamid, M.A., Saha, S.K., Rahman, M.A. and Khan, M.A.J. (1978) *Irrigation Technologies in Bangladesh: A Study in Some Selected Areas*. Rajshahi: Rajshahi University, Department of Economics.

Haque, B.A. and Hoque, M.M. (1990) 'Faecal Pollution of Surface Water and Diseases in Bangladesh', in Rahman *et al.* (eds), pp.180–200.

Harcourt, G.C. (1972) *Some Cambridge Controversies in the Theory of Capital*. Cambridge UK: Cambridge University Press.

Hasan, S. (1996) 'Environmental Governance in Bangladesh: Problems and Issues', in M. Alauddin and S. Hasan (eds.), pp.227–46.

Hasan, S. and Mulamsottil, G. (1994) 'Environmental Problems of Dhaka City', *Cities*, 1(3), pp.195–200.

Hayami, Y. and Herdt, R.W. (1977) 'Market Price Effects of Technological Change on Income Distribution in Semi-Subsistence Agriculture', *American Journal of Agricultural Economics*, 59(2) pp.245–56.

Hossain, M. (1984) 'Employment and Laour in Bangladesh Rural Industries', *Bangladesh Development Studies*, 12(1–2), pp.1–24.

Hossain, M. (1987) 'Agricultural Growth Linkages: The Bangladesh Case', *Bangladesh Development Studies*, 15(1), pp.1–30.

Hossain, M., Mannan, R., Rahman, H.Z. and Sen, (1994) 'Bangladesh', in Quibria (ed.), pp.73–187.

Hunter, W.W. (1876) *A Statistical Account of Bengal; Distinct of Rajshahi, Maldah*. New Delhi: Concept Publishers.

Huq, S., Rahman, A.A. and Conway, G.R. (eds. 1990) *Environmental Aspects of Agricultural Development in Bangladesh*. Dhaka: University Press Limited.

Hussain, S. (1993) *The Bangladesh Textile Complex: Focus on Readymade Garment Industry*. MBA Research Report. Brisbane: University of Queensland.

Ishikawa, S. (1978) *Labour Absorption in Asian Agriculture: An Issues Paper*. Bangkok: ILO, ARTEP.

Islam, A. (1983) 'A Report on Aquatic Culture in Bangladesh', *Fisheries Information Bulletin* 1(2), Bangladesh Fisheries Resource Survey Systems.

Islam, A. (1989) 'A Review of Some Aspects of Fisheries Sub-sector' in Bangladesh Agricultural Sector Review, *Bangladesh Agriculture Performance and Policies*, Compendium Volume II: Sub-Sectors of Agriculture, United Nations Development Program, Dhaka, pp.110–173.

Islam, M.N. (1991) *Towards Sustainable Development: Energy and Natural Resources of Bangladesh*. Dhaka: Ministry of Environment and Forestry and National Conservation Secretariat.

Islam, N. (1996) 'City Study of Dhaka', in J Stubbs and G. Clarke, *Megacity Management in the Asia Pacific Region*, Vol. 1. Manila: Asian Development Bank, pp.39–94.

Islam, S. (1990) 'The Decline in Soil Fertility', in Huq *et al.* (eds.), pp.96–118.

IUCN–UNEP–WWF (1991) *Caring for the Earth: A Strategy for Sustainable Living*. IUCN, Gland, Switzerland.

Ives, J.D. and Messerlie, B. (1989) *The Himalayan Dilemma: Reconciling Development and Conservation*. London: Routledge.

Jacobs, P. (1989) 'Foreword' in Berkes (ed.), pp.vii–viii.

Jayasinghe, J.M.P.K. 'Sri Lanka', Country Paper, in FAO/NACA, pp.357–76.

Jayasuriya, S. and Shand, R.T. (1986) 'Technical Change and Labour Absorption in Asian Agriculture: Some Emerging Trends', *World Development*, 14(3), pp.415–28.

Jha, L.K. (1995) *Advances in Agroforestry*. New Delhi: APH Publishing.

Jodha, N.S. (1985) 'Population Growth and the Decline of Common Property Resources in Rajasthan, India', *Population and Development Review*, 11(2), pp.247–64.

Jodha, N.S. (1986) 'Common Property Resources and Rural Poor in Dry Regions of India', *Economic and Political Weekly*, 21(27), pp.1169–81.

Johnston, B.F. and Cownie, J. (1969) 'The Seed-Fertilizer Revolution and Labor Force Absorption', *American Economic Review*, 59(4), pp.59–82.

Jones, G.W. (1991) 'Urbanization Issues in the Asian-Pacific Region', *Asian-Pacific Economic Literature*, 5(2), pp.2–33.

Jones, S. (1984) 'Agrarian Structure and Agricultural Innovations in Bangladesh: Panimara Village, Dhaka District', in Bayliss-Smith and Wanmali (eds.), pp.194–211.

Karim, M. and Aftabuzzaman (1995) 'Brackish and Marine Water Aquaculture Development and Management', a paper presented at a seminar on the occasion of Fish Fortnight 1995, Dhaka: August 29.

Karim, M. and Ahsan, A.K.M. (1989) 'Policy Recommendations for Fisheries Development in Bangladesh', Dhaka: Ministry of Fisheries and Livestock, Government of Bangladesh (mimeo.)

Khan, A.R. and Hossain, M. (1989) *The Strategy of Development in Bangladesh*. London: Macmillan.

Khan, L.R. (1990) 'Round Ground Water Abstraction', in Huq *et al.* (eds.), pp.125–153.

Khan, S. and Hasan, S. (1996) 'Urban Settlement in Bangladesh: Problems of Administration', in Alauddin and Hasan (eds.), pp.211–25.

Kumar, M.S. (ed. 1987) *Energy Pricing Policies in Developing Countries: Theory and Empirical Evidence*. Geneva: International Labour Office.

Leibenstein, H. (1957) *Economic Backwardness and Economic Growth: Studies in the Theory of Economic Development*. New York: Wiley.

Lele, S. (1991) 'Sustainable Development: A Critical Review', *World Development* 19(6), pp.607–21.

Leopold, A. (1966) *A Land Country Almanac: with Other Essays on Conservation from Round River*. New York: Oxford University Press.

Lewis, W.A. (1954) 'Economic Development with Unlimited Supplies of Labour', *Manchester School of Economic and Social Studies*, 20, pp.139–91.

Lianzela, S. (1995) *Four Decades of Planning in Mizoram*. Aizawl: Khuangkungi.

Lindquist, A.C. (1989) 'Project Aid in Agriculture: Major (Surface Water) Flood Control, Drainage and Irrigation Projects', in Bangladesh Agriculture Sector Review, *Bangladesh Agriculture Performance and Policies*, Compendium Volume III: Land, Water and Irrigation, United Nations Development Program, Dhaka, pp.1–41.

Lipton, M. (1985) *Land Assets and Rural Poverty*, World Bank Staff Working chapter No. 744. Washington, D.C.: World Bank.

Mahmood, N. (1986) *Effects of Shrimp Farming and other Impacts on Mangrove of Bangladesh*. Bangkok: IPEC Workshop.

Mahmud, I., Rahman, K. and Omar, K.I. (1991) *Towards Sustainable Development Industries of Bangladesh*. Dhaka: Ministry of Environment and Forest and National Conservation Strategy Secretariat.

Mahtab, F. and Karim, Z. (1992), 'Population and Agricultural Land Use: Towards a Sustainable Food Production System in Bangladesh', *Ambio*, **20**(1), pp.50–55.

Mäler, K.G. (1974) *Environmental Economics: A Theoretical Inquiry*. Baltimore: Johns Hopkins University Press.

Marglin, S.A. (1976), *Value and Price in the Labour-Surplus Economy*. Oxford: Clarendon Press.

Markandya, A. (1995) 'Technology, Environment and Employment in Third World Agriculture', in Ahmed and Doeleman (eds.), pp.69–92.

Marx, K. (1956) *Capital*. Moscow: Progress Publishers.

Mazid, M.A. (1995) 'Bangladesh', Country Paper, in FAO/NACA, pp.61–82.

McGillvray, M. (1991) 'The Human Development Index: Yet Another Composite Development Indicator?', *World Development*, **19**(10), pp.1461–68.

Meadows, D.H., Meadows, D.L. and Randers, J. (1992) *Beyond the Limits: Global Collapse or a Sustainable Future*, London: Earthscan.

Meadows, D.H., Randers, J. and Beherens, W. (1972) *The Limits of Growth: A Report of the Club of Rome's Projection on the Predicament of Mankind*, New York: Universe Books.

Meir, G.M. (1976) *Leading Issues in Economic Development*, 3rd Edition. New York: Oxford University Press.

Meltzoff, S.K. and LiPuma, M. (1986) 'The Social and Political Economy of Coastal Zone Management: Shrimp Mariculture in Ecuador', *Coastal Zone Management*, **14**(4), pp.349–380.

Ministry of Forestry and IUCN (1991) *Towards Sustainable Development: The National Conservation Strategy of Bangladesh*. Glauds, Switzerland: Ministry of Environment and Forestry, Dhaka, Bangladesh and IUCN.

Minkin, S.F. (1988) 'Steps for Conserving and Developing Fish Resources', in *Bangladesh Agricultural Sector Review*. Dhaka: United Nations Development Programme.

Mishra, H.R. (1982) 'Balancing Human Needs and Conservation in Nepal's Royal Chitwan National Park', *Ambio*, **11**(5), pp.246–51.

MOF and FAO (1992) 'National Fishery Development Programme', TSS-1 Fishery Sector Programming Mission to Bangladesh. Rome: Ministry of Fisheries and Livestock, Bangladesh and Food and Agriculture Organisation of the United Nations.

MPO (1986) *Final Reports (Vols. I–III)*. Dhaka: Master Plan Organisation.

Mujeri, M.K., Alauddin, M. and Tisdell, C.A. (1993) 'Consumption, Savings and Investment by Social Class in Bangladesh: Does the Urban Sector Support the Urban Sector?', *Journal of Development Studies*, **30**(1), pp.226–45.

Myers, N. (1992) 'Population/Environmental Linkages: Discontinuities Ahead', *Ambio*, **21**(1), pp.116–18.

Myrdal, G. (1971) *The Challenge of World Poverty*. Harmondsworth, UK.: Penguin.

Nath, G.B. (1993) *Origin Growth and Condition of Living of Agricultural Labourers in Orissa – A Village Study*, Unpublished Ph.D Thesis. Sambalpur, India: Sambalpur University.

Ng, Y.K. (1986) 'Social Criteria for Evaluating Population Change: An Alternative to the Blackorby-Donaldson Criteria', *Journal of Public Economics*, **29**, pp.375–81.

Nishat, A. (1989) 'Large Scale Water Development in Bangladesh', in Bangladesh Agriculture Sector Review, *Bangladesh Agricultural Performance and Policies*, Compendium Volume III: Land, Water and Irrigation, United Nations Development Program, Dhaka, pp.75–105.

North, D.C. (1981) *Structure and Change in Economic History*. New York: Norton.

North, D.C. (1990) *Institutions, Institutional Change and Economic Performance*. Cambridge, UK.: Cambridge University Press.

North, D.C. and Thomas, R.P. (1973) *The Rise of the Western World: A New Economic History*. Cambridge, UK.: Cambridge University Press.

ODA (1990) *Report and Recommendations of The ODA Fisheries Project Identification Mission to Bangladesh Under Fisheries and Flood Action Plan*, March 3–May 1. London: ODA.

Ogawa, N. and Tsuya, N.O. (1993) 'Demographic Change and Human Resource Development in the Asia-Pacific Region: Trends of the 1960s to 1980s and Future Prospects', in N. Ogawa *et al.*, pp.21–65.

Ogawa, N., Jones, G.W. and Williamson, J.G. (eds. 1993) *Human Resources in Development Along the Asia-Pacific Rim*. Singapore: Oxford University Press.

Oldfield, M.L. (1989) *The Value of Conserving Genetic Resources*. Sunderland, Mass.: Sinavaur Associates.

Osmani, S.R. (1990) 'Structural Change and Poverty in Bangladesh: The Case of a False Turning Point', *Bangladesh Development Studies*, **18**(3), pp.55–74.

Ostrom, O. (1990) *Governing the Commons: The Evolution of Institutions for Collective Actions*. Cambridge, UK.: Cambridge University Press.

Panayotou, T. (1995) 'Environmental Degradation in Different Stages of Development', in Ahmed and Doeleman (eds.), pp.13–36.

Parikh, J.K. (1988) 'Bangladesh: Agriculture, Biomass and Environment', in Parikh, J.K. (ed.) *Sustainable Development in Agriculture*. Dordrecht: Martinus Nijhoff Publishers, pp.331–64.

Passmore, J.A. (1974) *Man's Responsibility for Nature: Ecological Problems and Western Traditions*. London: Duckworth.

Pearce, D. (1993) *Blueprint 3: Measuring Sustainable Development*. London: Earthscan.

Pearce, D., Barbier, E. and Markandya, A. (1990) *Sustainable Development: Economics and Environment in the Third World*. London: Earthscan.

Pearce, D.W. and Maler, K-G. (1991) 'Environmental Economics and the Developing World', *Ambio*, **20**(2), pp.52–54.

Perera, M. (1990) 'Impact of Development on the Environment Related Activities of Women', Colombo: Marga Institute.

Perrings, A.C. (1987) *Economy and Environment: A Theoretical Essay on the Interdependence of Economic and Environmental Systems*. New York: Cambridge University Press.

Perrings, C. (1995) 'Incentives for Sustainable Development in Sub-Saharan Africa', in Ahmed and Doeleman (eds.), pp.95–132.

Pingali, P., Moya, P.F. and Velasco, L.E. (1990) *The Post-Green Revolution Blues in Asian Rice Production – The Diminished Gap between Experiment Station and Farm Yields*, Social Science Division, Paper No. 90–01. Los Brafios, The Philippines: International Rice Research Institute.

Pingali, P.L. and Rosegrant, M.W. (1994) *Confronting the Environmental Consequences of the Green Revolution in Asia*, EPTD Discussion Paper No. 2. Washington, D.C.: International Food Policy Research Institute.

Pomeroy, R.S. (ed. 1994) *Community Management and Common Property of Coastal Fisheries in Asia and the Pacific: Concepts, Methods and Experience*. Manila: International Center for Living Aquatic Resource Management (ICLARM).

Primavera, J.H. (1991) 'Intensive Prawn Farming in the Philippines', *Ambio*, 20(1), pp.28–33.

Quasem, A.S.M., 'The Industry – A Look Ahead at EUROPE of 1992 – Opportunities and Problems', paper presented at *Seminar on Europe*. Dhaka: BGMEA.

Quibria, M.G. (ed. 1994), *Rural Poverty in Developing Asia 1*. Manila: Asia Development Bank.

Quibria, M.G. and Srinivasan, T.N. (1994) 'Introduction', in Quibria (ed.), pp.2–72.

Rahman, A., Islam, A., Roy, I., Azad, L. and Islam, K.M. (1995) *Shrimp Culture and Environment in the Coastal Region*, Working Paper New Series No. 8. Dhaka: Bangladesh Institute of Development Studies.

Rahman, A.A., Huq, S. and Conway, G.R. (eds. 1990) *Environmental Aspects of Surface Water Systems of Bangladesh*: Dhaka: University Press Limited.

Rahman, R.S., Chowdhury, I.H. and Chowdhury, M. (1984) 'Evaluation in Shrimp Culture in Satkhira and its Impact on Landless, Small and Marginal Farmers/Fishermen', in *Consultation on Social Feasibility of Coastal Aquaculture, Case material II*, United Nations Development Program, Dhaka, pp.72–81.

Ramakrishnan, P.S. (1992) *Shifting Agriculture and Sustainable Development of North-Eastern India*, UNESCO, Paris and Parthenon, Cornforth, U.K.

Rashid, H.E. (1989) 'Land Use in Bangladesh: Selected Topics', in Bangladesh Agriculture Sector Review, *Bangladesh Agriculture Performance and Policies*, Compendium Volume III: Land, Water and Irrigation, United Nations Development Program, Dhaka, pp.106–155.

Rashid, H.E. (1991) *Geography of Bangladesh*. Dhaka: University Press Limited.

Ravi, N. (ed. 1995) *The Hindu Survey of the Environment*. Madras: Kasturi and Sons.

Rawski, T.G. and Li, L.M. (eds. 1992) *Chinese History in Economic Perspective*. Berkeley: University of California Press.

Repetto, R. and Holmes, T. (1983) 'The Role of Population in Resource Depletion in Developing Countries', *Population and Development Review*, 9(4), pp.609–32.

Repetto, R., Magrath, W., Wells, M., Beer, C. and Rossini, F. (1989) *Wasting Resources: Natural Resource in National Income Accounts*. Washington, D.C.: World Resources Institute.

Robinson, J. (1969) *The Accumulation of Capital*. London: Macmillan.

Romer, P.M. (1986) 'Increasing Returns and Long-Run Growth', *Journal of Political Economy*, **94**(5), pp.1002–37.

Romer, P.M. (1994) 'The Origins of Endogenous Growth', *Journal of Economic Perspectives*, **8**(1), pp.3–24.

Roy, K.C. and Tisdell, C.A. (1992) 'Gandhi's Concept of Development and Nehru's Centralized Planning', in Roy *et al.* (eds), pp.1–16.

Roy, K.C., Blomqvist, H.P. and Hossain, I. (eds. 1997) *Development That Lasts*. New Delhi: New Age International.

Roy, K.C., Tisdell, C.A. and Blomqvist, H.C. (eds. 1996) *Economic Development and Women in the World Community*. New York: Praeger.

Roy, K.C., Tisdell, C.A. and Sen, R.K. (eds. 1992) *Economic Development and Environment: A Case Study of India*, Calcutta: Oxford University Press.

Roy, K.C., Tisdell, C.A. and Sen, R.K., Alauddin, M. (eds. 1991) *Economic Development of Poor Countries*, Calcutta: The World Press Private Ltd.

Ruttan, V.W. and Binswanger, H.P. (1978) 'Induced Innovation and the 'Green Revolution'' in Binswanger and Ruttan (eds.), pp.358–408.

Sandalo, R.M. (1994) 'Community-based-Coastal Resources Management: The Palawan Experience', in Pomeroy (ed.), pp.165–81.

Sathiendrakumar, R. and Tisdell, C.A. (1990), 'Technological Change and Income Distribution: Findings from Maldivian Fishing Villages', *Journal of Economics and International Relations*, **3**(3), pp.217–40.

Sen, A.K. (1981) *Poverty and Famines: An Essay on Entitlement and Deprivation*. Oxford: Clarendon Press.

Shand, R.T. (1973) 'Conclusion: An Interim Judgement', in R.T. Shand (ed.), pp.282–98.

Shand, R.T. (ed. 1973) *Technical Change in Asian Agriculture*. Canberra: Australian National University Press.

Siddiqui, M.H. and Nishat, A. (1990) 'Forecasts of Long Term Changes in Water Systems', in Rahman *et al.* (eds. 1990), pp.201–04.

Sinha, S. (1984) 'Growth of Scientific Temper: Rural Context', Gibbons *et al.*, pp.166–90.

Sobhan, R. (1993) *Bangladesh: Problems of Governance*. Dhaka: University Press Limited.

Solow, R.M. (1956) 'A Contribution to the Theory of Economic Growth', *Quarterly Journal of Economics*, **70**, pp.65–94.

Solow, R.M. (1957) 'Technical Change and the Aggregate Production Function', *Review of Economics and Statistics*, **39**, pp.312–20.

Solow, R.M. (1974) 'Intergenerational Equity and Exhaustible Resources', *Review of Economic Studies*, **41**, pp.29–46.

Solow, R.M. (1986) 'On the Intertemporal Allocation of Natural Resources', *Scandinavian Journal of Economics*, **88**(1), pp.141–49.

Stubbs, J. and Clarke, G. (1996) *Megacity Management in the Asian-Pacific Region*. Manila: Asian Development Bank.

Swan, T. (1956) 'Economic Growth and Capital Accumulation', *Economic Record*, **32**, pp.334–61.

Tabor, S.R., 'Agriculture in Transition', in Booth (ed.) pp.161–209.

Task Force Report (1991) *Report of the Task Forces on Bangladesh Development Strategies for the 1990s, Developing the Infrastructure, Vol. 3*. Dhaka: University Press Ltd.

Thomson, J.T., Feeny, D. and Oakerson, R.J. (1992) 'Institutional Dynamics: The Evolution and Dissolution of Common – Property Resource Management', in Bromley (ed.), s, pp.129–160.

Thorner, D., Kerblay, B. and Smith, R.E.F. (eds. 1966) *A.V. Chayanov on the Theory of Peasant Economy*. Homewood, Ill.: Richard D. Irwin Inc.

Tisdell, C.A. (1975) 'The Theory of Optimal City-Sizes: Elementary Speculations about Analysis and Policy', *Urban Studies*, 12, pp.61–70.

Tisdell, C.A. (1988) 'Sustainable Development: Differing Perspective of Ecologists and Economists, and relevance to LDCs', *World Development*, 16(3), pp.373–84.

Tisdell, C.A. (1990) *Natural Resources, Growth and Development*. New York: Praeger.

Tisdell, C.A. (1991a) *Economics of Environmental Conservation*. Amsterdam: Elsevier Science Publishers.

Tisdell, C.A. (1991b) 'Population Growth and Environmental Protection. The Situation of Developing Countries in Global Perspective', in Roy *et al.* (eds. 1991), pp.224–238.

Tisdell, C.A. (1993a) *Economic Development in the Context of China*. London: Macmillan.

Tisdell, C.A. (1993b) *Environmental Economics*. London: Edward Elgar.

Tisdell, C.A. (1994a) 'Conservation, Protected Areas and the Global Economic System: How Debt, Trade, Exchange Rates, Inflation and Macroeconomic Policy Affect Biological Diversity', *Biodiversity and Conservation*, 3, pp.419–36.

Tisdell, C.A. (1994b) 'Population, Economics, Development and Environmental Security', in N. Polunin and M. Nazim, *Population and Global Security*. Geneva: The Foundation for Environmental Conservation, pp.63–84.

Tisdell, C.A. (1995a) 'Asian Development and Environmental Dilemmas', *Contemporary Economic Policy*, 13(1), pp.38–49.

Tisdell, C.A. (1995b) 'Issues in Biodiversity Conservation including the Role of Local Communities', *Environmental Conservation*, 22 (3), pp.216–228.

Tisdell, C.A. (1995c) 'Biodiversity, Conservation and Sustainable Development, Challenges for North-East India in Context', *Biodiversity Conservation*, Working Paper No. 21, Department of Economics, The University of Queensland, Brisbane, 4072.

Tisdell, C.A. (1996a) 'Reconciling Economic Development, Nature Conservation and Local Communities: Strategies for Biodiversity Conservation in Xishuangbanna, China', *The Environmentalist*, 16, pp.203–211.

Tisdell, C.A. (1996b) 'Economic Indicators to Assess the Sustainability of Conservation Farming Projects: An Evaluation', *Agriculture, Ecosystems and Environment*, 57, pp.117–31.

Tisdell, C.A. and Alauddin, M. (1989) 'New Crop Varieties: Impact on Diversification and Stability of Yields', *Australian Economic Papers* 28(52), pp.123–40.

Tisdell, C.A. and Alauddin, M. (1992), 'The Ishikawa Curve and Agricultural Productivity in Bangladesh: Some New Findings', *Hitotsubashi Journal of Economics*, 33(1), pp.113–27.

Tisdell, C.A. and Roy, K.C. (1997) 'Good Governance, Property Rights and Sustainable Resource Use: An Institutional Perspective with Indian Ocean Rim Examples', *South African Journal of Economics* 65(1), pp.28–43.

Tisdell, C.A., Alauddin, M. and Mujeri, M.K. (1992), 'Environmental Spillovers, Poverty and Failure to Balance Societal Demand on Water Resources in Bangladesh', *Discussion Paper No. 103*. Brisbane: Department of Economics, The University of Queensland.

Tisdell, C.A., Roy, K.C., and Gannon, J. (1996) 'Sustainability of Tribal Villages in West Bengal: The Impact of Technological Change at Village Level', in Ghosh *et al.* (eds.), pp.231–52.

Turner, R.K., Pearce, D. and Bateman, I. (1993) *Environmental Economics*. Baltimore: Johns Hopkins University Press.

UN Population Division (1994) *World Urbanization Prospects 1994 Revision*. New York: United Nations.

UNDP (1991) *Human Development Report 1991*, New York: Oxford University Press.

UNDP (1994) *Human Development Report 1994*. New York: Oxford University Press.

UNDP (1996) *Human Development Report 1996*. New York: Oxford University Press.

UNDP-World Bank (1982) *Bangladesh: Issues and Options in the Energy Sector*, Report No. 3873-BD, Report of the Joint UNDP/World Bank Energy Sector Assessment Program. Washington, D.C.: World Bank.

UNDP-World Bank (1982) *Bangladesh: Issues and Options in the Energy Sector*, Report No. 3873-BD, Report of the Joint UNDP/World Bank Energy Sector Assessment Program. Washington, D.C.: World Bank.

United Nations (1987) *Population Growth and Policies in Megacities*, Population Policy Paper No. 10. Bangkok: Department of International Economics and Social Affairs.

WCED (1987) *Our Common Future*, World Commission on Environment and Developement. Oxford: Oxford University Press.

Wilson, E.O. (1992) *The Diversity of Life*. Cambridge, Mass.: Harvard University Press.

Woodhouse, P. (1992) 'Environmental Degradation and Sustainability', in Allen, T. and Thomas, A. (eds.) *Poverty and Development in the 1990s*. Oxford, U.K.: Oxford University Press.

World Bank (1982) *Bangladesh: Foodgrain Self-Sufficiency and Crop Diversification (Annexes and Statistical Appendix)*, Report No. 3953-BD. Washington, D.C.: World Bank.

World Bank (1991) *Bangladesh: Fisheries Sector Review*, Report # 8830-BD. Washington, D.C.: World Bank.

World Bank (1992) *World Bank Report 1992: Development and the Environment*. New York: Oxford University Press.

World Bank (1994) *World Development Report 1994*. New York: Oxford University Press.

World Bank (1995a) *World Development Report 1995*. Washington, D.C.: World Bank.

World Bank (1995b) *From Stabilization to Growth*. Washington, D.C.: World Bank.

World Bank (1995c) *Recent Economic Developments and Priority Reform Agenda for Rapid Growth*. Washington, D.C.: World Bank.

World Bank (1996a) *World Development Report 1996*. Washington, D.C.: World Bank.

World Bank (1996b) *Bangladesh: Government That Works – Reforming the Public Sector*. Washington, D.C.: World Bank.

WRI (1990a) *Bangladesh Environment and Natural Resources Assessment*. Washington, D.C.: Centre for International Development and Environment, World Resources Institute.

WRI (1990b) *World Resources 1990–91*. New York: Oxford University Press.

WRI (1996) *World Resources 1996–97*. Washington, D.C.: World Resources Institute.

WRI-UNEP-UNDP (1994) *World Resources 1994–95*. New York: Oxford University Press.

Zafarullah, H. (1996) 'Toward Good Governance in Bangladesh: External Intervention, Bureaucratic Inertia and Political Inaction', in Alauddin and Hasan (eds.), pp.145–62.

Zhuge, R. (1996) 'Land Use Issues and Sustainable Development of the Jingpo Communities of Yunnan, China: Impacts of Governance, Institutions and Culture of Resource Management'. Paper for the conference on Governance Issues and Sustainable Development in the Indian Ocean Rim Countries, 28–30 October. Perth: University of Western Australia.

Zhuge, R. and Tisdell, C. (1996) *Sustainability Issues and Socio-economic Change in the Jingpo Communities of China: Governance, Culture and Land Rights*, Economics Ecology and the Environment Working Paper No. 4. Brisbane: Department of Economics, The University of Queensland.

Zuberi, M.I. (1992) 'Natural Resource Management and Utilization in Bangladesh: Changes in Land Use Pattern in the Barind Tract', University of Rajshahi, Rajshahi: Centre for Environmental Research (mimeo.).

Zuberi, M.I. (1993) 'A Description of North Western Bangladesh', University of Rajshahi, Rajshahi: Centre for Environmental Research (mimeo.)

Index

Adger, N., 125
Africa, 11
Aftabuzzaman, 149, 154
agricultural productivity, 56
Ahmad, Y.J., 7, 28
Ahmed, I., 1, 45, 79, 95
Ahmed, M., 92
Ahmed, M.F., 92
Ahsan, A.K.M., 43
Alagarswami, K., 148
Alauddin, M., 7, 13, 47–8, 56, 75–6,
    79–80, 82, 85, 92, 94–5, 110,
    116–7, 123, 126, 145, 152, 158,
    168
Ali, M.Y., 37, 45
anthropocentric, 19, 28
aquaculture, 45–6
area-based, 78, 79
Arunachal Pradesh, 139, 140
Asia, 11, 13, 15, 22–4, 26, 33, 55, 132
Assam, 139, 140
Axelrod, R., 112

backward linkages, 74, 165
Bangladesh, 3, 5, 8–10, 19–26, 28, 32,
    34, 37, 39, 43, 45, 52, 61, 75, 77,
    80–7, 89, 91, 92, 110, 114–7,
    123–4, 126, 134, 136, 139, 145–7,
    150, 151, 154–5, 169–72, 175–6,
    180–1, 183–5, 188–90, 193–8
Barbier, E.B., 2, 33
Barker, R., 55
Bartelemus, P.L., 125
Becker, G., 188
Bell, L.S., 83
Berkes, F., 102, 107
Biggs, S.D., 92
Bihar, 140
Binswanger, H.P., 55
biodiversity, biological diversity, 6,
    11–3, 25–6, 29–30, 32, 52, 114,
    142, 197

biomass, 52, 170, 173–4, 183
Blackorby, C., 28
Blaikie, P., 106
brackish water, 45
Brahmaputra, 54
Brammer, H., 134
Brandon, C., 24
Bromley, D.W., 37
Brundtland report, 2
Buchdal, J., 198

Cao, Yang, 83
capital intensity, 60–1, 63–5, 85
Cernea, M.M., 37
Chakravarty, S., 12
Chambers, R., 115
Chayanov, A.V., 77
China, 10, 14, 19–24, 26, 28, 32, 54,
    77, 102, 196–8
Chong, K-C., 151
Chowdhury, M.A.M., 151
Ciriacy-Wantrup, S.V., 99
Clark, C., 186
Clarke, G., 193
Clay, E.J., 92
Club of Rome, 10, 15
co-management, 8, 102
commercial energy, 170, 173
common-property, 108
common-property resources, 108
communal property, 102
Conway, G.R., 2, 48, 92, 116, 129,
    130
Cook, N.L., 151
Cordova, V.G., 55
Cownie, J., 55, 95
cross-subsidisation, 182

Dalal-Clayton, C., 34, 41, 54
Daly, H., 20
Das, R.K., 151
Demsetz, H., 115

Denison, E.F., 15
deforestation, 22–3
Dev, M.S., 113
Dhikawa, 95
Doeleman, J.A., 1
Donaldson, D., 28
Douglass, G.K., 2, 130

East Asia, 20, 22, 33
ecocentric, 131
economic logic, 185
Ecuador, 46
Ehrlich, P.R., 20
electricity, 13, 181
electricity generation, 174
electricity consumption, 176
El Serafy, S., 7
energy, 9, 169, 174, 182–6
energy conservation strategy, 185
energy crisis, 169, 185
energy planning, 185
energy prices, 181
energy pricing, 181–2, 185
energy pricing policies, 181
energy resources, 169, 185
Engels, F., 14
environmental changes, 92, 95, 97,
    114, 120, 125, 186
  conditions, 92
  conflicts, 45
  considerations, 182, 185
  cycle, 115
  damage, 101
  degradation, 4, 54, 102, 110, 112,
    155, 168
  deterioration, 102
  disorder, 192
  effects, 105
  goods, 3
  governance, 110
  hazards, 192
  health problems, 188
  impacts, 186
  implications, 92
  loss, 124
  management, 185
  pollution, 47
  predicament, 54

problems, 47, 52, 80–1, 189, 191–3
quality, 2, 93, 95
refugees, 139
shock, 130
situation, 124
spillovers, 38, 93, 97, 132–3
stocks, 131
Europe, 22, 24, 26
exchange income, 48, 94, 117
extensive culture, 46
externalities, 47, 82, 102, 118, 132–3

Farakka barrage, 9
Farvar, M.T., 102
fertiliser production, 179
Firdausy, C., 121
forward linkages, 74, 165

Gadgil, M., 102, 106–7
Gandhi, M.K., 107
Ganges, 54
gas, 181
gas consumption, 178
genetic diversity, 95
Gill, G.J., 79
Gordon, H.S., 99
governance, 8, 98–9, 105, 111, 174
greenhouse gas, 10, 197, 198
Green Revolution, 7, 9, 23, 33, 35, 48,
    52, 55–7, 59–60, 63–5, 74–80,
    94–5, 114–8, 126
Green Revolution technologies, 76
gross power loss, 176
ground water, 9
Gunatilleke, M.G., 113

Hamid, M.A., 92, 94, 110, 152, 158,
    168
Haque, B.A., 83
Harcourt, G.C., 60
Hasan, S., 7, 49, 50, 98, 108–10, 193–5
Hayami, Y., 116
Herdt, R.W., 116
Hoque, M.M., 83
Hossain, M., 74, 76–7, 113
human capital, 16
Human Development Index, 27–8
human welfare, 2

Hunter, W.W., 136
Hussain, S., 74
hydroelectricity, 173

IMF, 12
import intensity, 170
income distribution, 8
India, 3, 5, 8, 21–2, 24–6, 28, 32, 54,
    82, 102, 111, 113–15, 126–7, 134,
    141, 145–6, 148, 170–2, 188–90,
    196–7
Indonesia, 12, 21–2, 24, 26, 28
intensive culture, 46
Ishikawa, S., 7, 55–6, 77
Islam, A., 44–5, 151
Islam N., 195
Islam, S., 82
Ives, J.D., 54
Iyer, P., 102, 106–7

Jacobs, P., 102
Jayasinghe, J.M.P.K., 48
Jayasuriya, S., 7, 55–6
Jodha, N.S., 48
Johnston, B.F., 55, 95
Jones, G.W., 190
Jones, S., 92

Karim, M., 149, 154
Karim, Z., 6, 43, 114
Khan, A.R., 74
Khan, L.R., 37
Khan, S., 193–4
Kumar, M.S., 182
Kuznets, S., 198

labour intensity, 56–7, 60, 63–5, 67,
    72, 78, 86–7, 89–91, 95
land productivity, 60
land rights, 107
Leanzela, S., 144
Leibenstein, H., 199
Lele, S., 2
Leopold, A., 28
Lewis, W.A., 83
Lindquist, A.C., 36–7
Lipton, M., 48
LiPuma, M., 46

loss of biodiversity, 197
low income countries, 190
Lutz, E., 7

Mahtab, F., 6, 114
Maler, K-G., 2, 15
Mahmud, I., 7
Mahtab, F., 114
Mangroves, 46
Manipur, 139–40
market failures, 100
Marglin, S.A., 83–4
Markandya, A., 33, 80, 97
Marx, K., 14
Mazid, M.A., 148, 167
McGillvray, M., 27
Meadows, D.H., 15, 20
Meghalaya, 139–40
Meltzoff, S.K., 46
Minkin, S.F., 44
Messerlie, B., 54
Mizoram, 139–40, 144
Mujeri, M.K., 77
Mulamsottil, G., 195
multiple cropping, 44
Myanmar, 139
Myrdal, G., 110

Nagaland, 139
Nath, G.B., 122–3
natural environmental capital, 16
natural environmental problems, 81
natural gas, 173, 179–81
natural resource changes, 120
nature index, 29
Nehru, J., 107
neo-Malthusian, 32
Nepal, 82, 189–90, 197
Nishat, A., 36–7
Ng, Y.K., 28
non-commercial biomass fuel, 173
non-commercial energy, 169
non-exchange income, 48, 94, 117
non-renewable resource, 97, 178
North, D.C., 112

Ogawa, N., 12
Oldfield, M.L., 59

Osmani, S.R., 79
Ostrom, O., 112

Pakistan, 3, 5, 21–2, 24–6, 28, 32,
    170–2, 188–90, 196
Parikh, J.K., 183, 185
Passmore, J.A., 28
Pearce, D.W., 1, 2, 7, 15–9, 27, 125,
    127
Perera, M., 113
Perrings, C., 15, 101
petroleum, 173
Philippines, 12, 21–2, 24–6, 28, 32
power generation, 175–6, 179
power generation capacity, 176
pricing, 182
pricing policy, 182
primary energy, 173
private property, 102
productivity, 57
productivity-based, 79
productivity growth, 2
Property rights, 8, 98–9, 100, 102, 107,
    110–2, 115, 144

Quasem, A.S.M., 74
Quibria, M.G., 8, 113, 124

Rahman, A., 148, 151, 155–6, 167
Rahman, R.S., 46
Ramakrishnan, P.S., 107, 134, 140–3
Ramankutty, R., 24
Rashid, H.E., 46, 134
Ravi, N., 193
Reazuddin, 45
Repetto, R., 7, 28, 150
rice–shrimp farming systems, 152
Robinson, J., 60
Romer, P.M., 15
Roy, K.C., 13, 98–100, 105, 107, 113,
    119
Ruttan, V.W., 55

Sandalo, R.M., 106
Sathiendrakumar, R., 121
Schmidt, V.W., 151
sectoral linkages, 166
Shand, R.T., 7, 55–6, 59

shrimp cultivation, 148, 151, 158, 164,
    167
shrimp culture, 146, 148, 155
shrimp farming, 151, 158–9, 167–8, 184
shrimp farming methods, 150
shrimp industry, 166
Siddiqui, M.H., 37
Sinha, S., 79
Sobhan, R., 110
Solow, R.M., 14
social cost-benefit, 47
South Asia, 10–12, 22, 33, 125–6, 132,
    169, 186, 188–9, 191, 193, 197–9
spillovers, 34, 82
Sri Lanka, 3, 5, 20–1, 24–6, 28, 113,
    169–72, 188–90, 197
Srinivasan, T.N., 113
Stubbs, J., 193
structural adjustment, 12
sustainability, 2, 3, 16–8, 95, 97, 102,
    105, 110, 116, 118, 126, 128–30,
    131–2, 134, 139, 141–2, 167–9
sustainability implications, 187
sustainable development, 52
systems loss, 174, 184
Swan, T.W., 14

Tabor, S.R., 77
Task Force Report, 174–5
Thailand, 21–2, 24, 28, 107, 112
Thomas, R.P., 112
Thomson, J.T., 107
Thorner, D., 77
Tisdell, C.A., 2, 7, 13–4, 26, 29, 32–3,
    37–8, 48, 56, 59, 77, 79, 82–3, 85,
    92, 94, 98–100, 102, 104–5, 107,
    110, 114, 116–19, 121, 126, 130,
    139, 143, 186
traditional fuel, 173
Tripura, 139–40
Tsuya, N.O., 12
Turner, R.K., 15, 19

underpricing of natural gas, 182
UNDP, 27–8, 169
urban-centric, 186
urban growth centres, 186
urbanisation, 13, 186–9, 193, 199

value of marginal product (VMP), 83

WCED, 32, 54
West Bengal, 114, 124, 134
Whitby, M., 125
Wilson, E.O., 32–3
Woodhouse, P., 1

World Bank, 2, 5, 12, 21, 38, 40, 151,
    169, 175, 177, 179, 189–90, 197
WRI, 22–4, 26

Zafarullah, H., 110
Zhuge, R., 102, 139
Zuberi, M.I., 136, 138